HOW TO BUILD Killer BIG-BLOCK CHEVY Engines

Tom Dufur

S-A DESIGN

CarTech®

CarTech®, Inc.
39966 Grand Avenue
North Branch, MN 55056
Phone: 651-277-1200 or 800-551-4754
Fax: 651-277-1203
www.cartechbooks.com

© 2012 by Tom Dufur

All rights reserved. No part of this publication may be reproduced or utilized in any form or by any means, electronic or mechanical, including photocopying, recording, or by any information storage and retrieval system, without prior permission from the Author. All text, photographs, and artwork are the property of the Author unless otherwise noted or credited.

The information in this work is true and complete to the best of our knowledge. However, all information is presented without any guarantee on the part of the Author or Publisher, who also disclaim any liability incurred in connection with the use of the information.

All trademarks, trade names, model names and numbers, and other product designations referred to herein are the property of their respective owners and are used solely for identification purposes. This work is a publication of CarTech, Inc., and has not been licensed, approved, sponsored, or endorsed by any other person or entity.

Edit by Scott Parkhurst
Layout by Monica Seiberlich

ISBN 978-1-61325-170-6
Item No. SA190P

Library of Congress Cataloging-in-Publication Data

Dufur, Tom.
  How to build killer big-block Chevy engines / By Tom Dufur.
      p. cm.
    ISBN 978-1-934709-28-3
1. Chevrolet automobile--Parts--Handbooks, manuals, etc. 2. Chevrolet automobile--Motors--Maintenance and repair--Handbooks, manuals, etc. 3. Chevrolet automobile--Motors--Modification-Handbooks, manuals, etc. 4. Chevrolet automobile--Performance-Handbooks, manuals, etc. I. Title.

  TL215.C48.D84 2012
  629.25'040288--dc23

                              2011022978

Printed in China
10 9 8 7 6 5 4 3 2 1

Front Cover:
This engine is a 555-ci big-block built by the author for drag racing in NHRA's Super Comp and Top Dragster classes, as well as in the K&N Super Eliminator Series.

Title Page:
Weiand 6-71 blower topped with two Holley carbs is big, obnoxious, noisy, and moves a lot of air–exactly what you want for a no-compromise, take-no-prisoners radical street and strip or race-only big-block. This one has nitrous too. If some is good, more is better, and too much is just right.

Back Cover Photos

Top Left:
Chevy main bearings have an oil hole and groove in one half, and this half always goes in the block and aligns with the oil supply hole.

Top Right:
Measure the ring end gap with a feeler gauge. If you are using +.005-inch rings, there might not be any gap at all before you begin filing, but you need to check to be sure.

Middle Left:
Competition big-blocks need serious valvetrain pieces: fat pushrods, shaft rocker arms, long valves (these are titanium), triple valvesprings, titanium retainers and matching keepers, valvespring locators, and good valvestem seals are standard fare for 1,000-plus-hp Rat motors with over .900-inch lift at the valves.

Middle Right:
The Pontiac Super Duty Pro Stock head was the predecessor to today's crop of spread port heads like these Brodix Big Duke cylinder heads with reduced intake valve angles and raised runners. You'll find spread port heads on most 1,000-plus-hp big-blocks.

Bottom Left:
Racing manifolds should be port matched to the cylinder heads, leaving the port exit about .050 inch smaller than the intake gasket.

Bottom Right:
The main studs are torqued to 95 ft-lbs (inner) and 85 ft-lbs (outer) in four steps (45, 65, 85, and 95) starting with the center cap and working toward each end.

OVERSEAS DISTRIBUTION BY:

Brooklands Books Ltd.
P.O. Box 146, Cobham, Surrey, KT11 1LG, England
Telephone 01932 865051 • Fax 01932 868803
www.brooklands-books.com

Brooklands Books Aus.
3/37-39 Green Street, Banksmeadow, NSW 2019, Australia
Telephone 2 9695 7055 • Fax 2 9695 7355

CONTENTS

Acknowledgments 4
About the Author 5

Chapter 1: Family Tree 6
   396 Engines 7
   402 Engines 7
   427 Engines 8
   454 Engines 8
   General Motors Performance Parts Crate Engines 9

Chapter 2: Cylinder Blocks 14
   Block Selection 14
   Maximum Bore Sizes 15
   Stock Blocks 15
   Mark IV Blocks 16
   Gen V and Gen VI Blocks 17
   General Motors Performance Parts Blocks 19
   Bowtie Blocks 19
   GMPP Drag Race Competition Engine Blocks 20
   Aftermarket Blocks 21
   Block Casting Dates 25

Chapter 3: Crankshafts, Connecting Rods and Pistons 28
   Crankshafts 28
   Project: Balancing the Reciprocating Assembly 33
   Connecting Rods 35
   Bearings 39
   Pistons 39
   Harmonic Dampeners 43
   Flywheels and Flexplates 46
   Starters 47

Chapter 4: Camshafts, Lifters and Valvetrain Components 49
   Types of Camshafts and Lifters 49
   Lift, Duration and Lobe Separation Angle 51
   Project: How to Degree-In a Camshaft 52
   General Camshaft Recommendations 55
   OEM Cam Fitment 56
   Lifters 57
   Replacement Big-Block Camshafts 60
   Oversized Cam Journals 60
   Alternative Firing Orders: 4-7 Swap 61
   Cam Drives: Chains, Gears and Belts 62
   Pushrods 63
   Rocker Arms 65
   Valvesprings, Retainers and Keepers 67

Chapter 5: Oil and Lubrication Systems 72
   Oil Pumps 73
   Oil Pans 75
   Oil Filters and Adapters 76
   Pan Evacuation Systems and Vacuum Pumps 77
   Accumulators, Coolers and Accessories 78
   Motor Oil 79

Chapter 6: Cylinder Heads 80
   Oval or Rectangular Intake Ports 81
   Open or Closed Combustion Chambers 82
   Mark IV, Gen V and Gen VI Heads 82
   Aftermarket Cylinder Heads 83
   Spread Port Heads 84
   What's Your (Valve) Angle? 84
   Modifications 85
   Aftermarket Cylinder Head Manufacturers 88

Chapter 7: Induction Systems 97
   Intake Manifolds 97
   Carburetor Spacers and Adapters 100
   Tunnel Ram Intake Manifolds 101
   Rochester Quadrajet Carburetors 102
   Holley-Style Modular Carburetors 102
   Carter/Weber/Edelbrock Square-Bore Carburetors 103
   Air Cleaners 105
   Fuel Pumps 105
   Fuel Injection 106
   Nitrous Oxide Injection 110
   Superchargers 112
   Turbochargers 114

Chapter 8: Exhaust Systems 115
   OEM Exhaust Manifolds 115
   Tubular Headers 116
   Mufflers and Exhaust Pipes 117
   An Exhausting Summary 117

Chapter 9: Ignition Systems 119
   Distributors, Coils and Spark Plug Wires 119
   Ignition Controllers 121
   Spark Plugs 123
   Batteries and Cables 124

Chapter 10: Cooling Systems 125
   Water Pumps 126

Chapter 11: Gaskets and Fasteners 127
   Cylinder Head Gaskets 127
   Big-Block Engine Gaskets and Seals 129
   Fasteners 130

Chapter 12: Engine Build-Up 132
   Short-Block Assembly 132
   Long-Block Assembly 138
   Final Accessory Installation 141

Source Guide 144

ACKNOWLEDGMENTS

This book would not have been possible without help from a lot of fine people, and I wish I could thank them all individually, but such a task would require another book just to list their names. If I forgot to mention anyone, please accept my apology and know that your contribution was appreciated. First on my list has to be K&N's Steve Williams and John Reedy, two gentlemen who prove once again that the smartest guys in the high-performance industry are also among the nicest and most generous. Steve is a multi-time NHRA national event winner in Super Comp and Super Gas drag racing as well as the vice president of marketing at K&N, and graciously invited me to tag along as John rebuilt their stable of big-block racing engines at the K&N Race Shop for the upcoming season. Working with John Reedy was like meeting an old friend for the first time when we started this project. He's been building and racing big-block Chevys pretty much since the wheel was invented, and his knowledge and skill are reflected in every project he tackles.

Edelbrock's Dr. Rick Roberts, Robert Jung, Curt Hooker, Smitty Smith, and Mike Eddy have all helped me to get more power and performance from my own big-blocks over the years, and hopefully some of their knowledge will turn out to be beneficial to your engine project as well. My racing partners over the years include Vic Hahn, Rick Dessinger, James Burkhalter, and Ron Glazebrook, and all have contributed financially, morally, and with plenty of late-night blood, sweat, and tears. OK, no tears, but it sounded good, right? Special thanks goes to Ron for his drawings throughout the book, which hopefully clarify my rather wordy explanations.

Kirk Peters of Scat Crankshafts and Shane Turner of JE Pistons both took time out of their busy schedules to show me around their respective establishments, and they are both more than businessmen; they are gentlemen and big-block Chevy racers themselves, and know exactly how to satisfy their customers' high-performance needs and wants.

These last few guys had more than a little influence on this book; they made it happen. My editor, Scott Parkhurst, had faith in me to tackle this job even though my last published editorial work was in the disco era. He cut me some slack when a small obstacle, in the form of open-heart surgery, added months to the completion date, and was always dead-on with his observations and suggestions. George Kettler is responsible for this tome in more ways than one: more than 25 years ago he sold me my first big-block Chevy, a faux-L88 from his Nova that ended up in my first Super Comp dragster. When Scott was scouting around for someone gullible enough to write this book, one of his initial contacts was Mike Lewis of Lewis Machine and Racing Engines in the Pacific Northwest, but Mike was far too busy with his own successful business machining and building big-blocks to spend the massive amount of time involved in a venture like this. Mike mentioned this to one of his contacts, my old friend George Kettler, who suggested my name, and the rest, as they say, is history. In the meantime, George had spent two decades serving our country in the U.S. Army in such venues as Korea, Germany, and Iraq, always waiting for the day he could return to his wife, kids, and 427-powered '68 Vette. Thankfully, he did all of that and more, building an 11-second budget 454-motivated El Camino to keep the Vette company. To SFC Kettler (U.S. Army retired) and all those who serve to keep our freedom intact so that we may pursue our enjoyment of high-performance vehicles, I salute you.

About the Author

Tom Dufur grew up in the Four Corners region of northwest New Mexico and cultivated an early allegiance to the Bowtie Marque fostered by a 1967 Camaro and lots of wide-open roads. In 1976 he moved to southern California, the birthplace of hot rodding, and became immersed in the local car culture and drag racing. He worked as a technical editor for *Car Craft* magazine and Petersen's now-defunct *Drag Racing* magazine before landing a position with the Edelbrock Corporation where he performed a variety of duties over the next 24 years.

Tom campaigns a big-block Chevy-powered dragster (what else?) in NHRA Super Comp and Top Dragster competition and races in the K&N Super Eliminator Series in southern California running on a 7.90-second index. He won the K&N Super Eliminator Series championship in 2005 and again in 2008, and is hoping to add a third championship to the list before hanging up the driving gloves.

Photo Courtesy C. J. Sofka.

He plays the trumpet in three Los Angeles–area symphony orchestras and performs in a host of local bands and other musical productions. He is also an avid reloader and enjoys competing in action pistol and tactical rifle matches.

CHAPTER 1

THE FAMILY TREE

This modern 500-ci Pro Stock engine is the product of hundreds of hours of preparation and thousands of hours of research and development in every aspect of normally aspirated (non-supercharged) big-block racing engine technology. Every system has been massaged, flowed, tested, and changed to yield the absolute best performance on the dragstrip. External modifications are apparent: two 4500 series Holley Dominator carbs on a fabricated sheet-metal tunnel-ram intake manifold; symmetrical-port raised-runner aluminum cylinder heads; stainless steel headers with merge collectors; crank trigger ignition system; belt-driven camshaft and front-drive distributor; and dry sump oil pump and pan with a full-length kick-out. The engine block is a GM DRCE (Drag Race Competition Engine) iron block with compacted graphite and 4.900-inch bore spacing (stock is 4.840 inches); the roller camshaft is a custom nine-bearing billet with more than 1 inch of lift at the titanium valves, pushing on oversized keyway-guided roller lifters. High-ratio shaft-mount rocker arms provide valvetrain stability at 11,000 rpm, and the compression ratio exceeds 15:1. The cylinder heads are NHRA-legal GM DRCE castings that are fully CNC machined to each team's custom specifications, and they are the key to this engine's 1,400-plus-hp output on racing gasoline. (Photo Courtesy Jegs)

Unlike lesser engines, the evolution of the big-block Chevy can be traced back to a prestigious great-great-grand pappy, the high-performance 425-hp L78 396, first available in 1965 Corvettes and Chevelles. Even though the big-block was destined to eventually find a home in trucks and family sedans, it started off as a serious high-performance piece sporting rectangular port heads, solid-lifter cam (in the Corvette), high-rise aluminum intake manifold and 780-cfm Holley carb, and forged pistons with an 11:1 compression ratio.

To further complicate matters, advertising and marketing strategies were manipulated to bolster sales of particular models. For instance, the same

THE FAMILY TREE

L78 396 engine was rated at 425 hp in Chevy's vaunted Corvette, but only 375 hp when installed in a Camaro or Chevelle. Although the Corvette did indeed boast superior exhaust manifolds and a free-flowing air cleaner (neither of which were on the dyno test engine anyway), the real tell-tale clue was that the Corvette engine was rated at 6,400 rpm and the Camaro and Chevelle versions were rated at only 5,600 rpm. So they were not really "fibbing"; they were just quoting horsepower numbers below the true peak power level in order not to steal any thunder from the prestigious (and more costly) Corvette.

In 1972, insurance companies began imposing strict premiums for high-horsepower vehicles. Combined with the switch to unleaded gasoline and attending lower compression ratios, Chevrolet switched to the more realistic net horsepower rating, which reflected the true "as delivered" power of the engines with all accessories and a stock exhaust system in place. Since the GMPP crate engines were not installed in production vehicles, their horsepower ratings reflect the gross horsepower output of these high-performance powerplants.

Here's a quick overview of the RPO (Regular Production Option) engine offerings through the years.

396 Engines

RPO L35: 325 gross hp at 4,800 rpm

Oval port cast-iron heads, Holley 4-barrel carb through 1967, Quadrajet 4-barrel starting in 1968, 10.25:1 compression ratio, two-bolt main caps, forged steel crankshaft (through 1967). Available in most full-size passenger cars, Camaros, and Novas through 1972.

RPO L34: 350 gross hp at 5,200 rpm

Same as the L35 with the following improvements: higher-lift hydraulic

The L34 396 was rated at 350 hp and came with an open-element air cleaner, higher-lift hydraulic cam, and dual exhaust for a factory-rated 25-hp increase over the more common L35 396.

lifter cam, open-element air cleaner, dual exhausts. Some had four-bolt mains, all had forged steel crankshaft. Oval port cast-iron heads, Holley 4-barrel carb through 1967, Quadrajet 4-barrel starting in 1968, 10.25:1 compression ratio. Available in Chevelles and Camaros from 1966 to 1970.

RPO L78: 425 gross hp at 6,400 rpm (Corvettes), 375 at 5,600 rpm (Camaros and Chevelles)

Rectangular port cast-iron heads, high-lift solid lifter cam, high-rise aluminum intake manifold, 780-cfm Holley carb, forged pistons with an 11:1 compression ratio, four-bolt main caps, and forged steel crankshaft. Available in Corvettes, Camaros, and Chevelles through 1970. The Corvette version featured high-flow exhaust manifolds and open-element air cleaner. Like most high-performance four-bolt big-blocks of the muscle car era, the block was tapped for an oil cooler above the oil filter boss.

RPO L37: 375 gross hp at 5,600 rpm

Same as the L78 except for the change to a hydraulic lifter camshaft: rectangular port cast-iron heads, high-rise aluminum intake manifold and 780-cfm Holley carb, forged pistons with an 11:1 compression ratio, four-bolt main caps, and forged steel crankshaft. Available in Z-16 Chevelles.

RPO L89: 425 gross hp at 6,400 rpm (Corvettes), 375 at 5,600 rpm (Camaros and Chevelles)

Same as the L78 except for the change to closed chamber rectangular port aluminum heads: high-lift solid lifter cam, high-rise aluminum intake manifold, 780-cfm Holley carb, forged pistons with an 11:1 compression ratio, four-bolt main caps, and forged steel crankshaft.

RPO L66: 265 gross hp

For one year only (1969) the engine was the only big-block offered with a 2-barrel carburetor. Oval port cast-iron heads, 9:1 compression ratio, and two-bolt main caps. Available in most full-size passenger cars and wagons.

402 Engines

RPO LS3: 330 gross hp (1970), 300 gross hp (1971), 210 gross hp (1972), 240 gross hp (1972 with dual exhaust)

Similar to the L35, but with the 402's larger bore (4.125-inch), oval port cast-iron heads, Quadrajet 4-barrel carb, 10.25:1 compression ratio in 1970 only (reduced to 8.5:1 in 1971 and later), and two-bolt main caps. Available primarily in Camaros and Chevelles. New SAE engine test procedures established in 1972 resulted in lower horsepower ratings.

CHAPTER 1

RPO L34: 350 gross hp at 5,200 rpm

Same as the L34 396 engine but with the 402's larger bore (4.125-inch), oval port cast-iron heads, higher-lift hydraulic lifter cam, Quadrajet 4-barrel carb, 10.25:1 compression ratio, open-element air cleaner, and dual exhausts. Most had two-bolt main caps, though some may have been equipped with four-bolt blocks.

RPO L78: 375 gross hp at 5,600 rpm

Same as the L78 396 engine but with the 402's larger bore (4.125-inch), rectangular port cast-iron heads, high-lift solid lifter cam, high-rise aluminum intake manifold, 780-cfm Holley carb, forged pistons with an 11:1 compression ratio, four-bolt main caps, and forged steel crankshaft. Available in Camaros and Chevelles.

427 Engines

RPO LS1: 335 gross hp

This pedestrian engine came with oval port cast-iron heads, mild hydraulic lifter cam, Quadrajet 4-barrel carb, 10.25:1 compression ratio, two-bolt main caps, and cast-iron crankshaft. Available in 1969 midsize passenger cars only.

RPO L36: 390 gross hp (Corvettes), 385 gross hp (full-size cars)

Same as the L34 396 engine but with the 427's larger bore (4.250-inch) but with oval port cast-iron heads, higher-lift hydraulic lifter cam, Quadrajet 4-barrel carb, 10.25:1 compression ratio, and dual exhausts. Corvettes received the open-element air cleaner.

RPO L68: 400 gross hp

Same as the L36 427 engine but with three 2-barrel carburetors and distinctive open-element triangular air cleaner: oval port cast-iron heads, higher-lift hydraulic lifter cam, 10.25:1 compression ratio, and dual exhausts. Available in 1967 through 1969 Corvettes only.

RPO L71: 435 gross hp at 5,800 rpm

Three 2-barrel carburetors and distinctive open-element triangular air cleaner, rectangular port cast-iron heads, high-lift solid lifter cam, forged pistons with an 11:1 compression ratio, four-bolt main caps, and forged steel crankshaft. Available in Corvettes only.

RPO L72: 425 gross hp at 5,600 rpm

Same as the L71 427 engine but with high-rise aluminum intake manifold and 780-cfm Holley carb: rectangular port cast-iron heads, high-lift solid lifter cam, forged pistons with an 11:1 compression ratio, four-bolt main caps, and forged steel crankshaft. Initially rated at 450 hp in Corvettes, later dropped to 425.

RPO L89: 435 gross hp at 5,800 rpm

Same as the L71 except for the use of rectangular port aluminum cylinder heads: three 2-barrel carburetors and distinctive open-element triangular air cleaner, high-lift solid lifter cam, forged pistons with an 11:1 compression ratio, four-bolt main caps, and forged steel crankshaft. Available in Corvettes only.

RPO L88: 430 gross hp at 5,200 rpm

This legendary engine was the undisputed king of the iron-block 427s. It featured an aluminum high-rise intake manifold and Holley 830-cfm carb, aluminum rectangular port heads with closed chambers in 1967 through 1968 and open-chamber heads in 1969 only. Special high-lift solid lifter cam, 7/16-inch pushrods, 12.5:1 forged aluminum pistons, four-bolt mains and forged steel crankshaft. The conservative horsepower rating was far below the L88s true peak power level. With a set of tubular exhaust headers, they were known to make around 550 hp at 6,400 rpm! Available in 1967 through 1969 in Corvettes only.

RPO ZL-1: 430 gross hp at 5,200 rpm

Essentially an all-aluminum version of the L88, this rare engine is the crown jewel of the muscle car era. In 1969, only two were sold in Corvettes, and 69 in Camaros. It featured an aluminum high-rise intake manifold and Holley 830-cfm carb, aluminum rectangular port heads with open-chamber heads, special high-lift solid lifter cam, 7/16-inch pushrods, 12.5:1 forged aluminum pistons, four-bolt mains and forged steel crankshaft.

454 Engines

RPO LS4: 345 gross hp at 4,600 rpm (full-size cars), 275 net hp at 4,400 (1973 Corvettes), 270 net hp (1974 Corvettes), 245 net hp at 4,000 (full-size cars)

Oval port cast-iron heads, Quadrajet 4-barrel carb, mild hydraulic lifter cam, two-bolt main caps, cast-iron crankshaft. Available in most full-size passenger cars, it was the last big-block offered in Corvettes in 1974.

RPO LS5: 390 gross hp (1970 Corvettes), 360 gross hp (1970 Chevelles and Monte Carlos), 365 gross hp and 285 net hp (1971), 270 net (1972–on)

Oval port cast-iron heads, Quadrajet 4-barrel carb, low-restriction air cleaner, high-lift hydraulic lifter cam, 8.5:1 compression ratio, two-bolt main caps, cast-iron crankshaft, dual exhaust. Corvettes and full-size cars used larger free-flowing exhaust manifolds.

RPO LS6: 460 gross hp (1970 Corvettes), 450 gross hp (1970 Chevelle SS), 425 gross hp (1971)

It featured an aluminum low-rise intake manifold and Holley 780-cfm carb, rectangular port heads with closed chambers in 1970 (11:1 compression ratio) and open chamber heads in 1971 (9:1 compression). High-lift solid lifter cam, forged aluminum pistons, four-bolt mains, and forged steel crankshaft.

RPO LS7: 465 gross hp

This bad boy of the muscle car big-blocks was supposed to be an over-the-counter off-road engine only, but it's rumored that some made it into production cars. It was basically a stroked version of the mighty L88 and featured an aluminum high-rise intake manifold and Holley 830-cfm carb, aluminum rectangular port heads with open-chamber heads, special "off-road" high-lift solid lifter cam, 7/16-inch pushrods, 12.5:1 forged aluminum pistons, four-bolt mains and 5140 forged steel crankshaft.

RPO LE8: 240 net hp (trucks only)

Small oval ("peanut") port cast-iron heads, Quadrajet 4-barrel carb, mild hydraulic lifter cam, two- or four-bolt main caps, cast-iron crankshaft. Available in trucks only through 1986 and some heavy trucks through 1989.

RPO L19: 230 net hp (trucks only)

This engine superseded the LE8 when General Motors switched from carburetors to computer-controlled 2-barrel TBI (throttle body injection) in 1987. Small oval ("peanut") port cast-iron heads, mild hydraulic lifter cam, two- or four-bolt main caps, cast-iron crankshaft. Available in trucks only from 1987 to 1990, this was the last production Mark IV engine.

7.4 Liter Gen V (454 ci)
RPO L19: 230 net hp (trucks only)

Even though General Motors switched to the newly designated Gen V block, heads, and crankshaft in 1991, this workhorse retained the same RPO number as its predecessor: small oval ("peanut") port cast-iron heads, TBI, mild hydraulic lifter cam, four-bolt main caps, cast-iron crankshaft. Available in trucks only from 1991 to 1995.

7.4 Liter Gen VI (454 ci)
RPO L19/L29: 290 net hp at 4,000 rpm (trucks only)

The Vortec 7400 featured more refinements including the use of MPFI (multi-point fuel injection) and hydraulic roller lifters: small oval ("peanut") port cast-iron heads, four-bolt main caps, cast-iron crankshaft. Available in trucks only from 1996 to 2000.

RPO L21: 265 or 270 net hp at 3,200 rpm (commercial trucks only)

Sometimes referred to as the Vortec 7400MD, this engine is similar to the L29, but with the addition of forged pistons and crankshaft, and a different PCM (powertrain control module) for use with the early Allison 4-speed automatic or manual transmissions: MPFI, hydraulic roller lifters, small oval ("peanut") port cast-iron heads, and four-bolt main caps. Available in 1998–2001 Medium Duty truck platforms, Workhorse Custom Chassis, and Kodiak/Topkick series.

8.1 Liter Gen VII (496 ci)
RPO L18: 225-340 net hp (trucks only)

The last production big-block is an entirely different animal than its predecessors, featuring symmetrical port cylinder heads with a unique 18-bolt pattern, tall-deck block, distributorless coil-near-plug ignition, newly designed MPFI, hydraulic roller lifters, and the same bore as the 7.4 (4.25-inch) but with an increase in stroke to 4.37 inches. Even the firing order was changed to 1-8-7-2-6-5-4-3. Available in trucks only from 2001 to 2006.

General Motors Performance Parts Crate Engines

While technically not RPO engines, GMPP offers over-the-counter big-block crate engines for everything from a pedestrian work truck to a race-only dragstrip warrior. Although the point of this book is to help you build your own Rat motor, you may find it to be a better use of your time and resources to buy the engine you desire as a crate engine if one of these options is exactly what you're after.

The LS5 454 featured cast-iron oval port cylinder heads, a low-restriction air cleaner, high-lift hydraulic lifter camshaft, and dual exhaust to generate 360 factory-rated horsepower.

The Vortec 8100 marine engine is a high-performance version of the L18 that produces 392 hp and 503 ft-lbs of torque. (Photo Courtesy GM)

CHAPTER 1

The Gen VI GMPP 502-ci crate engine slides right into this early Camaro, just like the 396 that was there. A high-flow K&N air cleaner ensures deep breathing, but the 4-inch-tall filter element requires a cowl induction hood for clearance.

Another possibility is to buy one of these GMPP motors from a previous owner. If you're lucky enough to find a used one of these crate engines, they make an excellent starting point for a high-performance rebuild. Most contain heavy-duty components such as a forged crankshaft and rods that are well suited for performance or competition applications. An ideal situation is to find a worn-out 502 HO (PN 12568778), originally rated at 450 hp at 5,250 rpm. A set of .030-inch-over forged pistons and file-fit rings, plus a new hydraulic or mechanical roller cam matched to your application, and you could conceivably be looking at 550 to 600 hp for less than the cost of buying all-new hardware. The possibilities are endless.

A high-energy ignition (HEI) distributor (PN 93440806) with melonized steel gear or aftermarket equivalent must be used with every steel-core roller camshaft used in these engines, or engine damage occurs. Melonized distributor gear (PN 10456413) may be used with standard HEI distributors, if desired.

ZZ427/480 (PN 19166393): 480 hp at 5,800 rpm

Offered as a contemporary replacement for the legendary L88, this new version features an iron-block (PN 19170538) forged steel crankshaft, and high-flow aluminum cylinder heads. Gen VI upgrades include a one-piece rear main seal and hydraulic roller lifter camshaft (0.527-inch intake/0.544-inch exhaust, 224/234-degree duration at .050 inch) for better street manners and a greater rev range. The forged aluminum pistons yield a compression ratio of 10.1:1 for use with premium unleaded gasoline, and the crank and rods are forged steel. It features 4.250-inch bores and a 3.750-inch-stroke crankshaft with a one-piece rear main seal. Aluminum high-flow oval port cylinder heads (PN 19211799) have 2.19-inch intake and 1.88-inch exhaust valves, and the aluminum intake manifold is topped with an 870-cfm Holley carburetor. Includes an aluminum water pump, HEI distributor, SFI (SEMA Foundation, Inc.) approved balancer, spark plug wires, and a 14-inch flexplate.

Anniversary Edition 427 (PN 19166392): 430 hp at 5,800 rpm

Just as the original ZL1 in the late 1960s was essentially an L88 with an aluminum engine block, this Anniversary Edition 427 is the same as the ZZ427/480 except for the Gen VI-style aluminum block (PN 88958696). The conservative power rating of only 430 hp is a nod to the original ZL1's modest 430-hp rating designed to avoid the scrutiny of insurance companies and racing associations. This limited-edition engine series includes serialized cast aluminum valve covers. Note that GMPP also sells a replacement Mark IV-style ZL1 aluminum block with traditional two-piece rear main seal, under PN 12370850. These aluminum-block Rat motors weigh about 100 pounds less than their iron-block brethren.

454 HO (PN 12568774): 425 hp at 5,250 rpm

The 454 HO features a cast-iron Gen VI-style block (PN 19170538) and rectangular port cylinder heads (PN 12562920) with 118-cc chambers, plus a hydraulic roller lifter camshaft (0.510-inch intake/0.540-inch exhaust, 211/230-degree duration at .050 inch). Forged aluminum 8.75:1 pistons are compatible with 92-octane pump gas and the crank and rods are forged steel. Sold without carburetor, ignition, or starter.

ZZ454/440 HO (PN 12498777): 440 hp at 5,250 rpm

Same short block as the 454 HO, topped with aluminum oval port heads (PN 12363392) with 110-cc combustion chambers. Compression ratio is raised to 9.6:1 due to the smaller chambers.

HT502 (PN 88890534): 377 hp at 4,500 rpm

The High Torque 502 (512 ft-lbs at 3,300 rpm) uses a Gen VI–type siamesed-bore (4.470-inch bore) cast-iron block

Anniversary Edition 427 (PN 19166392). (Photo Courtesy GMPP)

THE FAMILY TREE

Big-Block Chevy Engine Size Chart

The chart below is a quick reference to most commonly built engine sizes. Engine sizes listed are in cubic inches, rounded off to the nearest tenth. Note that the factory engineers always rounded up to the next whole number; for instance, a bore of 4.250 inch and a stroke of 3.76 inch was designated as the 427, even though the calculated size is 426.7. This can be important if you are racing in a class based on claimed engine size. If you say the engine displaces 520 ci, and the measured size calculates to 520.1, well, now the tech guy has you over a barrel. To a tech inspector, slightly exceeding your claimed size is like being a little pregnant. Just call it a 521 and save yourself some grief.

There are two short-stroke cranks listed mainly for comparative purposes, the very rare Can Am crank (3.47-inch stroke), and a nominal Pro Stock crank with 3.6-inch stroke. Remember, for most street- and sportsman-level racing engines, bigger is better, and you are generally best advised to build the largest-displacement big-block you can afford. Here's the bottom line: you can see at a glance that it's possible to build a 500-plus-ci big-block using an OEM (original equipment manufacturer) block, an almost-600-ci block using an aftermarket so-called clone block that accepts most stock-spec parts, and a block of nearly 700 cubes (or more!) with exotic so-called mutant blocks. Let the fun begin.

		Stroke						these cranks must be used with raised cam & widened pan rail blocks		
		3.470-inch rare Can Am	3.600-inch typ. Pro Stock	3.760-inch OEM 396 & 427	4.000-inch OEM 454 (7.4L)	4.250-inch stroker	4.375-inch stroker	4.500-inch stroker	4.750-inch stroker	5.000-inch stroker
	Bore							these engine sizes are not possible with OEM engine blocks		
	4.094-inch (OEM 396)	365.4	379.1	395.9*	421.2	447.6	460.7	473.9	500.2	526.5
	4.125-inch (OEM 402)	370.9	384.8	401.9*	427.6	454.3	467.7	481.1	507.8	534.5
	4.250-inch (OEM 427 & 454)	393.8	408.5	426.7*	453.9*	482.3	496.5	510.7	539.1	567.4
	4.280-inch (+ .030-inch)	399.4	414.3	432.8	460.4	489.2	503.6	517.9	546.7	575.5
	4.310-inch (+ .060-inch)	405.0	420.2	438.8	466.8	496.0	510.6	525.2	554.4	583.6
max bore with OEM 454 blocks	4.350-inch (+ .100-inch)	412.6	428.0	447.0	475.6	505.3	520.1	535.0	564.7	594.5
	4.375-inch (+ .125-inch)	417.3	432.9	452.2	481.0	511.1	526.1	541.2	571.2	601.3
	4.440-inch (rare Can Am block)	429.8*	445.9	465.7	495.4	526.4	541.9	557.3	588.3	619.3
	4.466-inch (OEM 502, not Bowtie)	434.8	451.1	471.2	501.2*	532.6	548.2	563.9	595.2	626.6
Bowtie and aftermarket blocks	4.500-inch	441.5	458.0	478.4	508.9*	540.7	556.6	572.5	604.3	636.1
	4.530-inch	447.4	464.1	484.8	515.7	547.9	564.1	580.2	612.4	644.6
	4.560-inch	453.3	470.3	491.2	522.6	555.2	571.6*	587.9	620.5	653.2
	4.600-inch	461.3	478.6	499.9	531.8	565.0	581.6	598.2	631.5	664.7
	4.625-inch (max recommended bore for most aftermarket blocks)	466.3	483.8	505.3	537.6	571.2	588.0	604.8	638.4	672.0
	4.700-inch (4.9-inch and larger spread-bore blocks)	481.6	499.6	521.8	555.1	589.9	607.2	624.5	659.2	693.9

* OEM or GM Performance Parts engine sizes

CHAPTER 1

ZZ502/502 Deluxe Engine (PN 19201332). (Photo Courtesy GMPP)

(PN 19170540) and forged 4.000-inch-stroke crankshaft combined with production small oval ("peanut") port cylinder heads to boost low-RPM power, making it ideal for tow trucks and RVs. Forged steel connecting rods and forged aluminum 8.75:1 pistons provide strength under tough operating conditions, and the modest hydraulic roller lifter camshaft (0.510-inch intake/0.540-inch exhaust, 211/230-degree duration at .050 inch) makes this a great "grunt and go" replacement for 1975-and-earlier Rat motored trucks. Sold without water pump, intake manifold, carburetor, ignition, or starter.

502 HO (PN 12568778): 450 hp at 5,250 rpm

The 502 High Output features a siamesed-bore (4.470-inch bore) cast-iron Gen VI–style block (PN 19170540) and rectangular port cast-iron cylinder heads (PN 12562920) with 118-cc chambers, plus a hydraulic roller lifter camshaft (0.510-inch intake/0.540-inch exhaust, 211/230-degree duration at .050 inch). The bottom-end features a forged 4.000-inch-stroke crankshaft, forged and shot-peened steel connecting rods, and forged 8.75:1 aluminum pistons compatible with 92-octane pump gas. Sold without carburetor, ignition, on starter. Note: Distributor PN 93440806 with melonized steel gear must be used with steel camshafts, or engine damage occurs.

ZZ502/502 Base Engine (PN 12496963): 502 hp at 5,200 rpm

Same short block as the 502 HO, topped with aluminum oval port heads (PN 12363390) with 110-cc combustion chambers. Compression ratio is 9.6:1 due to the smaller chambers.

ZZ502/502 Deluxe Engine (PN 19201332): 502 hp at 5,200 rpm

Same engine as the ZZ502 Base but complete from the oil pan to the carburetor. Includes an HEI distributor, plug wires, starter, water pump, balancer, and an aluminum intake topped with a 4-barrel Holley 870-cfm. Note that the included distributor (PN 93440806) comes with a melonized gear that is compatible with all steel roller camshafts.

Ram Jet 502 (PN 12499121): 502 hp at 5,100 rpm

Same engine as the ZZ502 but includes a GMPP two-piece multi-point EFI manifold/plenum assembly (PN 12499249), eight injectors, a throttle body, and an updated MEFI 4 controller for a plug-and-play installation. This impressive-looking tunnel-ram-style intake stands 11 inches tall, so hood clearance must be taken into consideration. You were looking for an excuse to put a scoop on your hood anyway, right?

Ram Jet 502 (PN 12499121). (Photo Courtesy GMPP)

ZZ572/620 Deluxe (PN 19201333): 620 hp at 5,500 rpm

The ZZ572/620 represents the General's biggest, baddest crate engine designed for street use. It is based on a tall-deck siamesed-bore Bowtie block (PN 19212195) with a bore of 4.560 inches and an internally balanced 4.375-inch-stroke forged steel crankshaft with a one-piece rear main seal. Forged aluminum pistons swing from 4340 steel H-beam connecting rods that are .400 inch longer than stock. High-flow rectangular port aluminum cylinder heads (PN 12499255) feature 2.250-inch intake valves and 1.880-inch exhaust valves to feed this hungry Rat, and 118-cc chambers produce a pump-gas-friendly 9.6:1 compression ratio. The hydraulic roller lifter camshaft features impressive 0.632-inch intake/0.632-inch exhaust lift at the valve with 254/264-degree duration at .050 inch, and aluminum roller rocker arms provide strength with no possibility of rocker stud binding. Comes complete with 850-cfm Holley carburetor, aluminum water pump, HEI distributor with melonized gear, spark plugs and wires, and 14-inch flexplate for use with automatic transmissions. Starter and fuel pump not included.

THE FAMILY TREE

ZZ572/720R Deluxe Engine (PN 19201334). (Photo Courtesy GMPP)

ZZ572/720R Deluxe (PN 19201334): 720 hp at 6,250 rpm

Make no mistake, the "R" in ZZ572/720R stands for race. This serious track-only Rat motor is the same as the ZZ572/620 street engine except for a mechanical roller lifter camshaft (0.714-inch intake/0.714-inch exhaust lift at the valve with 278/282-degree duration at .050 inch), and 12:1 compression pistons requiring a minimum of 110-octane race gas. A 1,090-cfm Holley Dominator series carburetor feeds the beast, and rectangular port aluminum cylinder heads (PN 88961160) are assembled with high-pressure valvesprings compatible with mechanical roller lifter cams only. Requires starter and fuel pump.

Big-Block Chevrolet General Specifications

The following specifications apply to production and GMPP crate engines.

Engine type: 90-degree V-8, single camshaft, pushrod-activated overhead valves (two per cylinder)
Displacement: 366, 396, 402, 427, 454 ci (production); 502, 572 ci (over-the-counter GMPP crate engines)
Years of production: 1965 to 1989 (Mark IV), 1990 to 1995 (Gen V), 1996 to 2000 (Gen VI)
Firing order: 1-8-4-3-6-5-7-2
Cylinder numbering front to rear: 1-3-5-7 left (driver's side), 2-4-6-8 right (passenger's side)
Induction system: single 4-barrel (1965 to 1986) or three 2-barrel (1967 to 1969 only), Throttle Body Injection (1987 to 1995), Multi-Point Fuel Injection (1996 to 2000)
Engine block material: cast iron (most), aluminum (ultra-high-performance)
Cylinder head material: cast iron (most), aluminum (high-performance)
Weight: approximately 590 pounds (iron block and heads), 522 pounds (iron block and aluminum heads) without starter, carburetor, or accessories
Deck height from crankshaft centerline to cylinder head surface: 9.800 inches (passenger cars), 10.200 inches (heavy-duty trucks, marine, and 572-ci GMPP crate engine)
Bore spacing (center-to-center): 4.840 inches
Bore size: 3.935 inches (366 ci), 4.094 inches (396 ci), 4.125 inches (402 ci), 4.250 inches (427 ci and 454 ci), 4.466 inches (502 ci), and 4.560 inches (572 ci)
Piston: Three-ring cast aluminum, hypereutectic aluminum, or forged aluminum (high-performance)
Crankshaft material: cast iron or forged steel (heavy-duty and high-performance)
Crankshaft stroke: 3.760 inches (366, 396, 402, and 427 ci), 4.000 inches (454 and 502 ci), 4.375 inches (572 ci)
Crankshaft main journal diameter: 2.750 inches
Crankshaft rod journal diameter: 2.200 inches
Main bore in block: 2.937 to 2.938 inches
Main cap attachment: two- or four-bolt (1965 to 1989), four-bolt (1990 to 2000)
Connecting rods: forged steel, 6.135 inches center-to-center, .9885-inch pin bore, 2.3247 to 2.3252-inch big-end bore
Cam bore in block: 2.140 inches (number-1), 2.130 inches (number-2, number-5), 2.120 inches (number-3, number-4)
Camshaft journal diameter: 1.948 inches
Crank-to-cam centerline: 5.152 inches
Camshaft drive: crank and cam sprockets with steel-link or double roller timing chain (1965 to 1989), single roller timing chain (1990 to 2007)
Lifters: .843-inch diameter, self-adjusting hydraulic or mechanical flat-tappet (1965 to 1974), hydraulic flat-tappet (1975 to 1995), hydraulic roller lifter (1996 to 2007)
Rocker arm ratio: 1.7:1
Distributor: rear mounted, camshaft driven, ignition points (1965 to 1974), HEI (1975 to 1987), computerized (1988 to 2007)
Lubrication system: wet sump, cam-driven spur-gear oil pump with five-bolt cover

CHAPTER 2

CYLINDER BLOCKS

These big chunks of iron or aluminum are indeed the building blocks upon which your entire engine is crafted. Like a raw canvas or flawless piece of marble awaiting the master's touch, the block is only as good as the casting itself.

Oil passages, lifter bores, and dozens of bolt-hole locations all factor into what makes a good block for a true high-performance or racing big-block Chevy. Most of these machining operations have been handled at the factory, and more often than not, they are going to be right on the money. When it comes time to select your block, you want to start with the right casting for your projected power level, and then find the best machine shop to bring everything to spec.

Block Selection

The first decision you need to make when it comes to selecting a block for your bruiser is whether to start with a factory production or aftermarket block. For the vast majority of people, the decision is an easy one: you plan to use a stock block, whether it's one you already own or plan to purchase at the right price. There's nothing really wrong with a stock block engine. It's just that the beefier aftermarket or Bowtie blocks have advanced features (such as siamesed bores that can safely be bored to 4.600 inches or more) that contribute to greater power potential.

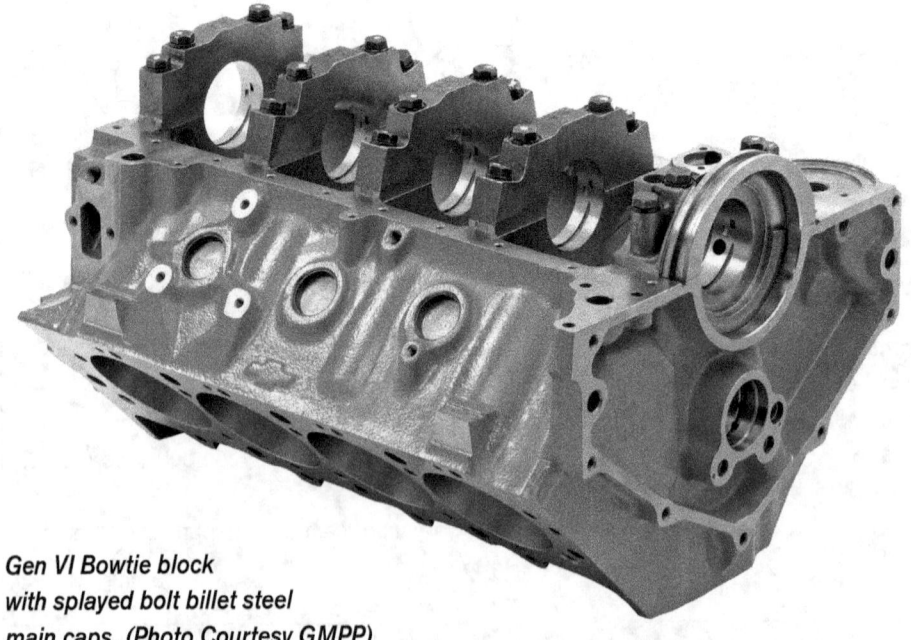

Gen VI Bowtie block with splayed bolt billet steel main caps. (Photo Courtesy GMPP)

This cutaway of a Merlin III block shows the beefy cylinder walls made possible with siamesed bores. This allows much larger bore sizes than stock 454 blocks and the thick cylinder walls promote better ring seal. Also note the additional head-bolt bosses in the lifter valley, which give extra clamping power for a better head gasket seal. (Photo Courtesy World Products)

CYLINDER BLOCKS

Here are the basics: if you plan to produce up to 650 hp (normally aspirated or "all motor" as the sport compact guys say) on the street or 750 hp on race gas, you can definitely get there with a stock-block four-bolt main engine. I limit power levels to 600 hp with a two-bolt main block. For higher power requirements, the aftermarket blocks start to look a lot better.

Let's look at some examples: say your target power level is 750 hp. You can get there with a stock block 467-ci engine (4.250-inch bore plus .060-inch overbore, and 4.000-inch-stroke crank), but to produce 1.602 hp per cubic inch may require better flowing CNC-ported cylinder heads, a larger camshaft, a full kickout oil pan and matching pump, and other such tricks to produce the power needed. And, you probably have to spin the engine up to about 8,000 rpm, which puts additional wear and stress on all components, especially the valvetrain.

But a 565-ci engine (4.600-inch bore x 4.250-inch stroke) only needs to make 1.327 hp per cubic inch. And you can easily get there by using less expensive heads and a typical high-performance oiling system. You make the power at a lower RPM, which eases wear and tear and takes less of a toll on the valvetrain. And the real kicker is how, when you decide to "step it up" to the next class, bracket, or you just want to go faster, the same parts you needed just to qualify with a 467 really wake up that 565.

Maximum Bore Sizes

When overboring your block, the best way to determine the maximum safe bore size is to use a sonic wall thickness tester, a very expensive piece of equipment that most high-end machine shops will have on hand. The minimum safe wall thickness is .200 inch, but you are better off with a slightly smaller bore (and thus thicker cylinder walls) if the engine will be used on the street or for endurance racing applications such as off-shore boat racing. Most production blocks will easily accommodate overbores of .030-inch or .060-inch as long as there is no evidence of extreme core shift. The best indicator of core shift during the casting process is to look at the lifter bore bosses: the lifter bores should be well centered in their bosses. If there is no visible core shift in the lifter bosses, many 454-based engines are bored to +.100-inch (yielding a bore size of 4.350 inches), and some brave souls have gone as far as +.125-inch, although that is usually best left to drag-race-only applications using some form of block filler in the water jackets to support the resulting thin cylinder walls.

502 engine blocks (8.2 cast on sides of block) will safely tolerate a 4.500-inch bore, which is only .034-inch over their 4.466-inch bore size as produced. The cylinder wall thickness of Bowtie and aftermarket blocks with siamesed bores has varied considerably over the years, but most can safely tolerate bores to 4.600 inches and some are rated up to 4.625 inches. For the amount of money being invested in an engine of that nature, you are best advised to have the cylinder walls sonically checked and hold to the minimum wall thickness of .200 inch.

Stock Blocks

When I refer to stock blocks, I'm talking about original-equipment cylinder blocks found in cars or trucks, as opposed to the Bowtie blocks, which, even though they are "Genuine GM Parts," were never available in a production vehicle. Always inspect a used engine for damage that is unrepairable, like cracks or excessive overboring, as well as flaws that can be fixed at additional expense, like stripped bolt-holes, main bore misalignment, and uneven deck surfaces.

All stock blocks are cast iron except the rare ZL-1 aluminum block, which saw limited production in 1969. It's a pretty safe bet that all of these jewels are well accounted for, and your chances of

Aftermarket blocks, like this Dart Big M cast-iron block, may cost more than stock blocks initially but can save you money in the long run as you search for more horsepower.

Original ZL-1 aluminum blocks are scarce as hen's teeth, but you can buy a brand-new version from GMPP (PN 12370850) with the Mark IV–style two-piece rear main seal. PN 88958696 comes with the Gen V/VI–style one-piece rear main seal. (Photo Courtesy GMPP)

CHAPTER 2

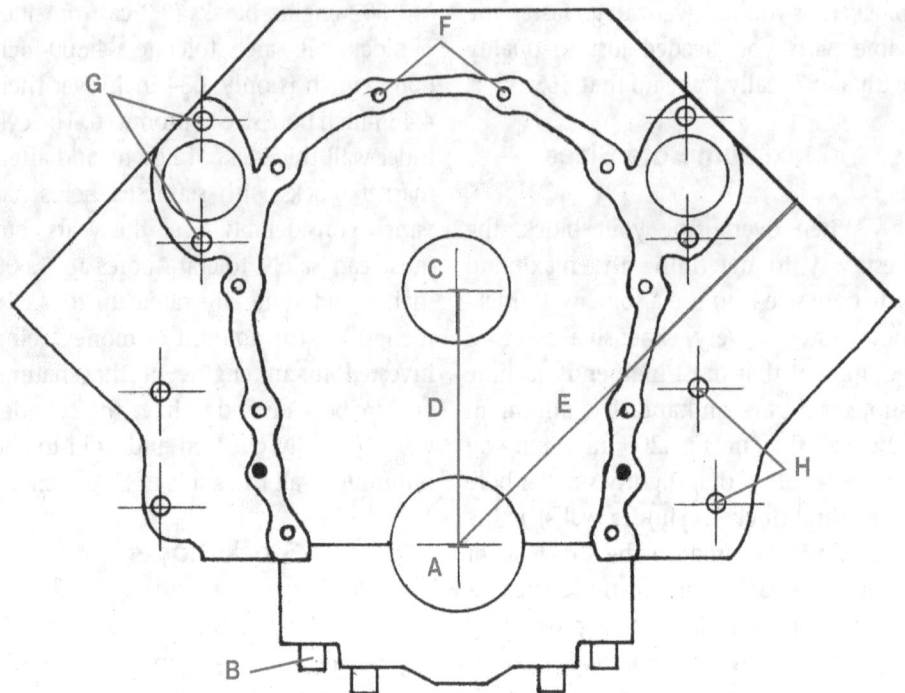

Here are the specifications of the front of the block:

A. Main Bore: 2.937 to 2.938 inches
B. Main Caps: (five) two- or four-bolt, 7/16-14 bolt holes
C. Cam Bore: 2.140 inches (number-1), 2.130 inches (number-2 and number-5), 2.120 inches (number-3 and number-4); cam bearing inside diameter: 1.950 inches
D. Crankshaft-to-Camshaft Centerline: 5.152 inches
E. Deck Height: 9.800 inches (standard), 10.200 inches (tall-deck Marine, Truck, and some High Performance)
F. Timing Cover Rail: ten 1/4-20 bolt-holes (Mark IV, Gen V), two .250-inch alignment dowels
G. Water Pump Pads: 3/8-16 bolt-holes, two each side
H. Accessory/Motor Mount Pads: 7/16-14 bolt-holes, two each side

stumbling across one in some salvage yard are fairly slim.

Mark IV Blocks

Stock blocks produced from 1965 to 1990 are the original Mark IV design, and were available with either two- or four-bolt main caps, and in three bore sizes (four, if you count the 366T tall-deck truck blocks with their miniscule 3.935-inch bores, but I'm not counting them because they are totally unsuitable for any performance big-block buildup). The 396 had a bore of 4.094 inches, the 402 was slightly larger at 4.125 inches, and 427s and 454s share a 4.250-inch bore. All else being equal, there is no reason to start with any stock block other than the larger 4.250-inch-bore blocks.

Very early Mark IV blocks had a couple of peculiarities you should be aware of. First, 1965 and 1966 blocks used a grooved rear cam bearing with a matching groove in the rear camshaft journal. This groove was designed to supply oil to the lifters, and if a non-grooved bearing or cam is used, there is no oil supply to the passenger-side lifters—this is not good. Second, all Mark IVs through 1967 used the 1950s-era oil canister with an oil filter cartridge inside. The 1968-and-later engines got the traditional spin-on oil filters that we all enjoy changing to this day.

Muscle-car era Mark IV blocks with four-bolt mains were drilled and tapped for oil cooler fittings just above the oil filter mount. Note the 1/8-inch NPT pipe plugs just above the oil pan rail. These are where the main oil gallery was cross-drilled to feed the main bearings.

Standard big-block deck height is 9.800 inches from the crank centerline to the deck surface, and tall-deck blocks like this one measure 10.200 inches. You can easily spot a tall-deck block by looking at the distance from the top water pump bolt-hole to the deck surface. With a standard-height block, the top of the water pump is nearly even with the deck, but a tall-deck block has .400 inch more material, about the same amount as the diameter of the 3/8-16 bolt-hole. Also, most tall-deck Mark IV blocks have a 1/8-inch NPT oil gallery tap in front of the manifold end rail, as shown here.

HOW TO BUILD KILLER BIG-BLOCK CHEVY ENGINES

Gen V and Gen VI Blocks

In 1991, General Motors changed several important design features of the Mark IV big-block with the introduction of the Gen V engine, most notably the addition of a one-piece rear main oil seal, and different coolant core passages in the deck surface of the block and heads. Gen V and Gen VI blocks are easy to spot in the wrecking yard; they all have a revised front core that features a distinctive continuous machined boss for the front cover, water pump, and front accessory mounting bosses, giving the appearance of having a frame around the front timing cover. All production engines were fuel injected by this time, so the mechanical fuel pump boss was also eliminated. Most of us "old timers" initially viewed this version of the big-block as something of a disappointment. The supply of good crankshafts, oil pans, and cylinder heads would no longer fit, which limited its performance potential.

Those performance challenges were addressed by a responsive aftermarket parts industry, and soon we had a choice of high-performance cylinder heads designed to work with either Mark IV or Gen V deck surfaces (with the appropriate head gasket for the block being used), two-piece seal adapters allowing the use of traditional Mark IV crankshafts, and performance oil pans designed for the wider rear main cap with its one-piece seal on the Gen V block.

With this kind of parts availability, there's no reason not to consider a Gen V or Gen VI block as a good starting point for your project engine, with a few caveats. For one thing, production-line Gen V blocks have no provision for mechanical fuel pumps or traditional clutch linkage. These obstacles can be overcome by using an electric fuel pump and hydraulic clutch linkage, but you have to factor in these additional expenses and see how they compare to simply buying a block that has the features you need in the first place. Also, consider the limited cylinder head availability for the Gen V deck surface. There were very few factory performance heads made for this engine family, and these were mostly for the over-the-counter 502 HO engine. The production Gen V heads were all low-performance "peanut" port heads designed to produce good low-end grunt for the truck applications these engines were used in.

There is a good assortment of aftermarket cylinder heads, both cast iron and aluminum, that work on the Gen V, but you have to factor in the additional cost of these premium parts. One often overlooked difference between the Mark IV and Gen V engines is that the taller rear main cap bolts required for the Gen V's one-piece rear main seal interferes with the original Mark IV oil pump. Gen V and Gen VI engines require matching oil pumps, along with a heavy-duty oil pump driveshaft like GM PN 3865886. On the plus side, all Gen V and Gen VI blocks were fitted with four-bolt main caps.

In 1996, the Gen VI was introduced with additional changes. Probably the easiest feature to spot when trolling for blocks at the salvage yard is the six-bolt

All Gen V and Gen VI blocks came with four-bolt main caps, like this Gen VI 502 block. Gen V/VI main caps are about .200 inch taller than Mark IV caps, and require different bolts or studs. This block has been drilled and tapped to accept a standard 10-bolt front cover; stock timing cover had six bolts.

OEM Block Features at a Glance

Features:	Mark IV	Gen V	Gen VI
Main Caps	2-bolt or 4-bolt	4-bolt	4-bolt
Rear Main Seal	2-piece	1-piece	1-piece
Freeze Plugs	1¾-inch	1⅝-inch	1⅝-inch
Timing Cover	10-bolt	10-bolt	6-bolt
Main Oil Gallery Passage	side-oiler	priority main	priority main
Cam Thrust Plate Bolt Pattern	horizontal	vertical	vertical
Lifters	solid or hydraulic flat tappet	hydraulic flat tappet	hydraulic roller (most)
Mechanical Fuel Pump Boss	yes	no	yes
Clutch Pivot Stud Boss	yes	no	yes
Oil Filter Boss to Pan Rail	recessed 7/8-inch	1/8-inch step	1/8-inch step

composite or aluminum front timing cover. Both the Mark IV and the Gen V used stamped steel front covers with 10 bolt holes. If the cover is missing, just look for the six-bolt pattern, compared to the 10-bolt pattern used on all Mark IV-style engines, including Bowtie and aftermarket blocks. Gen VI blocks also benefit from the reintroduction of the mechanical fuel pump boss and clutch pivot stud boss.

Production Gen VI blocks still have the large water passage and core holes in the deck surface, again requiring the use of Gen V or Gen VI cylinder heads or aftermarket heads designed to fit either the Mark IV or Gen V/VI blocks. Other refinements to the Gen VI include bosses in the lifter valley for the factory hydraulic roller lifter retainer, commonly called a "spider," although not all Gen VI blocks have this feature. This can be important if your plans call for the use of a hydraulic roller lifter camshaft, because the cost of the lifters is quite a bit more than the cost of the camshaft. If your core engine includes the original GM roller lifters, they may be reused (unlike conventional flat-tappet lifters) as long as they are in good condition, although the stock lifter and guide arrangement is limited to valve lifts of around .600 inch.

If your block does not have the factory roller lifter alignment bosses, there are aftermarket roller lifters available with self-aligning tie bars so you can still use a hydraulic or mechanical roller cam. If you use tie-bar roller lifters, the taller lifter bores require roller lifters that are .300-inch taller than Mark IV lifters, and they are readily available from most cam companies.

Gen V and Gen VI blocks feature a priority main oil gallery that runs parallel to the lifter-supply oil passage on the left (driver's) side of the block. This feature has two advantages: first, oil from the oil pump goes directly to the main bearings (after being filtered, of course) then on to the lifters and cam bearings; and second, relocating the oil gallery from the driver's-side oil pan rail (Mark IV location) means there is no chance of breaking into this passage when grinding the block for additional connecting rod clearance, or when fitting the block with splayed-bolt main bearing caps. This feature has proven to be so popular that it is now standard on most aftermarket cylinder blocks, as well as Gen V/VI blocks.

There is one more OEM block that was found in the last production big-block engines used in trucks from 2001 to 2006, and that is the 8.1L (496 ci). While General Motors is nearly mute about this engine, you could call it the Gen VII big-block, because it has substantial differences from all other big-blocks. It uses entirely different symmetrical-port cylinder heads, which are bolted to the block with 18 head bolts instead of the usual 16 found on Mark IV and Gen V/VI production blocks. And no, the 18-bolt pattern is not the same as the Bowtie or aftermarket 18-bolt pattern, both of which use two additional bosses in the lifter valley. This engine, designated the "Vortec 8100" or RPO L18, has a tall-deck block with a 4.25-inch bore and a cast crankshaft with a 4.37-inch stroke. It is fully computer-controlled, and features a distributorless coil-near-plug ignition system and multi-point electronic fuel injection (EFI). It relies upon crankshaft and camshaft position sensors, and has redesigned water pump and coolant passages.

In short, it is a unique animal in the big-block jungle, and very few other big-block performance parts fit. It does have both early- and late-model-style motor mount bosses, meaning it bolts into any engine compartment originally designed for the big-block, but its tall-deck design and different accessory mounting locations likely require some surgery with a cutting torch. There are aftermarket sources for powertrain control modules, if you really want to tackle something

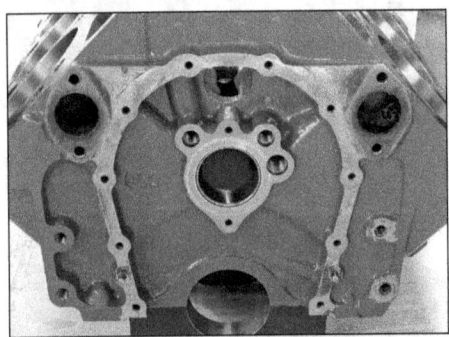

Gen V and Gen VI blocks feature a priority main oil gallery that runs parallel to the lifter supply oil passage on the left of the block. It is the larger hole at the 3 o'clock position next to the cam bore. The two lifter oil galleries are above the cam bore at the 10 and 2 o'clock positions.

Gen V/VI blocks have an abbreviated oil filter mounting pad with a 1-inch-wide reinforcing rib. The filter sealing surface is nearly flush with the oil pan rail, while it is recessed by 7/8 inch on Mark IV blocks.

502 blocks can easily be identified by the "8.2" designation cast into the side of the block. They feature siamesed cylinder barrels and the finished bore size is 4.466 inches. They can safely be bored to 4.500.

different in the world of big-block engine swaps. The block is readily identifiable by the "8.1" designation cast into the sides of the block.

Another block of considerable interest to hot rodders is the 502, sometimes referred to as the 8.2 liter, which is easily identified by the large "8.2" designation cast in the sides of the block. The 502 was never installed in production vehicles, though many were used by the marine industry, especially Mercury Marine. It features siamesed cylinder barrels and a finished bore size of 4.466 inches. They can safely be bored to 4.500 inches, which, even with the stock 454/502's 4-inch-stroke crank, yields a displacement of 509 ci. Drop in a 4.250-inch-stroke crank, and you're looking at 540 cubes (actually 540.7, but everyone calls them 540s). This makes the 502-ci block an ideal start for a moderately high horsepower street, marine, or drag race engine, but remember that it is basically a production-line block and does not tolerate large overbores. It is not the same casting as the factory-produced high-performance Bowtie blocks. These blocks are available from GMPP (PN 19170540).

General Motors Performance Parts Blocks

While never installed in production vehicles, General Motors Performance Parts (GMPP) offers several replacement four-bolt main blocks suitable for performance applications. PN 19170538 is a non-siamesed-bore block with a 4.250-inch bore that is a hybrid of the original Mark IV and the newer Gen V/VI designs. Because it is a production-based block, bore size should be limited to 4.310 inches. Like all Gen V/VI blocks, it has a one-piece rear main seal and must be used with a Gen V/VI crankshaft or adapted to the older two-piece rear main seal for use with Mark IV cranks. It is machined for the Gen VI 6-bolt front cover, but there is adequate material to drill and tap the block for use with traditional 10-bolt covers, if desired.

This block features traditional Mark IV features such as a machined fuel pump pad, clutch pivot stud bosses, and deck coolant passages that have been designed to seal properly with either Mark IV or Gen V/VI cylinder heads. It incorporates many of the Gen VI block's desirable features such as provisions for hydraulic roller lifters, redesigned priority main oil passages, and the standard Gen VI oil filter mount with oil cooler fittings in the pan rail surface. This block is used in the ZZ427, the 454 HO, and the ZZ454 crate engines offered by GMPP.

PN 19170540 shares the same traits as the PN 19170538 block, but has siamesed 4.466-inch bores that may be increased to a maximum bore size of 4.500 inches. This is the block that General Motors uses for all of its 502-ci crate engines, including the ZZ502.

GMPP block PN 19170538 is used in the 454 HO short block. This production-based non-siamesed-bore block with a 4.250-inch bore is a hybrid of the original Mark IV and the newer Gen V/VI designs. (Photo Courtesy GMPP)

Bowtie Blocks

Beginning in the 1980s, Chevrolet rewarded its legion of Pro Stock and other big-block racers with the introduction of the Bowtie blocks, which have substantial improvements over regular production-line blocks in terms of strength and potential bore sizes. The most notable of all these features was the introduction of siamesed bores, which have no water passageways between the individual cylinder barrels. The thickness of the cylinder barrels was increased enough to accept 4.500-inch and larger bores while still retaining a wall thickness of .200 inch or more. There have been many versions of the Bowtie blocks, in Mark IV, Gen V, and Gen VI configurations, so the maximum bore size varies with the individual block casting number. Many can be safely bored to 4.600 inches.

Mark IV Bowtie blocks still used the original oil passage design, which I like to call side-oilers (not to be confused with Fords of the same name), since the main oil gallery is a drilled passage along the left side of the block just above the pan rail surface. Gen V and Gen VI Bowtie and production blocks feature a priority main oiling system, in which the main journals receive the oil before the lifter bores, ensuring that the most critical components in the engine are the first stop on the oil supply route.

You can easily identify the difference between the side-oilers and the priority main blocks by looking for the four 1/8-inch national pipe thread (NPT) plugs along the bottom left side of Mark IV blocks. These plugs cover the opening where the factory drilled intersecting holes to feed the main bearings from the main oil gallery. This applies to production blocks, as well as the Bowtie blocks, so it is one more quick and easy way to distinguish Mark IV blocks from Gen V/VI blocks.

CHAPTER 2

Another major benefit of all Bowtie blocks is the extra-thick deck surface with blind cylinder head-bolt holes. The thicker-than-stock decks are more stable under high loads, such as ultra-high-compression ratios, nitrous, or supercharged applications. Any time power production goes up, the load on the cylinder head and block junction surface increases, and the thicker decks are simply more stable and provide a better clamping force for the head gaskets. The blind head-bolt holes require no thread sealant, and positively eliminate the age-old problem of engine coolant leaking into the engine through the head-bolt bores in the head. Most Bowtie blocks also feature additional head-bolt bosses in the lifter valley, providing six-bolt clamping around every bore for superior gasket seal. Compare this with the small-block, which has five bolts per cylinder, and Ford/Chrysler designs, which must get by with only four per hole. Those poor non-Chevy guys...

General Motors didn't stop there: Bowtie blocks have been beefed up in the main webs as well, some more than others. There are short-deck (9.8-inch) and tall-deck (10.2-inch) versions of the Bowtie blocks, and some feature splayed bolts on the center three main bearing caps for additional crankshaft support. This little luxury item won't add any performance to your basic 600- to 800-hp big-block, but it gives peace of mind when power levels exceed 900 hp.

GMPP Drag Race Competition Engine Blocks

GM Performance Parts currently offers two versions of this exotic iron block engineered to meet the specific needs of NHRA Pro Stock drag racers. Both are short-deck, semi-finished blocks with 4.900-inch bore spacing (4.840 inches is stock), and they are the spec blocks required by NHRA for GM competitors. They are supplied without head-bolt holes or lifter bores, allowing customization by the individual race teams to suit their needs. They may be machined to locate the starter on the left, allowing the use of oil pans with a full-length kick-out on the right side. The distributor-hole location has been moved to behind the lifter valley bulkhead and requires the use of special Drag Race Competition Engine (DRCE) camshafts. Side-motor mount pads have been eliminated, requiring the use of race-style front and rear motor plates.

The DRCE 2 (PN 24502572) is cast from traditional gray iron and comes with a 9.525-inch deck height that may safely be machined to 9.000 inches.

How do you know it's a Bowtie block? Well, you can carry this book around with you and check the casting numbers listed on pages 25–27, or, even easier, look for the prominent Bowtie logo cast into the side of the block.

Most Bowtie blocks feature splayed-bolt main caps on the three center mains for added bottom-end strength.

Gen V and Gen VI Bowtie blocks have been available with both the production-style one-piece rear main seal and with a two-piece adapter and Mark IV–style rear main cap for use with traditional Mark IV cranks and oil pans. Unlike their production counterparts, Gen V and Gen VI Bowtie blocks have small round coolant passages in the deck surface, and they accept all design cylinder heads, including traditional Mark IV heads. (Photo Courtesy GMPP)

DRCE 2 block (PN 24502572) for Pro Stock competition comes without head bolt-holes or lifter bores. It features a Chevy/Pontiac/Oldsmobile bellhousing bolt pattern and in-block distributor-hole location. Pro Stock racers use dry sump oiling systems and front-drive distributors, so this hole is usually blocked off. (Photo Courtesy GMPP)

The camshaft bore is raised to 5.750 inches (stock is 5.152 inches) and the semi-finished 4.500-inch bores may be enlarged to 4.700 inches. The oil pan rails are spread .400 inch per side.

The DRCE 3 block (PN 25534406) is cast from compacted graphite iron for its superior strength and resistance to bore distortion. The 9.250-inch deck height may be reduced to 9.000 inches and the cam bore has been raised to 7.067 inches. The semi-finished 4.590-inch bores can be bored to 4.700 inches and the oil pan rails are spread to 12 inches. Main bores are 2.500 inches (409 Chevy) and they accept a special nine-journal camshaft with 60-mm bearings.

Aftermarket Blocks

Aftermarket blocks are standard fare for most serious big-blocks built these days, not only for extreme competition but for high-end street and weekly bracket racers as well. They are available in cast iron, cast aluminum, and fully machined billet aluminum configurations. Most follow the Mark IV blueprint and accept original equipment–spec parts such as cylinder heads, oil pans, starters, and water pumps, but there are also "mutant" variety blocks with specialized features such as spread oil pan rails for long-stroke clearance, raised cam bore locations, and spread-bore blocks with a bore spacing of 4.900, 5.000, 5.200 inches or more (stock bore spacing is 4.840 inches).

Brodix, Inc.

Long known as a leader in the field of high-performance and racing aluminum cylinder heads, Brodix also manufactures A-356 virgin aluminum blocks for the big-block Chevy in a variety of stock-replacement or custom configurations. They feature splayed billet main caps made of 1044 steel and coated with black oxide, and additional head bolt lugs in the deck area provide additional head gasket clamping. The main bulkheads have been strengthened and the lifter valley includes reinforcing ribs to prevent flex under high-power, high-load conditions. The lifter oil gallery is easily restricted from the front using Brodix oil restrictors (available separately), and a plug kit is provided with these blocks.

The 8B 2000A block is available in short-deck (9.800 inches) or tall-deck (10.200 inches) versions, and is a direct replacement for conventional Mark IV blocks with 4.840-inch bore spacing and standard cam location. It accepts either stock or stroker oil pans. The cast-iron sleeves, available in two bore sizes (4.480 or 4.590 inches), are retained by 1/4-inch registers, and may be bored up to 4.600 inches (small-bore sleeves are available on request).

The 8B 2000C block features a .400-inch raised cam location and your choice of 9.800-, 10.200-, or 10.700-inch deck heights. The 8B 2100C block adds your choice of 11.100- or 11.200-inch deck heights, and the 8B 2200C block can be had in 11.500- or 11.625-inch deck heights.

The 8B 2000 series blocks may be ordered with conventional big-block Babbitt cam bearings, 50-mm roller bearings, 55-mm roller bearings, or 60-mm Babbitt bearings. Lifter bores are standard Chevrolet (.842 inch) or Chrysler (.903 inch) with larger sizes available. Stroke clearance is 4.750 inches with standard cam location blocks and 5.000 inches with the raised-cam blocks (additional machining required).

If a mountain motor Rat is in your sights, you want to take a good look at Brodix's fully CNC machined 5000 series aluminum blocks with 5.000-inch bore spacing. These blocks feature a 1.000-inch raised cam location and your choice of cam bearing and lifter sizes. Deck heights are 11.200 or 11.625 inches, and all are designed for dry sump oiling systems. Bore size as delivered is 4.585 inches, and the thick wall sleeves allow bore sizes up to 4.700 inches, which, combined with a 5.000-inch-stroke crank, gets you 694 ci of tire-frying power! Of course, Brodix also manufactures 5.000-inch bore space spread port cylinder heads that are the perfect match for these blocks.

CN Blocks

CN Blocks produces fully CNC machined aluminum blocks whittled out of a solid chunk of forged aluminum. According to CN Blocks, its billet aluminum blocks have more than 36-percent-higher tensile strength than a cast 356 aluminum block, with a yield strength that is 66 percent greater than cast blocks. As a result of the greater material strength of the billet aluminum, you can expect less cylinder liner distortion and a better piston ring seal, reducing blow-by

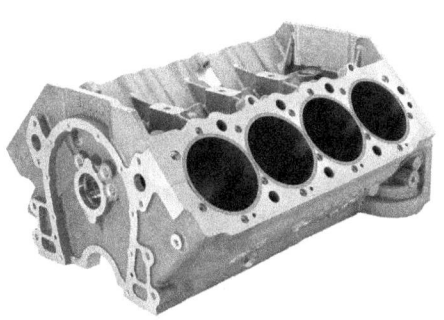

Brodix 8B 2000C tall-deck block. (Photo Courtesy Brodix)

Brodix 8B 5000C tall-deck block featuring 5.0-inch bore spacing and a 1-inch raised cam bore. (Photo Courtesy Brodix)

CHAPTER 2

and producing more force on the crankshaft and improved horsepower.

Obviously, the cost to produce a 100-percent CNC-machined block is far higher than traditional cast-aluminum blocks, but many top racers in the IHRA Pro Stock and Pro Mod ranks rely on these whittled aluminum gems when the need for maximum performance outweighs capital expenditure concerns. Most of these blocks are available as either "dry" or "wet" blocks. Dry blocks have no coolant passages and are used only for drag racing where the short running time does not require coolant circulation. You can custom order a block from CN Blocks to just about any specs you provide, but the following are some of its standard offerings.

A splayed-bolt main cap block is available in four configurations: a traditional Mark IV replacement-style block with standard 4.840-inch bore spacing, 9.8-inch deck height, and stock cam location; a tall-deck (10.2 inches) block with raised cam; a 4.900-inch-bore-spacing block with raised cam; and a 5.000-inch-bore-spacing block with raised cam location.

Cross Bolt blocks are intended for serious blower racers utilizing big-block Chevy-based engines. All five aluminum main caps are cross-bolted using 9/16-inch tool steel main studs and 1/2-inch side bolts; a custom Keith Black (KB) Olds or CN Blocks wide oil pan must be used with these blocks. Cam bearing sizes are standard BBC, 2.125 inches (460 Ford), 55 mm, 60 mm, or 65 mm. You also have your choice of lifter bores: .842, .904, .936, 1.00, or 1.062 inches. Blocks may be ordered with or without a distributor hole for racers who use a dry sump oil system and front-drive distributor.

The 1040Y can be used as a replacement block for KB Olds or Arias New Century blocks, and the 1041Y raises the cam .400 inch for larger cam cores and better pushrod geometry. The 1050Y and 1070Y feature 5.000-inch bore spacing, and the 1050Y features spread .160-inch mains and a +.400-inch-high cam. The 1070Y raises the cam +1.0 inch, and these blocks allow you to use bores of 4.600 to 4.750 inches. Dual starter bosses allow the use of full kick-out oil pans with left-mounted starters.

Dart Machinery

Founded by Richard Maskin, one of NHRA Pro Stock's pioneers, Dart has been making outstanding blocks for Rat racers for years. Most Dart blocks for big-block Chevy engines are patterned after the Mark IV block, but are designed for hard-core racing, addressing all the weaknesses of the factory castings. Extra-thick decks, siamesed bores, enlarged water jackets, priority main oiling, four-bolt main caps, and finished main bearing bores and cam tunnels make it easier to build superior racing and performance engines.

The Big M block is available with deck heights of 9.800 and 10.200 inches, and bore sizes of 4.250, 4.500, and 4.600 inches. The priority main oil system features a stepped main oil gallery (9/16 to 1/2 to 7/16 inch) to increase the flow of oil to the crank at high engine speed (RPM), and the front oil crossover eliminates internal oil leaks around the distributor shaft. There are two slotted head stud bosses on both sides of the lifter valley so you can use studs instead of hard-to-install bolts to take the place of the "missing" head bolts.

Big Ms are fitted with billet-steel four-bolt main caps for ultimate bottom-end strength, and they are machined on precision CNC equipment to ensure quality and to eliminate the need for additional machining. Another nice feature is the use of coated cam bearings, which have

CN Blocks' Cross Bolt billet aluminum blocks are intended for serious blower racers who need the ultimate in bottom-end strength. They are available with standard 4.840- or 5.000-inch bore spacing and cam bore locations up to +1.000-inch raised. (Photo Courtesy CN Blocks)

For mountain motor addicts, CN Blocks makes a series of 5.300-inch-bore-space billet aluminum blocks. These blocks are designed for a minimum bore size of 5.000 inches, yielding displacements in excess of 900 ci. The 5300 series features a 1.917-inch raised cam bore machined for 65- or 70-mm cam bearings and they may be ordered with head-bolt patterns to fit Alan Johnson, Sonny's GM Hemi, or Sonny's GM Wedge 5.3-inch cylinder heads. (Photo Courtesy CN Blocks)

CYLINDER BLOCKS

The Dart Big M Sportsman block is available with deck heights of 9.800 and 10.200 inches, and is fitted with ductile iron four-bolt main bearing caps. (Photo Courtesy Dart Machinery)

an annular groove on the back side and three oil holes to better lubricate the cam journals. The Big M Sportsman block was designed to be an even more affordable version of the Big M block, and is fitted with ductile iron four-bolt main bearing caps. All other features of the Big M are retained in the Big M Sportsman blocks.

The Dart Race Series block is for racers wanting to build real mountain motors—up to 763 ci—and it offers crank-to-deck dimensions of 10.600 and 11.100 inches, nearly 1 inch taller than the factory tall-deck block. The camshaft is raised .600 inch above the stock location for improved connecting rod clearance with stroker cranks, and the block is available with either 4.840- (standard big-block) or 4.900-inch bore spacing. The oil pan rails are spread to increase clearance for the connecting rods and crankshaft counterweights, and it can be ordered with various lifter locations and provisions for symmetrical or siamesed-port cylinder heads. You can specify 2.125-inch (standard), 55-mm, or 60-mm roller cam bearings, and the lifter bosses can be machined to accommodate a variety of valve layouts with a choice of .842- (standard Chevrolet), .904-, .937-, or 1.063-inch-diameter lifters, with bushings for either standard tie-bar or keyed lifters. This is a good foundation for one very serious racing engine.

Dart also makes lightweight (140-pound) aluminum blocks that feature extra strengthening in critical areas, increased displacement capacity, true priority main oiling, and precision CNC machining. Dart's Aluminum Big M block is a conventional Mark IV configuration that retains all production dimensions for compatibility with standard components. It is manufactured from virgin C355-T61 aerospace aluminum alloy and machined in-house to ensure absolute quality. Dart aluminum blocks feature ductile iron sleeves with extra-thick walls to promote excellent ring seal. Reinforcing ribs strengthen the lifter valley and bellhousing flange, and inboard head stud bosses provide additional head gasket sealing. The priority main oiling system delivers oil directly to the crankshaft bearings to enhance reliability at high engine speeds. These blocks include coated cam bearings, freeze plugs, and dowels.

Donovan Engineering

Donovan Engineering has been making aluminum racing engine blocks for more than 30 years, and each Donovan block is cast from strontium-modified B356 alloy with a special heat treat. These blocks may be ordered with full-water jackets, half-water jackets, or solid for drag racing use only.

The standard Donovan block weighs 140 pounds and is a traditional Mark IV replacement with oil filter and fuel pump bosses, standard motor mount and cam locations, and a custom 3/8-inch-wider oil pan rail. It is available in any deck height up to 10.300 inches, and with stock 4.840-inch bore spacing or custom 4.900- or 5.000-inch bore spacing. Chevy lifter bores (.842 inch) are standard, but any lifter bore diameter may be specified. For you marine types, you can even order the block anodized for corrosion resistance.

If you're headed for the mountains, you can specify one of Donovan's raised-cam blocks with options of .400- or 1.0-inch raised-cam location, 4.840- or 5.000-inch bore spacing, and deck heights up to 12.000 inches. These blocks all feature a 3/4-inch wider-than-stock

Manufactured from virgin C355-T61 aerospace aluminum alloy, Dart's Aluminum Big M block is a conventional Mark IV configuration that retains all production dimensions for compatibility with standard components. (Photo Courtesy Dart Machinery)

Dart's Race Series tall-deck block is available with deck heights up to 11.100 inches. (Photo Courtesy Dart Machinery)

CHAPTER 2

Most big-block Chevys used in racing cars are mounted with a 1/4-inch-thick mid-plate between the engine block and the transmission, and require longer-than-stock bellhousing dowel pins. The stock diameter is .619 to .621 inch, and some racers try to use common 5/8-inch (.625-inch) dowels. That's going to require a pretty big hammer, and may damage the block from the excessive force needed to drive them in. These dowel pins from Brodix and Speedway Motors (PN 91025840) are the correct diameter and are long enough for use with motor plates.

oil pan rail to clear long strokes. Weight is up to 180 pounds, depending on the deck height and water jacket configuration desired.

Merlin (World Products)

As one of Bill Mitchell's innovative companies, World Products has been producing its Merlin line of big-block Chevy engine blocks for years. They also follow the original Mark IV pattern in terms of parts fitment, and accept Mark IV spec cranks, heads, cams, oil pans, timing covers, etc. World's current version of the Merlin block is the Merlin III, easily identified by the name cast in 1-inch-tall letters on the front of the block.

Merlin III blocks are available in 9.800- and 10.200-inch (tall deck) versions, and can be ordered with nodular iron or billet steel splayed-bolt main caps. All versions include priority main oiling, expanded water jackets for improved cooling of the siamesed bores, and .600-inch-thick decks with blind tapped bolt-holes to prevent coolant leakage. The bottom end accepts standard Mark IV oil pans, and the crankcase has been clearanced to accept strokes up to 4.375 inches (up to 4.750 inches in the tall-deck blocks). The blocks are available in three bore sizes: 4.240, 4.490, and 4.590 inches, allowing you to finish hone the bores to your specs. Maximum bore size is 4.625 inches, and the minimum cylinder wall thickness is .240 inch at 4.600 inches.

World also sells its blocks fully race-prepped to your specifications, with finished bores and deck heights, cam bearings installed, etc., allowing you to do a fit-check and assemble the short block with no further machining required. Merlin blocks come with indexed stock location and diameter (.8437 inch) lifter bores. Approximate weight of these sturdy iron blocks is 270 pounds.

If an aluminum block is what you want, the Merlin X offers all the same features of the Merlin series in a 140-pound package. Cast from 357-A6 aluminum, these alloy blocks feature horizontal reinforcing ribs along the sides of the block and cross ribs in the lifter valley to stiffen the engine. Recommended maximum bore size is 4.600 inches, due to the use of cast-iron sleeves. The lubrication system features an integral boss for front-feed and a boss for rear scavenge. The rear main cap has provisions for a wet sump pump, and the block is also drilled for dry sump valley scavenge lines with cross-feed lines between left and right lifter oil galleries. The splayed-bolt main caps are made of 1045 alloy steel, attached with premium APR main studs and bolts.

Merlin III cast-iron blocks are available in 9.800- and 10.200-inch versions, and can be ordered with nodular iron or billet steel splayed-bolt main caps. All versions include priority main oiling, expanded water jackets for improved cooling of the siamesed bores, and .600-inch-thick decks with blind tapped bolt-holes. (Photo Courtesy World Products)

Cast from 357-A6 aluminum, Merlin X alloy blocks feature horizontal reinforcing ribs along the sides of the block and cross ribs in the lifter valley to stiffen the engine. (Photo Courtesy World Products)

CYLINDER BLOCKS

Block Casting Dates

Big-block casting dates are generally located on the rear ledge of the block on the passenger side, although occasionally you find these dates on the driver's side or even on the side of the block near the freeze plugs. The code is a simple alpha-numeric code such as "C 12 7." The first letter stands for the month of the year (A = January, B = February, etc.), so C would be March. The second numeral is the day of the month, and the last is the year of the decade. Which decade is not always clear, though it's pretty easy to decipher for the big-block Chevy.

Early Mark IV–style big-blocks were not produced until 1965, and by 1975 they were only found in trucks. By the late 1970s, big-blocks had the displacement in liters cast into the sides of the block, for instance, 7.0 (427 ci), 7.4 (454 ci), or 8.2 (502 ci), so the decade your block was produced is usually pretty easy to decipher. Gen V blocks were only produced from 1991 through 1996, and Gen VI blocks from 1996 to 2000.

Going back to our mystery "C 12 7" code, the block was cast (not necessarily assembled until later) on March 12 of some year ending in "7." If it were 1967, the block would accept an old-style canister oil filter housing, and might be a 396 (4.094-inch bore) or 427 (4.250-inch bore). If it were 1977, it would be 454 truck block with a 4.250-inch bore. By the 1980s, big-blocks had the engine size (in liters) cast into the side of the block, so a 1987 block from a truck would have "7.4" cast in. Simple, no?

This 454 block has the last three digits of the casting number, 445, repeated on the block just above the oil filter mount, along with the date code K 2 1, plus the words "Hi Perf" and "PASS." The "7.4" between the two freeze plug holes tell us it's 454 (7.4 liters) with an original bore size of 4.250 inches. K 2 1 indicates that it was cast on November 2 in 1981 (K = November, 2 = day of the month, 1 = the last digit of the decade). How do you know it's 1981 from the single digit "1"? In 1971 Chevy had not yet started using the metric designation 7.4, and by 1991 it would have been a Gen V block, which you can tell it's not from the recessed oil filter boss and the 1-3/4-inch freeze plug bores. "Hi Perf" and "PASS" means it could be either a two- or four-bolt main block; you just have to look to see which one it is. Nearly all big-blocks have both Hi Perf and PASS cast into them, so ignore that.

Big-Block Chevy Block Casting Numbers

Big-block casting numbers are located on either the left or right side of the block on the rear ledge just above the bellhousing bolt-holes. Remember that these are casting numbers, not part numbers, and the same casting might have been used to produce blocks with different features such as two-bolt or four-bolt main caps.

Often the rough cast numbers are difficult to read; for instance, a "6" and an "8" may look nearly the same, so you may have to look for other clues to positively identify your block. Most gearheads refer to blocks by the last three digits, which seldom repeat.

Casting No.	Engine	Years	Main Caps	Notes
0-326711	430		4-bolt	Alum., CanAm, 4.44-inch bores, steel cylinder liners
340220	427T	1968–1985	4-bolt	
345014	454	1970–1986		
346236	454	1975–1976	2-bolt	
359070	454	1970–1990		
361959	454	1973–1990	2- or 4-bolt	

HOW TO BUILD KILLER BIG-BLOCK CHEVY ENGINES   25

Big-Block Chevy Block Casting Numbers CONTINUED

Casting No.	Engine	Years	Main Caps	Notes
364776	427T	1968–1985	4-bolt	
364779	366T	1968–1990	4-bolt	
399204	509	1970–1971	4-bolt	Alum., CanAm, 4.5-inch bores, steel Cylinder liners
399293	366T	1977–1978	4-bolt	
473478	427T	1977–1990	4-bolt	
495102	509		4-bolt	Alum., CanAm, 4.5-inch bores
3782870	427T	1968–1976	4-bolt	
3824553	366T	1966–1967	4-bolt	1966 requires grooved rear cam journal
3855961	396	1965–1966	2- or 4-bolt	Requires grooved rear cam journal
3855961	427	1966	2-bolt	Requires grooved rear cam journal
3855962	396	1965–1966	4-bolt	Requires grooved rear cam journal
3855977	366T	1966–1973	4-bolt	1966 requires grooved rear cam journal
3869942	427	1966–1967	2- or 4-bolt	1966 requires grooved rear cam journal
3902406	396	1967	2- or 4-bolt	
3904351	427	1967	2- or 4-bolt	
3904354	366T	1966–1976	4-bolt	1966 requires grooved rear cam journal
3916319	366T	1968	4-bolt	
3916321	427	1968	2- or 4-bolt	
3916323	396	1968	2- or 4-bolt	
3925521	427T	1968–1985	4-bolt	
3935439	427	1968–1969	2- or 4-bolt	
3935440	396	1968–1969	2- or 4-bolt	
3937724	366T	1968–1985	4-bolt	
3937726	427T	1968–1984	4-bolt	
3946052	427	1969	4-bolt	Alum. ZL-1, Mark IV
3946053	427	1997–up	4-bolt	Alum. ZL-1, 2nd version, Mark IV
3955270	427	1969	2- or 4-bolt	
3955272	396	1969	2- or 4-bolt	
3955274	366T	1968–1985	4-bolt	
3955276	427T	1968–1973	4-bolt	
3963512	427	1969	2- or 4-bolt	
3963512	454	1970–1976	2- or 4-bolt	
3969852	366T	1968–1984	4-bolt	
3969854	396	1969	2- or 4-bolt	
3969854	402	1970–1972	2- or 4-bolt	
3969858	427T	1968–1984	4-bolt	
3999289	454	1971–1979	2- or 4-bolt	Some "CE" replacement blocks had four bolt main caps
3999290	396	1968–1969	2- or 4-bolt	Truck
3999290	402	1970–1972	2- or 4-bolt	Truck
3999290	402	1972	2 or 4-bolt	Passenger car
3999293	366T	1968–1990	4-bolt	
3999294	427T	1968–1984	4-bolt	
10051107	454		4-bolt	Bowtie, Mk IV, 9.8-inch deck, siamesed bores, 4.25-inch semi-finished bores, can be bored to 4.50 inches
10069282	366T	1990–1991	4-bolt	Mark IV, tall deck
10069284	427T		4-bolt	Mark IV, tall deck
10069286	454	1990–1991	4-bolt	Mark IV, short deck

CYLINDER BLOCKS

Casting No.	Engine	Years	Main Caps	Notes
10114182	454	1991–up	4-bolt	Gen V
10114183	366T	1991–up	4-bolt	Gen V
10114184	427T	1991–up	4-bolt	Gen V
10134366	454T		4-bolt	Bowtie, Gen V, tall deck
10185050	454		4-bolt	Bowtie, Gen V, short deck
10237297	454	1996–up	4-bolt	Vortec 7400, "L-29" Gen VI
10237299	427T	1996–up	4-bolt	Gen VI, 7.0L, truck
10237300	502	1996–up	4-bolt	Gen VI, 4.466-inch bore
	427T	1996-up	4-bolt	Gen VI, 4.250-inch bore, fuel pump boss, clutch linkage pivot boss
12550313	454	1991–up	4-bolt	Gen V crate motor, Gen VI 4.25-inch bare block, fuel pump boss
12556110	496	2001–1906	4-bolt	Gen VII 8.1L, "Vortec 8100," Truck
12561357	454	1996–up	4-bolt	Gen VI
12561358	502		4-bolt	Gen VI
14015443	454	1987–1990	2- or 4-bolt	Mark IV, Truck, Motorhome
14015445	454	1978–1990	2- or 4-bolt	
10051106	454		4-bolt	Bowtie, Mark IV, 4.250-inch bore, short-deck height
10185049	454		4-bolt	Bowtie, Gen V, 4.250-inch bore, 9.8-inch short-deck height, 1-piece rear main seal
10134367	454T		4-bolt	Bowtie, Gen V, 4.250-inch bore, 10.2-inch tall-deck height, 1-piece rear main seal
12370833	454		4-bolt	Bowtie, Mark IV, 4.495-inch bore, short-deck height
12370834	509T		4-bolt	Bowtie, Mark IV, 4.495-inch bore, tall-deck height
14044807	454T		4-bolt	Bowtie, Mk IV, CNC prep, tall deck, 4.25 or 4.495-inch bore
14044808	454T		4-bolt	Bowtie, Mark IV, 4.250-inch bore, 10.2-inch tall-deck height
14096859	502		4-bolt	Gen V, HO
24502500	454		4-bolt	Bow Tie, Gen V, CNC prep, 4.250-inch bore, 9.8-inch short-deck height, 16-degree splayed main caps
24502502	454T		4-bolt	Bowtie, Gen V, CNC prep, 4.250-inch bore, 10.2-inch tall-deck height, 16-degree splayed main caps
24502504	454		4-bolt	Bowtie, Gen V, Race prep, 9.8-inch short-deck height
24502504B	454		4-bolt	Bowtie, Gen VI, CNC prep, 9.8-inch short-deck height, 1- or 2-piece rear main seal
24502506	454T		4-bolt	Bowtie, Gen V, Race prep, 10.2-inch tall-deck height
24502506B	454T		4-bolt	Bowtie, Gen VI, CNC prep, 10.2-inch tall-deck height, 1- or 2-piece rear main seal
88958695	427	1997–up	4-bolt	Alum. ZL-1, 2nd version, Gen VI, 1-piece rear main seal
1A626			4-bolt	4.5-inch bore Olds DRCE 2, 9.525-inch deck height, PN 24502572
–			4-bolt	4.590-inch bore Olds DRCE 3, 9.25-inch deck height, PN 25534402
CG			4-bolt	4.590-inch bore Olds DRCE 3, 9.25-inch deck height, compacted graphite, PN 25534406

Notes
T = tall deck, 10.2-inch deck height.
1991-and-later Gen V, VI, and VII production big-block Chevy motors have one-piece rear main crank seals.

CHAPTER 3

Crankshafts, Connecting Rods and Pistons

The crankshaft, connecting rods, and pistons are frequently referred to as the rotating assembly, although, technically speaking, only the crank rotates during engine operation. The pistons are actually reciprocating parts, traveling up and down the bores with great alacrity while the rods connect the two and are partly rotating and partly reciprocating parts. When it comes to cranks, rods, and pistons, here's the bottom line: light is good, strong is better, but strong and light is best.

Crankshafts

Stock big-block Chevy crankshafts were available in only two strokes: 3.760 inches (in 396, 402, and 427 engines) and 4.000 inches (in 454 and 502 V-8s), and were made from either cast iron or forged low-carbon steel like AISI (American Iron and Steel Institute) 1053, although a few 4.000-inch-stroke cranks were produced from 5140 alloy steel. When the 396- and 427-ci Rat motors appeared in the mid 1960s, all were equipped with forged steel cranks that were dimensionally interchangeable, although they had slight differences in the counterweights and were balanced to different specs. If you want to use a 396 crank to build a 427, you won't have any problems other than having to re-balance the rotating assembly, which should always be done anyway. All 396, 402, and 427 engines were internally balanced and used neutral balance harmonic dampeners and flywheels or flexplates.

Cast-iron cranks started showing up when the Rat motor was tapped into service for non-high-performance passenger cars. When the 454 made its debut in 1970, most were equipped with forged steel cranks, but it was subsequently relegated to duty in trucks only after 1974 and most then featured cast-iron crankshafts, which are most commonly found when searching through a pile of crank cores at your local auto parts recycler (fancy talk for junkyard).

It's easy to tell the difference between a stock cast and forged steel crank by looking at the parting line, which is visible between the machined surfaces of the crank. A thin line indicates a cast-iron crank; and all forged steel cranks have a hefty 3/4- to 1-inch-wide parting line. Also, forged steel cranks ring like a bell when tapped lightly with a small hammer or other mallet. This is also a tried-and-true method of detecting cracks in forged cranks: when most of the counterweights ring clearly, and one produces a muffled "clunk," it's a pretty safe bet than there is a crack in that area.

High-quality 4340 forged steel stroker crankshaft, H-beam connecting rods, and forged aluminum pistons are a wise investment for any high-performance big-block.

All factory-produced 4.000-inch-stroke engines were externally balanced and used specific harmonic dampeners and flexplates (or flywheels) with extra balance weight built into them. You must always use the appropriate balancer and flexplate for your engine, or the resulting imbalance quickly helps you to disassemble the engine, maybe even without using tools.

Gen V and Gen VI cranks are readily identified by the large rear seal/flywheel flange developed for use with the one-piece rear main seal. The flywheels and flexplates used with these cranks have the same six-on-3.58-inch bolt pattern as Mark IV wheels, but they require specific flywheels or flexplates that are balanced differently than the Mark IV engines. Also, Gen V/VI engines used flywheels or flexplates with a cast crank different than those with a forged steel crank. The bolt pattern is the same, but they are balanced differently. All high-performance big-blocks should be equipped with an aftermarket flywheel or flexplate meeting SFI specs anyway, so just be sure you order the wheel that fits your crank. All other critical dimensions such as main journal diameter (2.750 inches), rod journal diameter (2.200 inches), overall length, journal spacing, and crank snout diameter (1.600 inches) are the same for production Mark IV and Gen V/VI cranks.

Harmonic dampeners are interchangeable among Mark IV and Gen V/VI engines, but you must be sure to use the correct balance for your rotating assembly, whether neutral balance (396/427 style) or externally balanced (454/502 style). Note that most aftermarket cranks intended for competition use are neutrally balanced, and must be used with matching neutral-balance dampeners and flywheels/flexplates.

The automotive aftermarket has really stepped up to the plate in terms of big-block crankshafts suitable for all levels of performance, offering economical cast cranks, forged steel cranks made from superior alloys, and even billet steel cranks for the ultimate in material strength and custom features. There are a plethora of high-quality crankshafts for the big-block Chevy from manufacturers such as BRC, Bryant, Callies, Cola, Crower, Eagle, K1 Technologies, Lunati, Ohio Crankshaft, Winberg, Scat, and probably others by the time you read this.

Of course, the primary benefit of going to an aftermarket crank is to increase the stroke (the distance which the pistons travel up and down the bore), which increases the displacement of your engine and always generates more torque and horsepower, unless you select engine parts that are so mismatched that even the stroker crank doesn't help.

An example might be to select a quarter-inch stroker (stock plus 1/4 inch, or 4.250 inches) for your car-hauler truck engine with small port heads and an extremely short-duration/low-lift "mileage" cam. The small ports and short cam timing might have worked well to pump up the low-end power of the stock 454. But the stroker crank further increases the velocity of the air/fuel charge and the extra displacement also increases the compression ratio (if the piston top design remains the same as before), so now it is likely that this 496 combo is prone to pre-ignition from excessive compression for the pump gas being used.

The simple solution is to change the cam to a design that is matched to this new combination, and change the heads to aftermarket aluminum pieces with bigger ports and better combustion chamber heat dissipation characteristics. But other than this obscure example, installing a stroker crank in your hot rod or competition big-block is a win-win proposition.

Aftermarket cranks typically use a larger fillet radius where the journal meets the sides of the counterweight to reduce the stress concentration at this critical point. This requires that you select rod and main bearings designed with additional clearance for the larger radius, or you have to clearance the bearing yourself. Old-timers are familiar with the concept of scraping bearings: the

The Mark IV crank (left) is designed for use with two-piece real main seals, and the Gen V/VI crank (right) is for use with a one-piece rear main seal. Both of these Scat 4340 cranks are balanced for use with neutral-balance flywheels; note the prominent balance pad at the rear of the Mark IV crank, which negates the need for stock-spec externally balanced wheels.

Cast-iron cranks are easily identified by the thin casting line visible on the counterweights and rod throws. This Gen V/VI 454 crank has a one-piece rear main seal and a steel trigger wheel on the nose for a crank position sensor. Use the trigger wheel for correct harmonic dampener spacing, even if you are building a non-EFI Gen V/VI engine. If you remove the wheel, your crank pulley does not line up correctly with the water pump and alternator pulleys. Note that Gen V/VI cast-iron cranks require a different flexplate or flywheel than forged steel Gen V/VI cranks due to differences in the balance.

bearing material is soft enough that you can carve it into shape with a bearing knife. (Now you know why they taught you to carve in Boy Scouts.) You're generally better advised to just order performance bearing inserts, which are narrower than stock bearings. Your crank manufacturer can advise you which part numbers work with the radius on your particular crank, but even so, you should always check to be sure the bearings aren't binding against the oversized fillet radius.

In normally aspirated applications for maximum effort, it's common

This high-quality Scat 4.250-inch-stroke crank is a traditional Mark IV design for use with two-piece rear main seals, and it is forged from 4340 alloy steel and fully nitrided for improved strength. It has several design improvements over stock cranks, including lightening holes in all four rod journals, scalloped cuts at the flywheel flange, and streamlined counterweights with bullet-shaped leading edges and tapered trailing edges to reduce oil windage. All external surfaces have been smoothed to reduce stress risers and improve oil shedding, thus the typical wide forging line is no longer visible. The counterweights have been specifically designed to allow use with neutral-balance (396- and 427-style) harmonic dampeners and flywheels.

Aftermarket cranks feature much-larger-than-stock journal fillet radii for increased strength, plus chamfered oil holes for improved lubrication. This rod journal also has been through-drilled to reduce weight for quicker acceleration.

Big-block Chevy cranks may have either one, two (left), or three (right) keyways in the crank snout, which are used to align the crank timing sprocket or gear and the harmonic dampener. Some shops offer the option of larger-than-stock 1/4-inch keyways located 180 degrees apart for supercharged engines, due to the tremendous strain put on the bottom blower pulley. Stock woodruff keys are 3/16 inch wide x 3/4 inch long.

This 4340 Scat crank features counterweight profiling to reduce windage and drag as the crank rotates through the suspended oil in the crankcase. The leading edges are rounded (left), and the trailing edges are tapered (right), which is the correct aerodynamic shape for best reducing frictional losses. Some cranks have counterweights that are knife-edged on the leading edge, but that's not the shape you see on the nose of a nuclear-powered submarine, is it?

This Manley connecting rod has been fitted with an HN series Clevite bearing designed to give more clearance with a large fillet radius crank. The generous chamfer on the rod always goes against the cheek of the crank throw, so odd-numbered cylinders get the rod installed with the chamfer toward the front of the engine, and even-numbered cylinders have the chamfer facing the rear.

to reduce the crank journal diameters to reduce bearing drag and free up a little more power. This kind of effort pays very little power dividends and does so at the expense of some crankshaft strength, so it's certainly not a good idea for the average street or bracket race engine or any competition engine with power adders such as nitrous oxide injection, blowers, or turbochargers.

Reducing the rod journals from the stock 2.200-inch diameter to 2.100 or even 2.000 inches is easily accomplished using custom connecting rods with small-block Chevy rod bearing inserts.

Pro Stockers typically go even further, reducing the journal diameter to 1.889 inches and running Honda bearings. Pro Stockers also typically run 409 Chevy main bearings with a 2.500-inch main journal. While it is possible to fabricate bearing spacers to adapt the 409 main bearings to a standard block, doing it the right way requires a custom block supplied with undersized main bores—not for the faint of heart, or light of wallet.

Inspection, Preparation and Repair

The first step in crank inspection is to just look it over carefully, checking for obvious cracks, deep scoring, heat-blackened journals, stripped bolt-holes, etc. Cracks large enough to be visible to the naked eye are grounds for dismissal of any crank; they normally can't be repaired. Other problems can usually be corrected by a reputable crank repair shop, but you have to weigh the cost versus the value of the crank. Generally, stock 3.760- and 4.000-inch-stoke cranks that have any of these problems, other than minor scoring on the journals, should not be used because they are going to cost more to repair than they are worth. More costly aftermarket

This 4.500-inch-stroke fully counterweighted Crower super-light crankshaft has small-block Chevy rod journals measuring 2.100 inches, compared to the standard big-block size of 2.200 inches. Smaller journals reduce bearing speed and allow a connecting rod with a smaller big end for more crankcase and camshaft clearance with the long stroke. Although it adds extra weight, center counterweights are beneficial for controlling crank harmonics and achieving better balance of the rotating assembly.

It's a World Market

Lately there has been an influx of crankshaft and connecting rod forgings from overseas sources, which has been the subject of many heated debates, typically involving the sentiment of "us versus them." When it comes to building big-block Chevy engines, I, like many of you, have to allocate my resources carefully, and if I can get a 4340 forged crank for a substantial savings over the premium brand, I'm certainly going to be tempted. I have also seen some so-called performance parts, especially intake manifolds, which were produced overseas, that exhibited absolutely horrible engineering, fit, and finish.

However, as far as cranks and rods are concerned, the trend I see is that less costly raw forgings are imported, and then finish machined at the manufacturer's facility in the United States. I've seen and used some pretty good parts produced by this collaborative method. You could even make the argument that these low-cost stroker cranks and forged connecting rods have had a significant effect on the growth and popularity of the big-block Chevy, making a 500-plus-ci Rat affordable for nearly every gearhead who wants to build one.

So why buy American? Let's not forget that all forgings are not created equal. There are many processes and controls involved in smelting and forging steels, some better (and more expensive) than others. This is not to say that just because a crank was forged in the United States it is automatically better than the offshore piece, but in reality, American manufacturers are usually held to higher standards of purity and process control, and many have the documentation to back it up. Our defense and aerospace industries are largely responsible for raising the bar in terms of metallurgical advances, and at the higher ends of racing and competition most Pro teams want to control every aspect of engine design and manufacturing. I don't think you'll see any offshore crankshafts in the NHRA Pro Stock ranks. But for the budget-minded performance enthusiast and sportsman drag racer, economical cranks and rods offer a lot of bang for the buck.

It's your choice.

CHAPTER 3

Cast, Forged or Billet: Don't Be "Cranky," Just Pick One!

In traditional hot rod lore, crankshafts have been made from ferrous (iron-based) alloys in one of three configurations: cast nodular iron, forged steel, or billet steel. Each method has its strengths and weaknesses.

Cast

Starting at the low end of the scale, nodular iron has been used for the majority of stock big-block cranks, and it offers adequate strength for most street-duty performance big-blocks up to about 500 hp. I'm sure somebody out there will tell you about the 800-hp engine he built with a cast crank, but unless you're the kind of person who likes to go ice skating on a 1/4-inch layer of ice over a deep lake, you may want to avoid taking that kind of unnecessary risk.

Other than low cost and ready availability, cast-iron cranks have two more redeeming features that may benefit your engine: first, the cast iron is actually quite hard (and brittle), and does not require costly hardening processes that are commonly used on forged steel cranks, even after re-grinding the journals. Second, they absorb harmonic vibrations much better than forged or billet cranks, and are actually a very good choice for low-RPM heavy-duty engines like the truck engines in which most cast-iron cranks are found.

Forged

Next up on the strength scale are forged steel cranks, and there are plenty of material choices. Most factory forged cranks are made from 1053 carbon steel, and some were produced from 5140 alloy steel. In the aftermarket, some manufacturers offer the more economical 5140 cranks, but the majority are produced from high-quality 4340 alloy steel. Some manufacturers offer cranks in EN-30B, an expensive upgrade with even better strength and durability. So which one do you need? I've used factory 1053 cranks on 800-plus-hp big-blocks spinning more than 8,000 rpm, but I consider that the maximum performance level for these cranks. Anymore, I sleep better at night with a top-notch 4340 forging in any engine making 800 hp or more.

Billet

Billet cranks are machined from a single bar of alloy steel billet (typically 4340) and have none of the residual stresses that may be present when forgings are violently "smacked" into shape with tons of pressure. Obviously, there is a tremendous amount of machining required to whittle an entire crank from a very heavy piece of solid steel, but as they say, you get what you pay for. When do you need a billet? Considering that billet cranks can cost $8,000 or more, you'll probably know when it's time get one–usually when your engine budget is in the $50,000 or more category.

Still not sure which is the right choice? Just call the manufacturer of your choice and discuss your options with them—they do this every day, so let their experience be your guide.

It takes a lot of machining to carve a 70-pound big-block crankshaft out of a 300-pound chunk of billet steel. This Scat billet crank has had the first roughing cuts completed and is ready to move on to the next machining center.

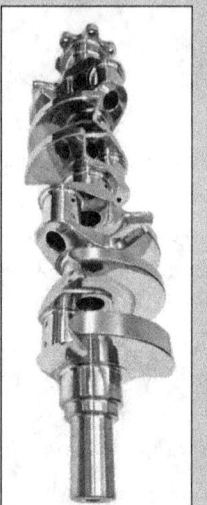

This Bryant Racing billet steel crankshaft for DRCE 4.900-inch bore spacing Pro Stock engines is designed to handle the abuse of 1,400-plus-hp at 11,000 rpm, yet it weighs only 49 pounds. It is machined from a 4330 Modified steel billet with a tensile strength 40 percent greater than 4340 steel, and it incorporates every advanced feature possible to reduce friction, windage, and weight. All eight undercut counterweights are streamlined with rounded leading edges and tapered trailing edges, and the counterweight diameter is as small as possible to minimize polar moment of inertia for quicker revs. Rod throws and mains are drilled, and the flywheel flange is scalloped to reduce weight. The finish is Bryant's REM Isotropic Superfinish, a two-step micro-polishing process that eliminates stress risers and improves oil shedding. Most Pro Stock racers order the crank with 2.500-inch (409 Chevy) mains, 1.889-inch (Honda) rod journals, and a stroke of 3.600 inches. (Photo Courtesy Bryant Racing)

CRANKSHAFTS, CONNECTING RODS AND PISTONS

cranks might be worth repairing, and a good shop should be able to give you an estimate for repairs before you commit to the job.

Regardless of whether or not the crank appears to need other work, you should always have it Magnaflux tested to reveal any cracks, which are a deal breaker as far as that crank goes. A good crank shop can straighten your crank, weld up badly scored journals, re-grind to fit standard or undersize bearings, Helicoil stripped bolt-holes, true the flywheel flange, re-harden the crank, and just about anything else you can think a crank might need, but cannot fix deep cracks. So do the Magnaflux thing first, and save yourself a lot of grief and wasted money. If the crank doesn't pass this first step, consider it money well spent, knowing that a crank failure in a running engine usually destroys the entire short block, and sometimes even damages the upper end of the engine.

If your crank passes the visual inspection, the next area of concern is whether the journals can be used as-is, with just a polish, or if they need to be ground undersize. Oversize bearings are available in .001-, .010-, .020-, .030-, and .040-inch sizes, and you should measure the journals with a dial caliper or micrometer to see if they are standard (2.750-inch mains, 2.200-inch rod journals) or have already been undercut. In gearhead lingo, cranks are described as "standard/standard, ten/ten (.010/.010 inch)" or some combination of sizes indicating how much (in thousandths of an inch) the crank has been ground undersize on the mains and rod journals. Excessive undercuts are generally viewed as a negative, because they indicate that the crank has had a long, hard life, and if the crank was induction hardened, you may be getting into the softer core layer of steel, requiring the crank to be re-hardened after further grinding. Remember, most aftermarket cranks were hardened by nitriding, Tufftriding, or some other method which usually only penetrates to a depth of a few thousandths of an inch, so re-hardening is mandatory after grinding the journals. Cast-iron cranks do not need to be hardened, even after regrinding.

Project: Balancing the Reciprocating Assembly

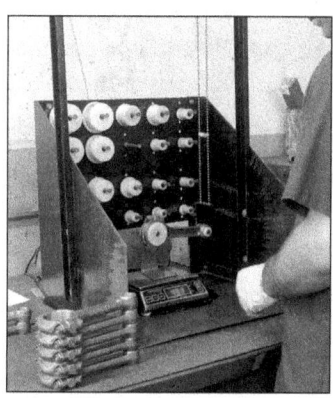

1 Each end of the connecting rods must be balanced separately. This machine supports one end at a time (the small end in this case). Then the seven heavy rods have metal removed to match the lightest rod. Most aftermarket connecting rods come pre-balanced, but your engine balancer checks them to be sure.

2 Some of the aluminum is removed from the piston skirts with a milling machine to reduce weight and equalize all eight pistons.

3 After all eight pistons and rods are balanced to each other, a formula is used to determine the weight of bob weights that get clamped to the crank rod journals. Modern crank balancing machines, like this one at Scat, digitally measure and display imbalance after spinning the crank so that the operator knows how much metal needs to be removed from the counterweights with the drill press. The operation is repeated until everything is spot on.

4 This 5-inch-stroke mountain motor crank had to have lots of heavy-metal slugs added to achieve a neutral balance. Most 4- or 4.250-inch cranks just need one or two.

HOW TO BUILD KILLER BIG-BLOCK CHEVY ENGINES

CHAPTER 3

Stock Crankshaft Casting Numbers

The following apply to two-piece rear main oil seals with 3.76-inch stroke used on 1965–1990 Mark IV 366T, 396, 402, 427, or 427T big-block Chevy engines:

Casting	Engine	Notes
6223	396, 402, 427	Forged, 1053 steel
7115	396, 402, 427	Forged, nitrided, cross-drilled, 5140 steel
3804816	396, 402, 427	Cast
3856223	396	Forged
3863114	402	
3863144	396, 402	
3874874	396, 402	
3879621	427	Forged
3882841	396	Forged, cross-drilled, nitrided
3882842	427	Forged, cross-drilled, nitrided
3882847		
3882848		
3882849	427	Forged
3887114	396	Forged, nitrided, 5140 steel
3904815	396, 402	Cast, nodular iron
3941180		
3942411		
3965746		Semi-finished, forged
3993804		Raw, 5140 steel

The following apply to one-piece rear main oil seals with 3.76-inch stroke used on 1991–up Gen V and Gen VI 366T, 427T big-block Chevy engines:

Casting	Engine	Notes
10114186	427T	Forged, 1053 steel
10114187	366T	Cast
10114189	427T	Cast

The following apply to two-piece rear main oil seals with 4.00-inch stroke used on 1970–1990 Mark IV 454 or Mark IV 502 big-block Chevy engines:

Casting	Engine	Notes
3520	454	Forged, cross-drilled, 1053 steel
3521	454, 502	Forged, cross-drilled, 5140 steel
3524	454	Forged
7416	454, 502	Forged, cross-drilled, 1053 steel
7463	454	Forged
336782	454	Cast
353039	454	Cast
353638	454	
359730	454	
3962523	454	Forged
3963523	454	
3963524	454	Forged
3967416	454	Forged
3967463	454	Forged
3975945	454	
3963521	454	Forged, cross-drilled, 5140 steel
3965753		semi-finished, Forged, 5140 steel
3975495	454	
3993878	454	Forged
10051169	454	Forged raw casting

The following apply to one-piece rear main oil seals with 4.00-inch stroke used on 1991–up Gen V and VI 454 or 502 big-block Chevy engines:

Casting	Engine	Notes
10114188	454	Cast
14097044	454, 502	Forged, 1053 steel

Restoring Balance

The need to balance any spinning mechanism that rotates at high speeds is pretty obvious, but when part of that assembly is actually reciprocating (moving up and down along the centerline of the bore) instead of rotating, it complicates matters. You can't simply balance a crank in the same fashion that you spin balance your wheels and tires, for instance, but instead you or your engine balancer uses a formula to determine the bob weight, or effective weight of the rods, bearings, pistons, wrist pins, and rings as they affect the balance of the crankshaft.

The standard formula is:

Bob Weight = Rotating Mass + (Reciprocating Mass ÷ 2)

CRANKSHAFTS, CONNECTING RODS AND PISTONS

Where:

Rotating Mass = weight of the rod bearings plus the big end of the rod

Reciprocating Mass = weight of the pistons, rings, wrist pins and retainers, plus the small end of the rod

Because two piston/rod assemblies attach to each crank journal, the final calculated weight is doubled and then clamped onto each crank rod journal using carefully weighed bob weights to duplicate the forces acting on the crank as it spins.

In addition to the crank and piston/rod assembly components, you also need to supply the engine balancer with your harmonic dampener and flywheel or flexplate. While externally balanced big-blocks like the 454 and 502 are commonly used in high-performance street applications, most high-end performance and racing engines benefit from having a neutral- or internal-balance condition. You can achieve correct balance with external weights on the harmonic dampener and flywheel, but the resulting vector forces and harmonic vibrations are transmitted along the length of the crankshaft to the counterweighted parts hanging off each end of the crank, and that can have detrimental effects on bearing life and crankshaft integrity.

To achieve a neutral balance with long-stroke crankshafts, it is usually necessary to add heavy-metal weights to the counterweights by drilling and reaming large holes in the counterweights, then pressing in a slug of Mallory metal to add weight where needed. The holes must be parallel to the crank axis so that centrifugal force doesn't dislodge them at high engine speeds. This adds cost to the balancing operation, but is well worth it in the long run.

Connecting Rods

Stock big-block Chevy rods are I-beam designs (the cross-section of the main beam resembles a capital letter I), and they were all made from forged steel with the same basic dimensions: .990-inch-diameter pin bores (the small end), 2.324-inch-diameter big end to accept the 2.2025-inch inside diameter rod bearings, with a hole center-to-center length of 6.135 inches. Two threaded fasteners on each side of the big end allow the rod cap to be removed for installation on the crankshaft journal.

Stock rod bolts were either 3/8 (most passenger car and truck applications) or 7/16 inch (high-performance applications), have a shaped head to register securely against a shoulder on the main section of the rod, and are knurled to tightly align the main section of the rod with the rod cap. There have only been three types of big-block rods in production engines: the standard passenger car rod ("dog-bone" rods, named after the shape of the forging relief on the beam section), truck rods (with their Q-Tip–shaped relief on the beam), and high-performance "dot" rods (with a distinctive dot cast into the upper portion of the beam relief). These high-performance rods are often erroneously referred to as "dimple" rods, but that is not accurate. Dimples go in, not out. Let's agree to call them dot rods or hi-po rods. The high-performance rods initially used 3/8-inch rod bolts in the 1960s, but subsequently changed to 7/16-inch bolts, which are stronger.

All original equipment big-block rods are physically interchangeable. The standard passenger car rods (dog-bone) are adequate for mild performance street engines up to about 500 hp. The truck rods (Q-Tip–shaped relief) are a bit stronger, and the hi-po rods have been used successfully on many 700-plus-hp engines. But (and this is a big but), it is usually not the rod itself that fails, it is the relatively weak-by-design rod fastener hardware. The OE (original equipment) design uses two nuts with a limited amount of thread engagement to

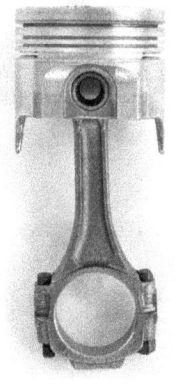

Stock cast piston with a press-fit pin. Note that no pin retainers are necessary with this setup. This four-ring piston is from a heavy-duty 427 truck engine, and that's why Chevrolet went with tall-deck (10.200 inches) blocks for those applications. The connecting rod is the standard "dog-bone" design with 3/8-inch rod bolts.

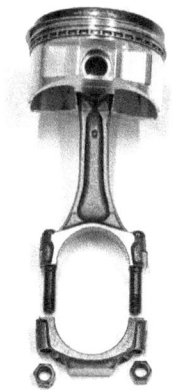

Chevy high-performance "dot" rod with 7/16-inch rod bolts is still a good choice for engines up to about 700 hp. There were three versions of these rods: one with 3/8-inch rod bolts and pressed pins (1965–1969), one with 7/16-inch rod bolts and pressed pins (LS-6 and LS-7), and a version with 7/16-inch boron rod bolts and full-floating pins, which was used in Chevy's killer big-blocks, like the L88 and ZL-1.

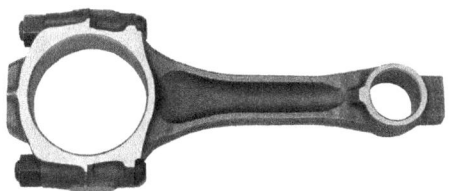

GMPP PN 19170198 is a Magnafluxed 4340 steel rod with heavy-duty 7/16-inch bolts. It is a pressed-piston pin design used in Gen V and Gen VI 454 and 502 engines.

secure the rod cap, and this is the weak link in the connecting rod chain. If you decide to use stock rods, invest in premium rod bolts and nuts from a reputable aftermarket company, such as ARP. Along with conventional replacement rod bolts made from superior steel, ARP has developed the Wave-Lok rod bolt. It features an undulating surface in place of the stress-inducing knurling of conventional rod bolts.

Before the advent of affordable aftermarket rods, it was standard practice to rebuild stock rods for performance applications. The usual procedure was to Magnaflux the rod to detect any cracks, grind and polish the forging lines on the side of the beam, shot-peen the rod to harden and improve the surface finish, bore and ream the small end for a bronze bushing (for full-floating pins), recondition the big-end to restore roundness and proper bearing crush, and then install high-quality rod bolts. Whew! That's a lot of work and money to sink into parts that are still not as strong as the aftermarket rods that are readily available today. And to top it off, you can get the aftermarket rods in a variety of lengths (typically .250 or .400 inch longer than stock, plus many more) to take advantage of better rod/stroke ratios.

Most OEM rods used in passenger cars and light-duty trucks with cast pistons were installed with press-fit wrist pins. This is a very durable system of pin retention, but disassembly requires pushing the pin out with a hydraulic press, which usually damages the piston. Connecting rods for full-floating pins usually have the small end bored out for a bronze bushing that is then honed to a very precise clearance, usually less than .001 inch. The pin is retained in the piston with pin locks that snap into pin retainer grooves

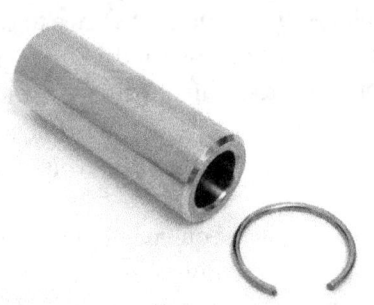

Round wire pin locks must be used with correctly sized and chamfered wrist pins.

These JE pistons are getting the pin bores precisely honed to fit with the supplied wrist pins.

Wrist pin walls may be straight in various thicknesses, or internally tapered on each end to reduce weight.

Since tapered pins weigh less, they are popular for professional competition, but not as strong as straight-wall pins. If you see evidence of scuffing or cracks in the piston pin bores, the pins are flexing under load, and you should change to a stronger pin. Generally you're better off to go with a pin that is stronger than you think you need, rather than take a chance on the lightweight part. This is especially true in high-output engines or with heavy nitrous oxide or supercharged engines.

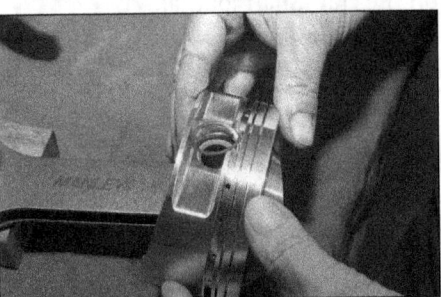

Spirolox rings are a good choice for wrist pin retention. They are a little tough to install and much harder to remove, which is what makes them so good; they want to stay in place. They can be spiraled into the lock groove easily with a little practice, but be sure not to stretch them out of shape during installation. Most piston manufacturers use two per side. Be sure to lube pin with assembly lube before final assembly, and replace Spirolox rings with new ones every time they are removed.

Forged aluminum piston, billet aluminum connecting rod, and heavy-wall wrist pin from a 1,200-plus-hp blown alcohol big-block. Aluminum buttons are normally used to retain the wrist pin in competition engines with blowers and nitrous. Note the step in the buttons, necessary because the pin bore intersects the oil ring groove.

CRANKSHAFTS, CONNECTING RODS AND PISTONS

This high-quality, lightweight Crower I-beam rod is made from 4340 steel and is easily capable of handling more than 1,000 hp. Note that the shoulders of the beam section are profiled for clearance with long stroke big-blocks. It uses 2.100-inch small-block Chevy rod bearing inserts, which not only reduce friction, but allow the rod bolts to be moved closer together for improved rod-to-cam and rod-to-block clearance.

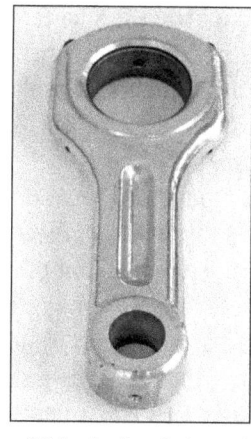

This vintage Bill Miller Engineering (BME) aluminum connecting rod features 2.100-inch small-block Chevy bearings. In addition to reduced bearing speed, the most important benefit of this design is how the standard forging is used, but with a smaller bore in the big end, resulting in a stronger cap-to-main-body junction. Note wrist pin oil hole in top of rod. All full-floating pins must have an oiling provision.

in the piston pin bore. Most street high-performance pistons and all racing pistons utilize full-floating pins, and there are several methods of retaining the pins.

Tru-Arcs are simple snap rings that are quite easy to install and remove, but most aftermarket pistons these days use Spirolox rings to retain the wrist pins. They are a pain to install and even harder to remove, and that's what makes them an excellent choice for wrist pin retention: you don't want your pins to come loose during engine operation. Round wire locks are another popular method of pin retention, but they require special wrist pins that are chamfered on the ends.

With full-floating pins, the pin-to-lock end clearance is critical, since excessive clearance lets the pin batter against the locks, possibly knocking them out. Typical pin-to-retainer clearance is .0000 to .0005 inch. Wrist pin buttons are popular with builders of engines with extremely high horsepower, since they are very easy to install or remove, and absolutely can't be knocked loose. The downside to buttons is that they add weight to the reciprocating assembly, but pistons designed for use with a supercharger or lots of nitrous are usually pretty heavy already, and frequent piston changes are much easier with the buttons.

Because the fit between the wrist pin, piston pin bore, and pin retainers is so critical, most engine builders opt to buy pistons "pin fitted," meaning that the manufacturer has carefully machined and checked these clearances, and supplied the correctly sized pins with the piston. All that remains is to verify the pin-to-connecting-rod clearance, which normally runs from .0008 to .0012 inch. Engines with vacuum pumps may require a bit more clearance, since the pump tends to reduce the amount of oil available to lube the pin bore.

Aftermarket rods for the big-block are available in a variety of shapes and materials to suit various applications from manufacturers such as Bill Miller Engineering, BRC, Carillo, Crower, Eagle,

Due to the greater thermal expansion rate, aluminum rods must use pinned bearings in the cap to prevent spun bearings. Serrated parting line where the cap meets the beam section ensures positive registration. Note that hardened washers have a chamfered side, which must be installed facing the bolt head to clear the large under-head radius.

Rods with full-floating pins require an oil hole to provide splash lubrication to the pin. This hole must be drilled before the small end is honed to final size. You can just barely see the pin oiling hole in the top of this Scat H-beam rod. Note the two relief cuts for the bearing tangs of the big-end bore. These two notches are always on the same side of the bore.

A connecting rod vice holds rods securely for torquing or loosening bolts on the workbench. You can use your shop vice with non-marring aluminum or brass inserts in a pinch.

GRP, Howard's, Lunati, Manley, Ohio Crankshaft, Oliver, Scat, Venolia, and others. There are steel rods available, usually made from very strong 4340 alloy steel, in I-beam and H-beam configurations; aluminum rods that are exclusively used for very-high-RPM drag racing; and even titanium rods for those of you with unlimited budgets. Titanium offers the strength of steel with the light weight of aluminum, but they are so expensive, the vast majority of big-block performance and racing engines are outfitted with either steel or aluminum.

I'm going to venture a rough estimate that 90 percent or more of today's performance and racing big-blocks use steel connecting rods for their brute strength and longevity. Yes, aluminum is lighter, but because it is not as strong as steel, aluminum rods must be physically much larger than steel rods, which limits their use in very-long-stroke engines because there just isn't enough room in the crankcase. Additionally, aluminum rods must be replaced regularly, usually after no more than 200 runs down the quarter-mile. Pro racers replace them even sooner.

One positive attribute of aluminum connecting rods is their ability to dampen severe shock loads, such as those that are common in supercharged, exotic fuel-burning engines, or with massive amounts of nitrous oxide. Aluminum rods are used in those types of engines to save the crankshaft and bearings from frequent failure, and replacement is just seen as part of the regular maintenance schedule for these fire-breathers. Also, aluminum rods expand more when they get hot, so rod bearings must be drilled for an anti-rotation dowel (which is pressed into the cap), and minimum piston-to-head clearance must be at least .050 inch (consult with your piston/rod manufacturer for their specs) to allow for the aluminum rod growth.

Rod Length

In this section, I'm going to butcher and barbecue a few sacred cows that have been worshiped for the past few decades. I'll get right to the point: the job of the connecting rod is to connect the piston to the crank journal, and the center-to-center length has very little effect on the engine's power production. Much has been written about the importance of longer-than-stock connecting rods—how they have a better rod angle, produce less piston skirt loading, have more "dwell time" at top dead center (TDC), and the importance of the rod-to-stroke ratio. Balderdash. I can hear your teeth gnashing now. Good. Let's try some new ideas.

First, I use longer-than-stock rods in all of my racing engines, but not for any of the reasons listed above. Remember, your primary goal with the rotating assembly is to make it as light as possible, while still retaining adequate strength to do the job. And longer rods lead to shorter pistons that weigh less than the tall pistons used with short rods. As much as I'd like to take credit for coming up with this radical anti-establishment statement, I can't. The credit belongs to noted Chevrolet engine builder and Pro Stock pioneer David Reher, of Reher-Morrison Racing Engines. Author of many technical articles on big-block Chevy racing engines. Here's what David has to say on the subject:

"Many books and technical articles have been written concerning the supposed importance of connecting rod length to racing engine performance. Rod length actually has very little impact on power output. Choose your

The reason tall-deck blocks and long rods are needed with long-stroke engines has little to do with the piston/rod angle after TDC, and a lot to do with how far the piston skirt extends below the bore at BDC. The more the piston sticks out the bottom of the bore, the less stable it becomes, which not only affects ring seal but also increases piston skirt wear. These long rods (6.800 inches) provide piston-skirt-to-crank-counterweight clearance with this 4.500-inch-stroke crank in a tall-deck (10.200 inches) block.

This +.400-inch Manley H-beam 4340 steel rod is typical of the high-quality aftermarket rods that are readily available in a variety of lengths for the big-block Chevy. They are nominally rated to 900 hp, but routinely end up in engines making in excess of 1,000 hp with no problems.

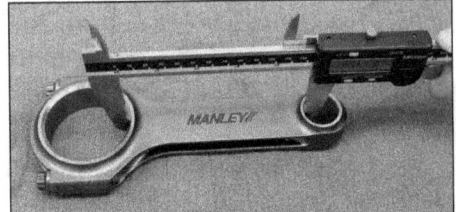

To get rod center-to-center length, just measure the beam section and add 1/2 of the pin bore diameter and 1/2 of the big-end diameter. Standard pin bores are .990 inch and the big end should be 2.324 inches. Add them and divide by two to get 1.657 inches. Stock Chevy rod length is 6.135 inches, so 6.135 − 1.657 = 4.478 inches. This beam section measures 4.878 inches, so this is a "+.400-inch" rod.

CRANKSHAFTS, CONNECTING RODS AND PISTONS

crankshaft and pistons first; they dictate the rod length you need.

"Conventional racing engine theory states that long-rod engines have significantly different torque and horsepower profiles than do short-rod engines. The theory is that the rod length affects the position and speed of the piston. Statements are often made that the piston lingers (dwells) near TDC on a long-rod engine and that this affects breathing. This turns out to be largely untrue.

"At 10-degree ATDC (the time when the most pressure is present in the cylinder on a power stroke), the difference in piston location between the longest (6.535 inches) and shortest (6.135 inches) rod engines is only .0004 inch. Even at 45 degrees of crank rotation, the difference is only .010 inch. This amounts to only .16 ci per cylinder in a 502-ci engine. Rod length and angularity have very little real impact on engine performance."

Bearings

Automotive engines use plain bearings, which are sized so precisely to the crankshaft journals that they literally float the crank and rods on a hydrodynamic wedge of oil supplied by the oil pump. What we gearheads call bearings are really bearing inserts, which can easily be changed when worn and sized to accommodate changes in the crankshaft; for instance, when the crank journals are ground undersize.

Most bearings feature a tri-metal design: a hard steel backing to retain the shape, a layer of copper for thermal conductivity, and a layer of soft Babbitt that can embed small particles without damaging the crank journals. Some performance engine bearings offer an additional coating of some type of polymer or Teflon for even greater friction reduction.

Chevy engine bearings are split into two halves that get clamped together when you tighten the main caps in the block (main bearings) or the connecting rod cap (rod bearings). The bearings are slightly larger than the bore so that they are securely clamped when you tighten the caps. This is called bearing crush, and is one of the reasons that bearings are thinner at the ends. Another reason is that the high loads in a performance engine tend to elongate the opening in the bearing bore, and this action pulls the sides of the bearing inward. Consequently, when you measure bearing diameter and clearance, always measure at a point 90 degrees from the parting line.

Locating tabs align the bearing inserts with matching notches in the block and the rods. Chevy main bearings have an oil hole and groove in one half, and this half always goes in the block and aligns with the oil supply hole. The bearing insert in the main caps has no oil hole or grooves. In the past, some thought that grooving the bearings all the way around (360 degrees) ensured more oil supply to the main journals, but that has since proven to be faulty logic. Such a bearing only lessens the load-carrying ability of the oil wedge, and should never be used. Connecting rod bearings are the same for the upper (beam section) and the lower (rod cap), except that aluminum connecting rods require a hole in the cap bearing for a locating dowel. Because of aluminum's high thermal expansion rate, the dowel prevents the bearing from spinning in the bore, which destroys the engine in short order.

Most performance bearings are slightly narrower than passenger car bearings to provide needed clearance with the larger fillet radius in a high-performance crankshaft. Bearing inserts are available in many sizes, usually standard (OEM spec), and undersizes of .001, .010, .020, .030, and .040 inch. Custom cranks may require entirely different bearings; for instance, many big-block cranks are offered with small-block Chevy rod journals of either 2.100 or 2.000 inches. Pro Stock engines use Honda rod bearings measuring 1.889 inches (48 mm) and 2.500-inch main bearings from a 409 Chevy.

Stock big-block bearing specs call for clearances of .002 to .0025 inch, but most performance engine builders prefer slightly larger clearances of .003 to .004 inch. This is one of the reasons that most performance big-blocks are equipped with high-volume oil pumps, because larger clearances result in more internal oil leakage.

Pistons

Although those shiny new pistons are well hidden inside your big-block, their importance in the engine's power production is paramount. Remember that other modifications (such as a bigger cam, aluminum heads and intake manifold, exhaust headers, double throw-down carburetor, and flame-thrower

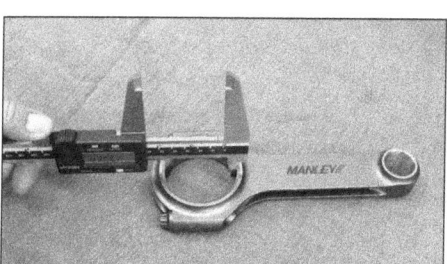

When measuring bearing clearance, always measure at a point 90 degrees from the parting line.

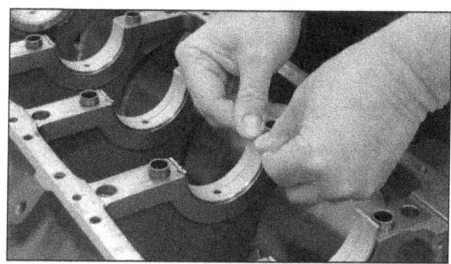

Chevy main bearings have an oil hole and groove in one half, and this half always goes in the block and aligns with the oil supply hole.

CHAPTER 3

ignition) are of little or no value if they don't lead to higher pressure on the piston during the power stroke. The piston, ring, and cylinder wall must all work together to harness the energy of combustion, letting as little as possible escape in the form of blow-by (gas leakage past the rings) and frictional losses.

The piston design can also be a source of additional power through higher compression ratios, which extract more thermal energy from each drop of fuel, but there are limits to how much can be gained with a particular type of fuel. An engine with a 14:1 compression ratio makes more power than the same engine with 9.5:1 compression, if the fuel has a high enough octane rating to prevent pre-ignition and detonation; that means race gas. But for street use, 92-octane premium pump gas generally does not tolerate more than a 9.5:1 compression ratio (higher with aluminum heads and other "tricks"). The first general rule here is to go for all the compression you can get within the boundaries of the fuel you use. More compression is as close as you can get to "free" horsepower in an internal combustion engine.

Big-block Chevy pistons are either cast or forged aluminum. Most production engines were equipped with cast pistons, which are actually an aluminum casting over a steel strut, which serves to strengthen the relatively weak cast part. The biggest advantage of cast pistons is that they expand less than forged pistons when hot, so they may be fitted to the bores with less piston-to-wall clearance. This offers the benefit of less noise and piston clatter upon start-up, and very good ring seal and longevity because tighter clearances mean less piston rock in the cylinder bore.

A variant of cast pistons are hypereutectic pistons, which are cast from an aluminum alloy containing more silicon than traditional cast pistons. They also can be fitted tightly to the bore, with typical piston-to-wall clearances of .002 inch. They are stronger than regular cast pistons, but still do not provide the extreme strength of forged pistons, and should not be used in racing big-blocks or with more than a small amount of nitrous, typically up to 150 hp.

Forged aluminum pistons are the best choice for any serious performance engine, and all of Chevy's potent factory high-performance engines came with forged pistons. Even within the forged piston ranks, different aluminum alloys are used depending on the application. Most high-performance street and moderate strip engines are best served with

JE SRP 4032 forged aluminum piston with a high-compression dome for open chamber heads has 1/16-inch top rings and a 3/16-inch oil ring. Note oil drainback holes in oil ring groove. Piston diameter should be measured 1 inch up from bottom of the skirt, perpendicular to the pin bore.

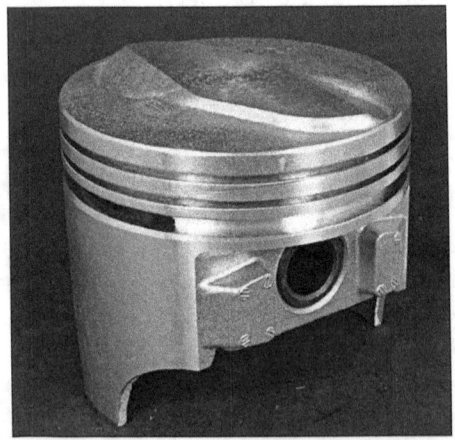

Most OEM pistons are cast aluminum, like this Silv-O-Lite stock replacement 427 piston. The offset pin location reduces piston "slap" and results in quieter engine operation. With a .140-inch dome, it makes 9.5:1 compression with closed-chamber heads and accepts stock spec 5/64-inch top rings and 3/16-inch oil rings.

This KB Performance hypereutectic piston for a 454 big-block has a net dome volume of 12 cc. Because piston-to-wall clearance is so tight (.002 inch), it offers a very stable platform for excellent ring seal and long life in a street Rat motor. Compression is 9.1:1 with 119-cc open combustion chambers, and 9.9:1 with 108-cc closed chamber heads.

Some piston manufacturers offer the option of digitizing your cylinder head combustion chambers and machining the piston domes to match perfectly, with the valve reliefs in exactly the correct position, angle, and depth to match your heads. This JE Pistons engineer is designing a custom big-block piston using sophisticated computer-aided design and manufacturing software.

This JE piston has a CNC-machined max piston dome to match Edelbrock Victor 24-degree heads. Note lateral gas ports in the top ring groove, and accumulator groove between the top and second ring grooves. An oil ring support rail is used where the oil ring intersects the pin bore.

As supplied by the piston manufacturer, piston domes may have sharp edges from the many machining operations; these cause hot spots, which can cause pre-ignition. These should be smoothed by hand, removing as little material as possible to retain compression.

pistons forged from 4032 aluminum, a high-silicon alloy providing good lubricity and less expansion due to heat. Typical piston-to-wall clearance with 4032 is .0045 to .006 inch. For supercharged, heavy nitrous, or all-out racing applications, most manufacturers use 2618 aluminum for its tremendous strength and durability under high-heat/high-load conditions.

However, the downside is that piston-to-wall clearances must be opened up to .0065 to .008 inch due to its higher thermal growth rate. Careful warm-ups are definitely called for before any full-throttle loads are put on the engine because the pistons are quite loose until operating temps are realized, and excessive blow-by and oil consumption may result as the cold piston/ring package rattles around the bore.

Like most other performance parts for the big-block Chevy, we enjoy an almost embarrassing number of good aftermarket piston manufacturers that can supply pistons for virtually any bore, stroke, rod length (compression height of the piston), dome shape and volume, valve reliefs, and ring package you can imagine. You may choose from a dizzying array of stock replacement or custom pistons from Arias, BRC, Diamond, Federal-Mogul/Speed-Pro/Sealed Power, JE, Keith Black/Silv-O-Lite, Probe, Ross, Venolia, Wiseco, and others.

Piston Rings

The most important function of the piston is to provide a stable platform for the rings to achieve the best possible seal with the cylinder bore. Careful attention to the ring selection, cylinder bore preparation, and ring fit inside the piston ring grooves is just as important to your high-performance engine as the latest camshaft, carburetor, or cylinder head.

Modern pistons for the big-block have three rings; a top compression ring, a second compression ring, and an oil control ring, which is really an assembly of two steel rails and a wavy spacer designed to scrape excess oil from the cylinder walls on the down stroke. Ring material is usually cast iron, ductile iron, or steel, and high-performance rings typically have a plasma-molybdenum face for better sealing and reduced friction with the cylinder walls. Chrome rings are available for engines that are subjected to dirty operating conditions, such as off-road racing, but they require a different cylinder wall finish and do not conform to the cylinder bore as well as high-performance rings. Low-tension oil rings are popular to reduce ring drag, but should only be used if the engine has some type of crankcase pressure reduction system such as a vacuum pump, dry sump oil pump, or pan evacuation system in the headers.

Stock cast aluminum big-block pistons are machined for rings that measure 5/64, 5/64, and 3/16 inch (oil ring). They are typically made from cast iron. Nearly all high-performance pistons for the street and modest racing applications use 1/16-, 1/16-, and 3/16-inch rings. Narrower rings have less mass than the fatties, and are able to maintain a good seal in the ring groove without fluttering at high engine speeds. High-end racing engines often use top rings measuring .043 inch, and Pro Stockers may use rings as thin as .7 mm (.0275 inch) with 3-mm (.118-inch) oil rings. As with everything, there is a trade-off. Narrow rings cannot handle as much heat as thick rings, and they wear out quicker.

Obviously your ring choice is influenced by your application; you don't use the same rings in a street engine that you hope can survive for 100,000 miles as you use in an 8,000-rpm race Rat.

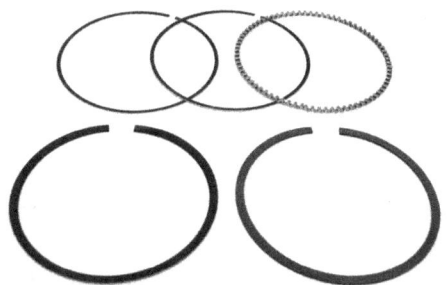

A typical ring package for high-performance pistons would include 1/16-inch top and second rings with a 3/16-inch low-tension oil control ring. This set has a barrel-face moly top ring, tapered cast-iron second ring, and three-piece oil ring assembly consisting of two steel rails and a wavy steel expander. Most engine builders order rings that are .005-inch over the finished bore size, then file fit each ring to a specific end gap for reduced blow-by.

CHAPTER 3

Engine Preparation - Iron Cylinders
Finish hone cylinder walls with torque plates installed if available. Recommended hone grit specification: moly-face or cast iron top ring 280-320 grit. Chrome face top ring: 220-280 grit. Finished hone with a 22 to 24 degree cross-hatch pattern off horizontal axis.

If this crosshatch angle pattern differs from the O.E. makers' recommendations please follow the O.E. specifications.

Cylinder Deck Surface

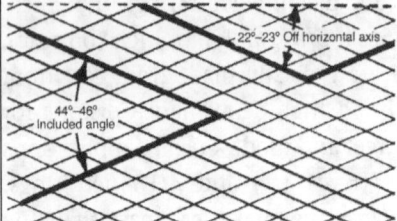

Plateau Honing - call

Nikasil® or Coated Cylinders - call

RING INSTALLATION
See gapping chart for recommended ring end gap and procedures.

Total Seal Gapless® Top Ring
1) Install machined ring first with groove side down and gap 180° from 2nd ring end gap (see fig. 1).
2) Install rail into groove machined in ring with gaps opposed 180°.

Top Rings (Conventional)
1) If ring has a dot or laser mark, install that side up.
2) Unmarked rings with inner bevel are installed bevel side up.
3) Rings without dot or inner bevel install either side up.

Total Seal Gapless® 2nd Ring
1) Install machined ring first with groove side down and gap 180° from top ring end gap (see fig 1).
2) Install rail into groove machined in ring with gaps oppose 180°.

Non Gapless (Conventional) 2nd and 3rd Rings
1) If ring has a dot or laser mark, install that side up.
2) Unmarked rings with an inner bevel install bevel side down.
3) Rings without a dot or inner bevel install either side up.

Oil Control Ring
1) Three piece type - install as shown in figure 1.
2) **Do not attempt to modify expander in any way.**

Fig. 1

*If piston has more than 2 compression grooves, subsequent rings should be positioned 180° apart in descending order.

Helpful Tips for Ring Fitting and Seating
All pistons (including new ones) should be checked for proper ring to groove clearances.

Ring to piston groove back clearance should be a MINIMUM of .005" deeper than radial wall dimension of piston ring. When rings are installed and bottomed out in the ring groove they should not protrude past the edge of the ring land. Due to variations in piston manufacturing it is the end users responsibility to check for proper fitment prior to final assembly.

Fig. 2

Ring to groove side clearance should be a minimum of .0015 to a maximum of .003" (see fig. 2).

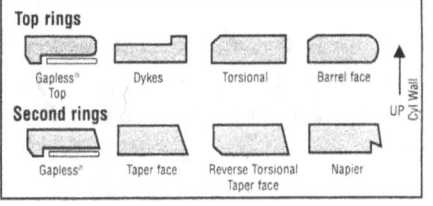

Fig. 3

All GMPP 502-ci crate engines use a unique ring package measuring 2, 1.5, and 4 mm (oil ring). The production 4-mm oil ring is a low-drag version that may cause excessive oil consumption in some applications. If you are re-ringing the original pistons and are not using some sort of crankcase evacuation system, it is a good idea to replace it with a conventional 4-mm oil ring.

There are many top ring face designs, but the most popular for performance is

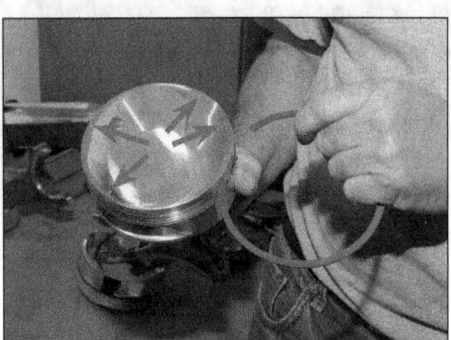

It's easy to check ring back clearance by rolling the ring around the groove. Note the vertical gas ports drilled in the piston top, which intersect the back of the top ring groove.

With a long stroke and/or long connecting rods, it's common for the pin bore to intersect the oil ring groove. JE supplies a support rail to span the gap and support the oil ring. The support rail's radial tension pulls it in toward the piston, while the oil ring rails are designed to push out against the cylinder wall for a better ring seal. Note the locating dimple on the bottom of the rail, which must be positioned in the pin bore gap.

Cross-sections of typical high-performance and racing ring designs. Gapless top or second rings feature a steel rail under the main ring section, which closes off the end gap for greatly reduced blow-by and more power. (Illustration Courtesy Total Seal)

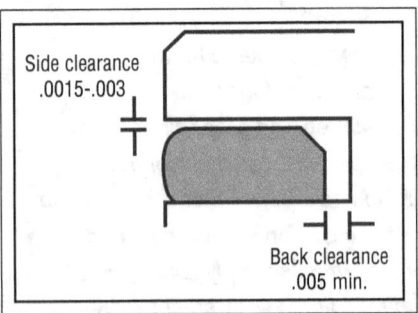

Piston ring-to-groove clearance is just as important as piston-to-wall clearance for maximum power. The correct clearance lets combustion gases behind the ring push it tighter into the cylinder bore for a better seal. Many competition pistons have gas ports drilled into the top ring land for the same effect, only more so. Back clearance is necessary to prevent rings from bottoming in the groove and to provide the needed volume for combustion gases to pressurize the ring. Some manufacturers offer back-cut rings to fit in a shallower ring groove, which may be necessary with very high ring locations and deep valve relief notches. (Illustration Courtesy Total Seal)

CRANKSHAFTS, CONNECTING RODS AND PISTONS

the barrel-face plasma-moly. Dykes top rings have an L-shaped cross-section that uses combustion pressure to seal tightly against the cylinder walls, although most Rat racers these days accomplish the same thing by using traditional rings with gas ports in the piston to pressurize the back side of the ring. Second rings may have a reverse taper or Napier design, which has an undercut to reduce the width of the tapered face to aid in scraping oil off the cylinder wall on the down stroke.

Harmonic Dampeners

That big chunk of metal on the front of your crankshaft serves a much more important function than just a place to bolt on the front pulley. Sometimes called a harmonic balancer, or just balancer, its real function is to dampen harmonic vibrations from the crankshaft. Without one, or with one that is not matched to your engine, the crankshaft eventually develops cracks and fails.

Big-block dampeners fall into two categories: internally balanced or externally balanced. All 3.76-inch-stroke engines (396, 402, and 427) came with an internally balanced dampener, and 4.000-inch-stroke engines (454 and 502) came with externally balanced dampeners. Stock harmonic dampeners were available in 7- and 8-inch diameters. If you look closely, you see that the dampener is actually two pieces of metal—a center hub that bolts to the crank and an external metal ring that is bonded to the hub with rubber. That is why you must use the proper dampener installation and puller tools for removal and installation. If you were to use a common gear puller, you would pull the outer ring off the hub and destroy the unit. Likewise, installation should never be done by hammering on the dampener as that also destroys the bond between the two parts. Stock dampeners are subject to deterioration of the rubber bond, which leads to inaccuracies when setting the ignition timing if the outer ring has shifted its position.

All high-performance and racing big-blocks should be equipped with an aftermarket harmonic dampener that is designed to control these damaging harmonic vibrations much better than the stock units. If you are going take your car to the dragstrip, an SFI-approved dampener is mandatory for cars running quicker than 10.0 seconds in the quarter-mile. Even if your car isn't that quick, the benefits of longer crank and internal parts life is worth the investment. Note that GM's big-boy 572-ci crate engines come with an SFI dampener (PN 88962814), which is available through GM Performance Parts. This is an internally balanced dampener, and works well on any 396-, 402-, or 427-cube motor as well.

This stock externally balanced 454 harmonic dampener has a large counterbalance weight on the back side.

Fluidampr's CT Gold dampeners use centering technology to improve the control of torsional vibrations above 6,000 rpm. Targeted at drag race big-blocks, this new technology allows the inertia ring to remain centered in the housing cavity, even when the unit is at rest. This one has a counterbalance weight for use with 454/502 externally balanced engines. (Photo Courtesy Fluidampr)

GMPP's harmonic dampener PN 12361146 is standard equipment on the 572-ci crate engines. This 8-inch-diameter internally balanced dampener is SFI-certified and works on any neutral-balance engine. (Photo Courtesy GMPP)

The Rattler by TCI takes a unique approach to vibration control. Pendulum weights inside the dampener are designed to move to counteract the crankshaft harmonics. The principle is similar to a deadblow hammer, which uses moveable shot to prevent bounce-back. (Photo Courtesy TCI)

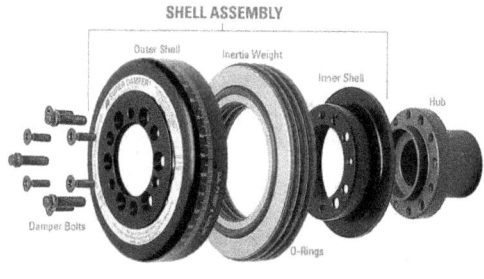

Exploded view of ATI's Super Damper shows the internal inertia weight with tunable O-rings for specific engine combinations. The outer shell bolts solidly to the hub so there is no chance of the timing marks shifting position, which is a common failure of stock harmonic dampeners. (Photo Courtesy ATI)

Ring End Gap

Piston rings must have an opening so that they can be expanded for installation over the piston, and that leaves a gap when they are installed in the engine. Stock replacement rings are sized to provide a generous end gap when installed in the bore, due to variations in bore sizing. A change of .001 inch in bore diameter produces a change of .003 inch in the gap, and standard rings may have as much as .030-inch or more end gaps. The smaller that opening, the less combustion pressure is lost, so high-performance rings are offered in +.005-inch bore sizes that require filing of the end gaps to fit the exact bore. Compression rings operate in a very hot environment, so the minimum end gap must not be so small that the ends butt together, which causes ring and/or piston land failure.

Is it worth the trouble to file-fit rings? You bet! Results vary, but some builders have seen 20-hp gains over conventional pre-gapped rings. Gapless rings are also available, and they are capable of even further power increases with reduced blow-by. Gapless rings are actually two rings in one assembly, designed so that their gaps never line up during engine operation. They still must be file-fitted by hand; in fact, you may have to file-fit both ring segments. Gapless rings are typically installed in either the top or second ring grooves, but not in both.

You could file ring gaps with a traditional file, but commercial ring filers are available that range from reasonably priced hand-cranked models to elaborate motorized units with built-in dial indicators for the high-volume shop.

You should always consult with the manufacturer for specific ring end-gap specifications, but the following guideline from JE Pistons is a good reference. Note that the second ring gaps are generally larger than the top ring, while some manufacturers recommend tighter second ring gaps. That is because the top ring is subject to higher heat from combustion, so the ring expands more. You can indeed run the second ring gaps tighter, but the larger gap helps to give combustion pressure (which gets trapped between the two ring grooves) somewhere to go, and it helps the second ring do a better job of removing oil from the cylinder walls. This is also why many racing pistons have an accumulator groove between the top and second ring grooves; it delays the build-up of pressure that gets past the top ring.

Ring End Gap Table*

Application	Top Ring Minimum Gap per Inch of Bore	Second Ring Minimum Gap per Inch of Bore	Oil Ring Rail Minimum Gap
High-performance Street & Strip	Bore x .0045 inch	Bore x .0050 inch	.015 inch
Street Moderate Turbo/Nitrous	Bore x .0050 inch	Bore x .0055 inch	.015 inch
Late Model Stock	Bore x .0050 inch	Bore x .0053 inch	.015 inch
Circle Track/Drag Race	Bore x .0055 inch	Bore x .0057 inch	.015 inch
Nitrous Race Only	Bore x .0070 inch	Bore x .0065 inch	.015 inch
Supercharged Race Only	Bore x .0060 inch	Bore x .0060 inch	.015 inch

* Use as a guideline only.

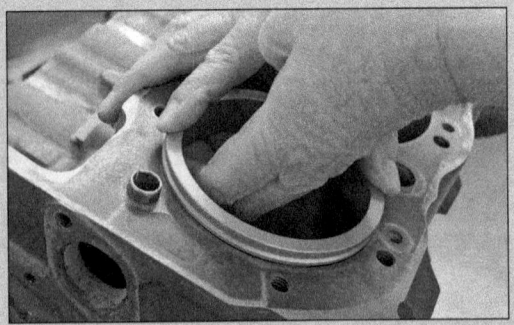

1 *The first step in filing ring gaps is to square the ring in the bore. You can use a commercially made tool like this one, or an inverted old flat-top piston of the correct bore size. A nice feature of the purpose-made tool is that you can make sure the ring is flush against the tool face with your fingers.*

CRANKSHAFTS, CONNECTING RODS AND PISTONS

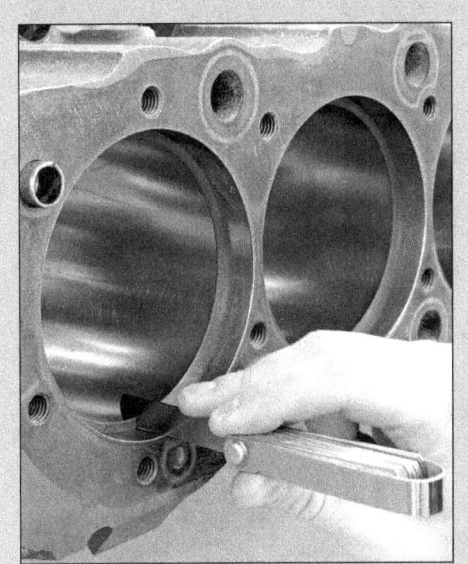

2 Measure the ring end gap with a feeler gauge. If you are using +.005-inch rings, there might not be any gap at all before you begin filing, but you need to check to be sure.

3 This motorized ring filer makes the job go much quicker, but you still need to take a little off the ring at a time and measure between each filing. Most casual engine builders use a hand-crank model that still gets the job done, but it takes a little longer. With the hand-crank filer, be sure to turn the cutting wheel into the ring from the outside so you don't chip the moly facing on the ring. Plan on spending an entire afternoon on this project.

4 The last step is to de-burr the edges of the cut with some emery cloth over a hard backing or machinist's stone. Don't bevel the edges, just knock off any small burrs.

While there are SFI-certified externally balanced dampeners, most racing engine builders prefer to have the crankshaft internally balanced by adding heavy metal to the crank counterweights during the engine balancing operation. This likely adds several hundred dollars to the cost of balancing, but the results are a much more balanced and stable rotating assembly. Of course, the flywheel or flexplate must also match the crank and dampener combo, whether internally or externally balanced.

Aftermarket dampeners use various methods to control harmonic vibration. Many refine the OEM elastomer-to-metal bonding technique to prevent deterioration of the bond, but Fluidampr uses an inertia weight dampened with viscous fluid inside a sealed unit to control engine harmonics. Another approach is taken by the TCI Rattler, which has internal pendulum rollers that move to counteract crankshaft vibration in a running engine. All SFI-certified dampeners have passed stringent tests to ensure safe operation at high engine speeds, and may be relied upon to deliver excellent performance.

Aftermarket harmonic dampeners are available in 6-, 7-, and 8-inch diameters (approximately) to satisfy the requirements of different big-block engine combinations. In general, the larger dampeners are needed with long strokes, and the smaller dampeners allow a competition engine to rev quicker. Most are all steel, but some are available with aluminum components to reduce weight, again for quicker acceleration. Before you automatically go for the smallest, lightest dampener to get your hot rod down the racetrack quicker, remember that the dampener's most important function is to reduce damaging crankshaft harmonics and improve the lifespan of your engine. Check with the manufacturer for specific recommendations, and you and your crankshaft will both be happy.

ATI Super Damper being installed on an all aluminum big-block racing engine. Always use the correct damper installation tool; never hammer on the damper.

CHAPTER 3

Flywheels and Flexplates

Big-block Chevy flywheels are available in two diameters, 14 and 12.75 inches, although the vast majority use the larger 168-tooth size. Flexplates, so-called because they allow the torque converter a small amount of flex to properly center itself on the transmission input shaft, are only available in the larger 168-tooth configuration. Big-block flywheels and flexplates are either neutral balance for use with 396-, 402-, and 427-ci engines, or have external balance weights for use with 454- and 502-ci engines. Engines with one-piece crankshaft seals require externally balanced flywheels or flexplates (except for GMPP ZZ427, ZZ572/620, ZZ572/720R, and the Anniversary Edition 427).

Check the charts below to find the correct GM parts for specific engine applications.

Flexplates are thinner than flywheels and require different-length bolts. Stock flexplate bolts PN 3727207 (six required) are 7/16-20 x 27/32 inch, and flywheel bolts PN 12337973 (six required) are 1.0 inch long. High-performance and racing big-blocks put a tremendous load on these six fasteners and it's always a good idea to upgrade to specialty aftermarket flywheel or flexplate bolts, such as those offered by ARP. A flywheel dowel (GM PN 10046031, 7/16-inch OD x 7/8-inch long) is also a good idea with any high-output Rat motor.

Remember that these are original equipment flywheels and flexplates, and

GM Performance Parts Big-Block Flywheels

Part Number	Year of Engine	Outside Diameter (inches)	Crank Flange Bolt Pattern	Clutch Diameter (inches)	Starter Ring Gear Teeth	Technical Notes
14085720	1965–present	12.75	3.58	10.40	153	Lightweight nodular iron; weighs approximately 15 lbs; for internally balanced engines
3991469	1965–present	14.00	3.58	11.00	168	Use with internally balanced engines and balancer PN 3879623
3993827	1970–1990	14.00	3.58	11.00	168	Counterweighted for externally balanced 454 Mark IV 2-piece rear seal engines; use with balancer PN 10216339
14096987	1991–present	14.00	3.58	11.00	168	Lightweight nodular iron; for externally balanced engines
12582964	1965–present	14.00	3.58	11.50	168	Used with 427 or 572 crate engine; internally balanced

GM Performance Parts Big-Block Flexplates

Part Number	Year of Engine	Outside Diameter (inches)	Crank Flange Bolt Pattern	Converter Bolt Pattern (inches)	Starter Ring Gear Teeth	Technical Notes
10185034	1991–up	14.00	3.58	10.75 and 11.50	168	Use with forged steel crank; has dual converter bolt pattern (502 & 454 1-piece rear main seal)
12561217	1991–up	14.00	3.58	11.50	168	427-ci crate engine production internally balanced, .100 thick
471598	1965–present	14.00	3.58	10.75 and 11.50	168	For internally balanced engines; use with 572/620 crate engine; has dual converter pattern, .120 thick
14001992	1970–1990	14.00	3.58	11.50	168	For externally balanced 454 Mark IV 2-piece rear main seal engines

CRANKSHAFTS, CONNECTING RODS AND PISTONS

Stock 454 flexplate has a large counterbalance weight next to the starter ring gear. This externally balanced flexplate must be used with matching harmonic damper and externally balanced crank (454 and 502).

GMPP flexplate PN 12561217 is .100 inch thick for internally balanced engines. (Photo Courtesy GMPP)

GMPP flywheel P/N 14096987 is lightweight nodular iron for externally balanced engines. (Photo Courtesy GMPP)

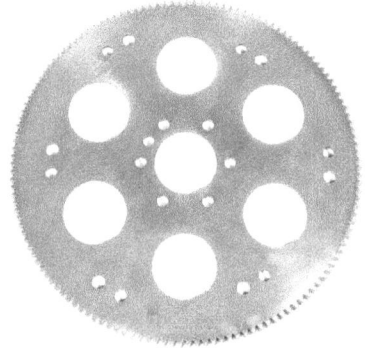

Meziere billet steel flexplate is machined from solid 4340 steel for maximum strength with minimum runout. They are available with standard 12-pitch gears (168-tooth), or new 10-pitch tooth design with 139 teeth, which must be used with a matching 10-pitch starter. (Photo Courtesy Meziere Enterprises)

An SFI-certified scattershield like this Lakewood PN 15000 is required for any car running quicker than 11.50 in the quarter-mile, and it's a good investment for any standard transmission-equipped high-performance big-block car. (Photo Courtesy Lakewood)

An SFI-certified flywheel, like this Hayes 153-tooth steel flywheel, is also required for any car running quicker than 11.50 in the quarter-mile. (Photo Courtesy Hayes)

do not meet SFI specs required by most race sanctioning bodies. I urge you to equip your big-block with a high-quality aftermarket flywheel or flexplate meeting SFI specs. Those parts have been tested and approved for high-RPM use and are not likely to disintegrate with catastrophic results. If you have a Gen V or Gen VI engine, note that cast crank and forged crank engines require different flywheels or flexplates. When switching to an aftermarket wheel on Gen V/VI engines, you need to have the crank balanced with the new flywheel and harmonic dampener.

Starters

Stock starters are fine for stock engines, but high-compression and large-displacement Rat motors need all the cranking power they can get.

There are two basic OEM starter designs for the big-block that must be used with the matching 12¾- or 14-inch flywheels/flexplates. All generations of big-blocks use the same 3 x 3/8-16 bolt-hole pattern on the right side of the engine to accommodate either starter design. The majority of Rat motors are equipped with a 14-inch (168-tooth) flexplate, and the OE starter design uses the two staggered bolt-holes for mounting. The 12¾-inch flywheels had 153 teeth, and starters for these engines used the two bolt-holes perpendicular to the crank centerline in the block. There were no 12¾-inch (153 tooth) flexplates produced by Chevrolet, so these starters would only be used on vehicles equipped with standard transmissions. Production starters are adequate for most streetable big-blocks with up to 10.5:1 compression, but high-compression and large-cubic-inch motors need a high-torque aftermarket starter.

Full-size OEM-type starters use an engine brace to support the front of the starter, while the lighter mini-starters don't require a brace. Heat shields are available from many sources and may be constructed from sheet metal or some type of protective high-heat blanket.

The use of 16-volt batteries is common in racing applications, and this presents no problem to the starter. The extra kick from a 16-volt system results in a quicker start-up, so that the starter is actually working less than with a 12-volt system. There are even aftermarket starters wired for 24 volts that must be used with dual 12-volt batteries.

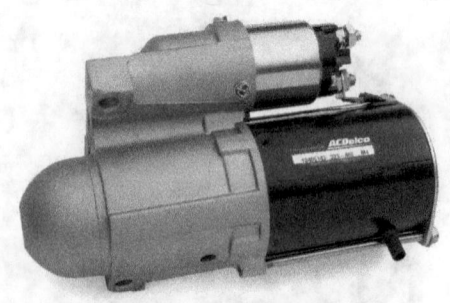

GMPP starter PN 10465143 is a lightweight starter suitable for street-performance big-blocks with a 153-tooth flywheel. Originally for 1993–1997 Camaros and Firebirds with the LT1 engine, the bolt pattern is inline and must be used with starter bolts PN 14097279 (1) and P/N 14097278 (1). (Photo Courtesy GMPP)

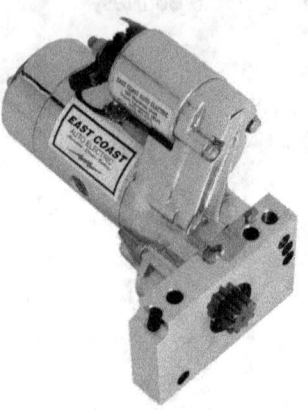

This high-torque Super Mini Starter from East Coast Auto Electric features a gear-reduction 2.4-hp motor, and the body can be clocked to provide extra clearance for your particular oil pan or headers. The dual mounting pattern works with either 12¾- or 14-inch flexplates. Chrome doesn't make your car any faster, but it sure looks good!

GM Performance Parts offers this mini-starter (PN 12361146) that weighs only 10.5 pounds and has a 3.75:1 gear reduction ratio. It works with both 12¾- and 14-inch flywheels or flexplates and includes mounting bolts, shims, gaskets, and electrical connectors. (Photo Courtesy GMPP)

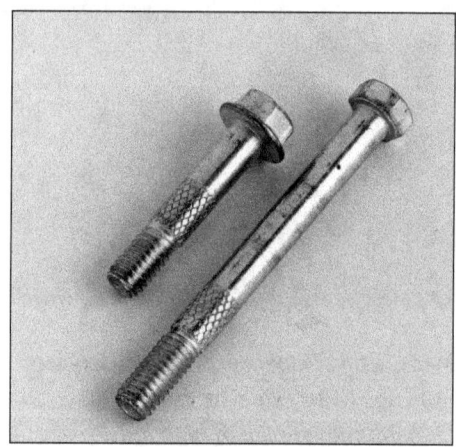

OE starter bolts are knurled to accurately locate the starter and must be used to prevent damage or failure of the starter and/or ring gear on the flywheel.

Meziere starter features 2.2 kilowatts of cranking power and is available with standard 12-pitch or larger 10-pitch gear for mountain motors with very high compression ratios. The 10-pitch starters must be used with matching 10-pitch flexplates. (Photo Courtesy Meziere Enterprises)

Most big-blocks produced before 1975 used ignition distributors with points, and those starters include an "R" terminal (the small terminal on the left) to by-pass the ballast resistor for more voltage to the spark plugs while cranking the engine. If you have an electronic distributor, including the HEI, this terminal is not needed. Most aftermarket starters do not have this provision, since modern engines all use electronic ignition systems.

A starter heat shield like this one from Moroso helps prevent heat soak. This unit fits stock Delco starters, but they are also available for most aftermarket starters. (Photo Courtesy Moroso)

CHAPTER 4

Camshafts, Lifters and Valvetrain Components

Choosing a cam profile and matching valvetrain parts is one of the most critical steps in building your high-performance big-block, and there are literally hundreds of choices available from the aftermarket manufacturers. That is both good and bad—it's good because somewhere out there is the perfect cam for your application, and bad because there are hundreds of wrong choices too. I'm going to try to steer you in the right direction when it comes time to select the cam for your rad Rat, but the best piece of advice I can give you right now is to consult with the manufacturer's tech consultants for the proper cam selection. There are dozens of variables when it comes to selecting a cam profile that matches not only your engine, but also your intended use of the car.

Types of Camshafts and Lifters

There are four types of lifter designs and matching camshafts currently available for the big-block Chevy: flat-tappet in either mechanical (fixed length) and hydraulic (self-adjusting), and roller lifters that have a roller bearing that follows the contours of the cam lobe, also in either mechanical or hydraulic. I'll cut right to the chase: the roller lifter designs are superior in every way to the traditional flat-tappet designs that we have been using since the big-block made its appearance in 1963. Obviously, roller tappets offer less friction during operation, but that is not their most redeeming quality.

The real benefit of roller tappets is twofold. First, because the contact patch between the roller and the cam lobe is so narrow, roller cam profiles can be much more aggressive than flat-tappet cams, and, second, due to the improved wear characteristics of the roller, much higher valvespring rates can be used. The more we modify our project Rat motor for higher power levels and higher RPM, the more important valvespring pressure becomes to eliminate valve float (which is defined as when the valves remain open beyond their engineered specification due to engine speed overcoming the valvespring's ability to close the

The camshaft and matching valvetrain hardware determine the "personality" of your engine, and must be carefully selected to complement the engine/vehicle combination. (Photo Courtesy Comp Cams)

HOW TO BUILD KILLER BIG-BLOCK CHEVY ENGINES 49

Flat-tappet cams are made from cast iron, then receive a surface treatment such as Parkerizing to ensure compatibility with hardened steel lifters. Some cam companies now offer more exotic treatments such as nitriding to harden the cam and lessen the chance of lobe/lifter failure with higher spring pressures. (Photo Courtesy GMPP)

Comp Cams' street roller and hydraulic roller camshafts are made from an austempered material, which is compatible with the standard distributor gear, but they recommend the new composite gear for best results. (Photo Courtesy Comp Cams)

Most racing roller cams are made from steel billet, which requires an upgraded distributor gear (bronze, composite, or melonized). If you think this isn't a big-block Chevy cam, you're half right. It's a Pro Stock cam for the GM DRCE 2 engine with 60-mm cam journals. If it had a distributor drive gear, it would be behind the rear cam journal. This one was ordered without the gear, since Pro Stockers use a front-drive distributor conversion. (Photo Courtesy Comp Cams)

valve). Roller lifters are the only choice when valvespring pressures start to climb above 200 pounds of pressure on the seat. Today's typical race-only engines with a roller tappet cam generally require valvesprings with 300 or more pounds of pressure with the valve seated, and rise to more than 1,000 pounds of pressure as the lifter rolls over the nose of the cam lobe at full lift.

Don't be alarmed: these are the outer limits of big-block technology, and there certainly is still room for traditional flat-tappet camshafts in most street-driven or street-and-strip big-blocks. The main attribute of flat-tappet cams and lifters is one of economy; they typically cost less than half what a roller set-up does, sometimes even closer to one-third the cost. So for a budget street Rodent, you still may want to consider one of the hundreds of flat-tappet (whether mechanical or hydraulic) cams, but there is a catch. Due to increasing awareness of the environment these days, most automotive motor oils have severely reduced or eliminated zinc (the actual compound is ZDDP, or zinc dialkyldithiophosphate) from their formula, and it is the zinc that provides the high-shear lubrication necessary for the overstressed junction between the cam lobe and the flat tappet.

These new-age lubricants have been responsible for a rash of cam/lifter failures in older vehicles as well as in high-performance engines using conventional lifters. The lesson is quite clear: if you are going to use an old-fashioned flat-tappet cam, you need to use motor oils that have been specially formulated with zinc and/or other wear-reducing additives. Thankfully, there are plenty of choices available, but most oils with these properties are designated as heavy-duty truck or racing oils with the normal markup in price over the bargain-bin brands. You get what you pay for.

Another characteristic of flat-tappet cams and lifters is that once the engine is broken-in, the lifters and cam lobes have been mated to each other and the lifters must be returned to their original bores if the engine is taken apart and reassembled. This is not necessary with roller lifter cams, although many engine builders still return the roller lifters to their original bores, too. Old habits die hard, and it's always a good idea to keep parts together that have been run-in before.

Steel billet roller lifter camshafts require the use of a bronze, composite, or melonized distributor gear. (Photo Courtesy MSD)

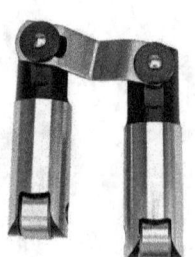

There are four types of cams and lifters used in big-blocks: self-adjusting hydraulic flat-tappets, mechanical flat-tappets, hydraulic roller lifters, and mechanical roller lifters. Mechanical and hydraulic flat-tappet lifters appear virtually identical; their difference is internal. (Photos Courtesy GMPP [left] and Comp Cams [right])

Lift, Duration and Lobe Separation Angle

It's important to know some basic camshaft terms commonly used to describe the qualities of the cam.

Lift is generally taken to mean "lift at the valve," which is the amount that the valve opens under ideal circumstances. It varies depending on the rocker arm ratio you use, though most cams are rated with the standard big-block rocker arm ratio of 1.7:1. To find the theoretical lift at the valve, you measure the lift at the cam lobe (how high the lifter is raised from the base circle of the cam) and simply multiply that by the rocker arm ratio. I say theoretical because, in practice, you have to deduct the amount of valve lash (with mechanical or solid lifters) plus the amount of deflection in the valvetrain (pushrods and rocker arms) to determine the actual valve lift.

Though few of us do it, it wouldn't be a bad idea to set up a dial indicator on the number-1 cylinder intake and exhaust valvespring retainer and check all 16 of your rocker arms to see what their actual ratio is, and to check for any variance. It is easiest to check lobe lift after the cam is installed in the block using a 0- to 1-inch dial indicator directly on the lifter, but it is also possible to check lobe lift before the cam is installed using a micrometer or dial calipers. Just measure the lobe at its smallest point, which is the base circle, then measure the largest point, which is across the nose of the lobe. The difference between these two dimensions is the lobe lift. Just multiply that by the rocker arm (RA) ratio (usually 1.7:1) and you have lift at the valve. One more thing: remember that the first lobe on a big-block Chevy cam (not counting the fuel pump eccentric) is the number-1 cylinder's exhaust,

Continued on page 55

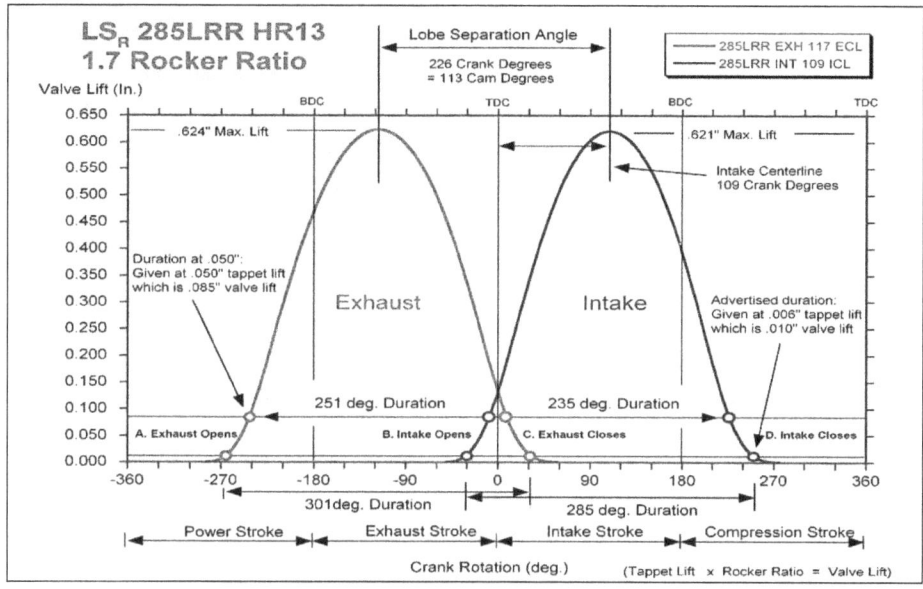

This graph clearly shows how the intake-and exhaust-valve events relate to engine rotation. Notice that 0 degrees on the baseline represents TDC on the exhaust stroke. At that position, the exhaust valve is not yet closed and the intake valve has started to open, which is called valve overlap. Also note that the exhaust centerline is measured before BTDC and the intake centerline is after ATDC. The distance in degrees between the two centerlines is the lobe separation angle (LSA). (Illustration Courtesy Comp Cams)

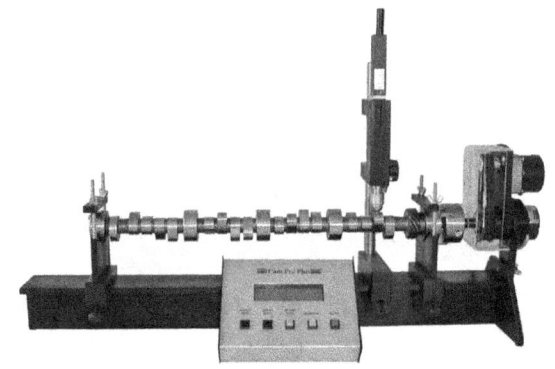

High-performance cams and lifters require high-performance motor oils and additives with high levels of ZDDP to protect them from wear and damage, especially during the engine's critical break-in period. (Photo Courtesy Comp Cams)

While it's probably not in your budget, top engine builders and race shops can make good use of a computer-integrated camshaft checking fixture like this one from Audie Technology. Cam Pro Plus tells you everything you could want to know about the cam. In addition to lift, duration at any checking clearance, and LSA, it digitally and graphically displays the lift curves and their derivatives, which include acceleration, "jerk" (change in acceleration), clearance ramps, and more. You might be able to accomplish the same thing by installing the cam in your engine and checking it with a degree wheel and dial indicator, but it would take you a solid week to accomplish what this computer-controlled machine can do in a few minutes. Cam checking fixtures and dedicated software packages are available from Audie Technology, Andrews Products, Inc., and Performance Trends, Inc.

CHAPTER 4

Project: How to Degree-In a Camshaft

Dialing-in a camshaft is viewed with great mystery and awe by some, but it's really a most rudimentary step in assembling any high-performance big-block. There are two distinct goals with dialing-in your cam: first, you want to verify that the cam's lift, duration, and lobe separation angle (LSA) are correct and agree with the specs on the cam card; second, you need to verify the cam's position relative to the crankshaft: is it advanced, retarded, or straight up, and where should it be for best performance?

The cam manufacturer has a pretty good idea where the cam should be installed, and you frequently see this listed in the cam specs. If a cam has a recommended intake centerline of 110 degrees and the LSA is 112 degrees, the cam is 2 degrees advanced (112 degrees – 110 degrees = 2 degrees). Remember that advancing the cam tends to improve low-RPM power, and retarding it improves higher-RPM power. Most cams work best within 4 degrees of the straight-up position, so if your engine runs best with more than 4 degrees advance or retard, you really should consider changing cam grinds.

To dial-in your cam you need a 0- to 1-inch dial indicator with a magnetic base, a degree wheel, a piece of stiff wire to fashion a pointer (a wire coat hanger works well), and a note pad to write down your numbers. The best time to degree the cam is before the heads and oil pan are installed, because you can get a precise measurement of TDC with the heads off, and if you need to change the cam timing position you usually have to remove the cam drive (timing chain, in this example), which cannot be accessed with the timing cover and oil pan in place. If you have a belt drive you can easily adjust cam timing even after the engine is assembled, but you should recheck piston-to-valve clearance if you change the cam timing, so dialing-in the cam before everything is buttoned up is still a good idea.

The three steps for cam degreeing are:

1. Locate TDC and zero the degree wheel.
2. Move the dial indicator to the lifter on the number-1 cylinder intake lobe to measure duration at .050 inch, lobe lift, and intake centerline.
3. Move the dial indicator to the lifter on the number-1 cylinder exhaust lobe (closest to the front of the engine) and measure duration at .050 inch, lobe lift, and exhaust centerline.

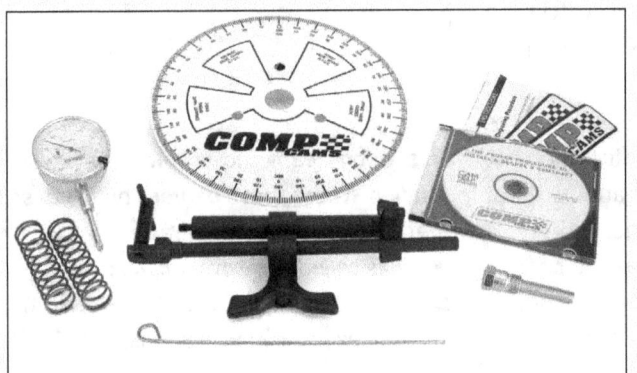

Most cam manufacturers offer degree wheels, and Comp Cams sells this cam installation kit with everything you need: degree wheel, dial indicator and indicator base, a positive stop (for finding TDC with the heads installed), wire pointer, checking springs, and an instructional DVD.

1 *Position the dial indicator probe over the flat surface (not the dome) of the number-1 piston and bring it to approximate TDC. Then install the degree wheel on the crankshaft and the wire pointer to one of the timing cover boltholes. This gets you close, but to establish true TDC, rotate the crankshaft until the piston is .020 inch down in the bore BTDC and write down the number on the degree wheel. Note that this indicator reads ".080-inch," which is .020 inch down from "0." Remember that you are measuring piston movement, so don't get confused by the raw numbers on the indicator.*

CAMSHAFTS, LIFTERS AND VALVETRAIN COMPONENTS

2 Rotate past TDC until the piston is again .020 inch down in the bore and write down that number. True TDC is exactly halfway between these two numbers. In this example, the first reading was 8 degrees BTDC, and the second was 9 degrees ATDC). 8 + 9 = 17; 17 divided by 2 is 8½, so just bend the wire pointer from 9 degrees to 8½ degrees. Spin the crank all the way around and double-check your readings. Also, it doesn't matter whether you use .020, .050, or any other distance, as long as the piston depth is the same before and after TDC. Important Note: If you are using the harmonic dampener bolt to attach the degree wheel to the crank, you must never try to turn the engine backward (counter-clockwise), or the bolt loosens and you lose the accuracy of your readings. Also, the cam drive mechanism (timing chain in this case) always has some amount of play, and reversing directions does not give accurate timing readings. If you over-shoot one of your checking points, just spin the crank around again two more times (the cam turns at half the crankshaft's speed) and be more careful!

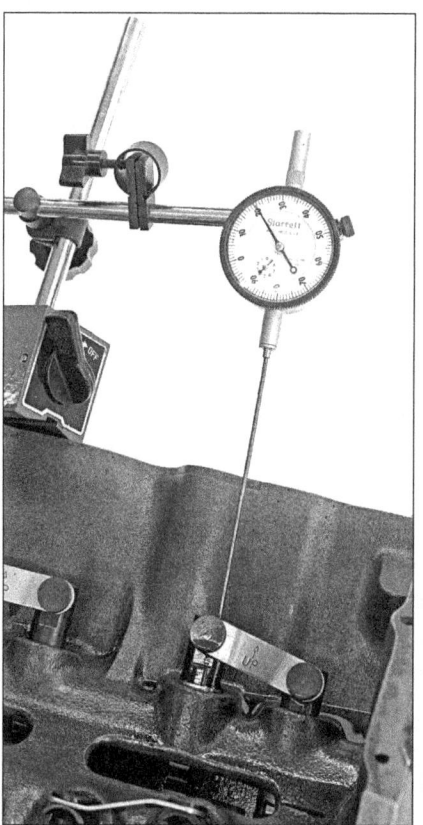

3 After zeroing the degree wheel, move the dial indicator to the intake lifter. It's easier to position the indicator if you use an extension on the probe, and you can buy a nice, expensive probe extension from the gage manufacturer or just fashion one from a stiff piece of wire, as shown here. If you make your own extension, be sure to file or grind a point on the tip for accurate indexing and repeatable results. I like to position the probe tip on the narrow top edge of the lifter body because it falls off if the lifter axis and probe axis are not accurately aligned, which affects the accuracy of the readings. Don't rest the probe tip in the pushrod cup of the lifter because the curved surface lets the probe move around.

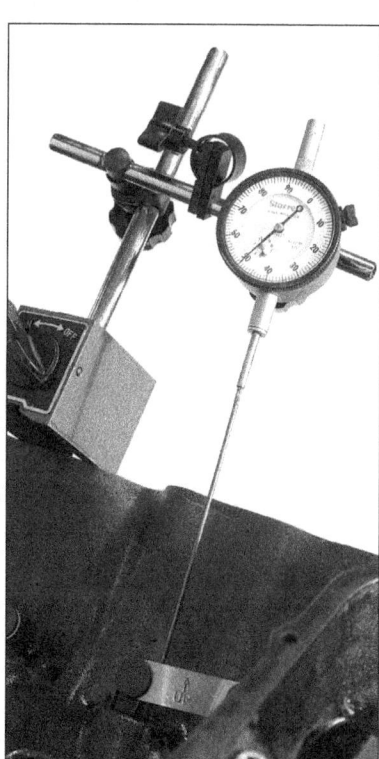

4 With the lifter on the base circle, set the dial indicator to .000 inch and rotate the crank until it reads exactly .050 inch. Stop and write down the reading on the degree wheel. In this case, it was 30 degrees BTDC. Continue rotating the engine and note the highest reading on the dial indicator, which is lobe lift. For this cam, it was .421 inch. Rotate the crank until the lifter is .050 inch from the base circle and note that reading; for this cam, it was 72 degrees ABDC. Adding up the valve opening and closing values plus 180 degrees that transpired between TDC and BDC equals the duration at .050 inch: 30 degrees + 72 degrees + 180 degrees = 282 degrees duration at .050-inch clearance for the intake valve.

Project: How to Degree-In a Camshaft *Continued*

5 To find the intake centerline, rotate the crank until the intake lobe is at full lift, then re-zero the dial indicator. You can now check the numbers on the degree wheel .020 inch before and after maximum lobe lift, just as on the piston to get TDC. For this engine the numbers were 84 degrees ATDC and 138 degrees ATDC. Add them and divide by two, which gives you an intake centerline of 111 degrees: (84 degrees + 138 degrees) ÷ 2 = 111 degrees.

6 Now move the dial indicator to the exhaust lobe and repeat the same measurements. Here we found 76 degrees BBDC exhaust opening at .050 inch and 37 degrees ATDC for the closing event, so duration at .050 inch is 293 degrees (76 degrees + 37 degrees + 180 degrees = 293 degrees). Lobe lift was .412 inch and exhaust centerline was 108 degrees.

We can now calculate the lobe separation angle:

LSA = (Intake Centerline + Exhaust Centerline) ÷ 2

(111 degrees + 108 degrees) ÷ 2 = 109.5 degrees

Considering that my measurements are probably not as accurate as the cam grinder's equipment, I'll round up the LSA to 110 degrees.

Now you know this cam's vital statistics:

288 degrees/292 degrees (intake/exhaust) duration at .050 inch
.714/.700-inch lift at the valve
(.421-inch x 1.7/.412-inch x 1.7)
110 degrees LSA

With the intake centerline reading 111 degrees, the cam is in the engine 1 degree retarded. You could advance or retard the cam in several ways. The easiest is to use a timing set with multiple keyways. This one has three: 0 degrees, 4 degrees advance, and 4 degrees retard. To change cam timing just pull the crankshaft sprocket off and re-install on the appropriate keyway.

If your timing set doesn't have multiple keyways or you want to change timing by some amount different than 4 degrees, there are offset cam timing bushings readily available from most cam companies. These require a few simple modifications to the cam sprocket: first drill out the dowel pin alignment hole to match the outside diameter of the offset bushing, then slot the three bolt-holes enough to allow proper bolt insertion with the offset bushing in place. These bushings have become less popular lately, due to the large selection of high-quality cam drives on the market, which feature either as many as nine offset keyways or variable cam timing choices.

I prefer to use the intake centerline as the primary reference point for verifying whether the cam is installed straight up, advanced, or retarded. Some engine builders just compare the intake opening at .050 inch to the specs on the cam card as the main checking point, and I agree that it's a good idea to check this event, but that number by itself doesn't mean much. Two very different cam profiles may have the same intake opening at .050 inch, so what does that information tell us?

If, on the other hand, the cam has a measured 114 degrees LSA, and the intake centerline is 116 degrees, I know that the cam is 2 degrees retarded. (If the intake centerline is smaller than the LSA, the cam is advanced; if it is larger than the LSA, it is retarded.)

Savvy engine builders re-check valve event timing after installing all 16 lifters, pushrods, and rocker arms, because the added tension of racing valvesprings stretches the timing chain or belt and causes the cam to lag behind a few degrees. This may be why most cam manufacturers grind their cams with a few degrees of advance built in. Also, the cam gradually retards with use and over time because the timing chain loosens up from normal wear.

and the third lobe from the front is the number-1 cylinder's intake.

Duration is simply a measurement of lobe lift in degrees of crankshaft rotation. The confusing part about duration when comparing one cam to another is that different checking clearances are used for different purposes. Advertised duration may be measured at various clearances from .006 to .020 inch of lifter rise, but it is not an accurate indicator of that lobe's profile. Remember, in a running engine, there is valve lash (clearance) and/or valvetrain deflection, so that the point when the valve opens sufficiently to allow flow (either intake or exhaust) lags far behind lifter rise of only .006 inch, so you typically measure duration at .050 inch of lifter rise.

Although it's not commonly listed in any spec chart, duration at .200 inch of lifter rise shows you the difference between two cams in terms of how "fat" the curve is near its mid-point. This is especially noticeable when comparing a conventional solid lifter cam lobe to a roller lifter lobe of similar lift. The roller lobe is 10 degrees (or more) larger, and this pays dividends in terms of improved airflow through the engine and more power production. Most cam manufacturers don't list duration at .200 inch for a good reason: just because one lobe is "fatter" at this point doesn't always mean it makes more power. Too much of a good thing is bad if the lobe profile is so aggressive that it causes valvetrain instability and/or valve float, so be careful if you choose to use duration at .200 inch to compare different cams. Obviously, you can't distill the entire lift curve of a cam lobe down to just one or two numbers, but these commonly used checking clearances give you some place to start. You're best advised to ignore advertised duration and look at the duration at .050-inch lift when judging between cam profiles.

Lobe separation angle (LSA) is a simple physical measurement of the angle between the intake lobe centerline and the exhaust lobe centerline. It can only be measured by installing the cam in the engine or by checking the cam with a sophisticated measuring tool like the Cam Pro Plus. You measure LSA in cam degrees, which is half of the crank degrees when measuring the cam in the block. Because of this, it is easy to determine if your cam is advanced or retarded in the engine, even without a cam spec sheet to guide you.

First measure the LSA and compare that number to the intake centerline. If the LSA is 112 degrees and the intake centerline is 116 degrees ATDC the cam is 4 degrees retarded; that is, the cam is 4 degrees behind its position midway between the two lobe centerlines.

In this example, the exhaust centerline is at 108 degrees before top dead center (BTDC), so to determine the LSA, you just add the intake centerline (ATDC) and exhaust centerline (BTDC) and divide by 2.

116 + 108 = 224 ÷ 2 = 112 degrees LSA

Typical LSAs for a big-block Chevy range from about 107 degrees (very tight) up to 118 degrees (very wide). The most obvious effect of wider LSAs is to reduce valve overlap, which generally improves manifold vacuum at idle and yields better low-end power production. However, remember that as you increase LSA, you are also changing the cam timing; the intake valve opens sooner, and the exhaust opens later. Not all engines like this, and for this reason wide LSAs are typically used on cams destined for use in "mountain motors" in excess of 600 ci, or in nitrous or supercharged applications. The most common LSAs for street and moderate racing use typically fall into the 110- to 112-degree range. Tighter LSAs are frequently used to improve the high-RPM power without excessive amounts of valve lift and duration, while wider LSAs are mostly found in very large cams (valve lifts over .800-inch, duration over 280 degrees at .050-inch) to improve the low-end power and effectively "fatten up" the torque curve.

General Camshaft Recommendations

The following are general cam selection guidelines for most 454- to 502-ci street-driven full bodied cars (larger engines can use more valve timing).

Matching Cam Duration to Other Engine Specs

Duration @ .050-inch	Expected RPM	Compression Ratio	Converter Stall Speed	Rear Gear Ratio	Intake Manifold
Up to 218 degrees	Idle to 4,500	Up to 9.0:1	Stock	3.08 to 3.42	Dual-Plane
218 to 235 degrees	1,500 to 6,000	9.0:1 to 9.5:1	1,500 to 2,500	3.42 to 4.11	High-Flow Dual-Plane
235 to 245 degrees	2,500 to 6,500	9.5:1 to 10.5:1	2,500 to 3,500	3.73 to 4.56	High-Flow Dual-Plane or Single-Plane
245 to 255 degrees	3,000 to 7,000	10.0:1 and up	3,500 to 4,500	4.11 or lower	Single-Plane
255 degrees and up	4,000 and up	11.0:1 and up	4,500 and up	4.56 or lower	Single-Plane or Tunnel Ram (2 x 4-bbl)

CHAPTER 4

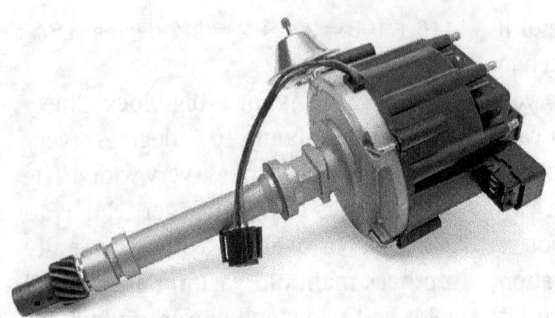

GMPP offers this HEI distributor (PN 93440806) with a melonized distributor gear for compatibility with the steel camshaft cores used for all GM roller-lifter camshafts. Aftermarket companies also offer bronze and composite distributor gears. You must use one of these gears with any steel-core roller lifter camshaft, as the standard steel distributor gear wears excessively and soon fails if used with a roller cam. (Photo Courtesy GMPP)

Comp Cams two-piece billet aluminum timing cover (PN 217) for Gen V/VI big-blocks has room for a double-roller timing chain. (Photo Courtesy Comp Cams)

Roller cams in Mark IV big-blocks must have a thrust button to control fore and aft movement of the cam in the block, and there are many roller thrust bearings on the market that are designed to butt against the inside of the front cover. I never seem to find a combination that gives exactly the clearance desired (no more than .010 inch), so I like to use Comp Cams nylon button (PN 205). It is .945 inch long and can easily be shortened to the desired length. It is difficult to determine the exact length for a particular front cover without a lot of cut-and-test fitting, and one time I cut one too short. Now, that one stays in my tool box. When I need to make a new one, I just put a small piece of clay on the nose of the short button and install the front cover. Remove the front cover and measure the thickness of the clay, and I have the new overall length needed for that combination, less the desired clearance. You must use an aluminum front cover to control cam thrust, as the stock stamped steel cover flexes too much to give adequate thrust control.

There are many more variables that influence your cam selection including vehicle weight, tire size and diameter, exhaust system, driving style and intended usage (daily driver, weekend warrior, etc.). Remember that other factors such as intake port volume and engine size are also closely tied to cam requirements. Large volume heads might necessitate less valve timing to keep flow velocity up, and larger displacement big-blocks can generally move up a step in cam size while retaining the milder characteristics of a smaller cam—better idle quality, more low-end torque, etc.

The chart on page 55 gets you "in the ballpark," but I still recommend that you contact the cam manufacturer for specific cam recommendations for your application.

OEM Cam Fitment

All Mark IV big-blocks accept the same dimension camshafts and attending cam drive hardware, although 1965 and 1966 396 and 427 engines came with a grooved rear cam journal and matching grooved rear cam bearing to supply oil to the right side lifter gallery. Most aftermarket cam companies can supply cams for these blocks or modify existing cams for this application, although I encourage you to use a newer block such as one of the numerous 454 blocks from the 1970s and 1980s as the basis for your engine project.

All factory Mark IV camshafts were of the flat-tappet design, most with hydraulic lifters although many of the early high-performance big-blocks were equipped with mechanical lifters, also known as solid lifters. Although solid lifter cams are avoided by many because they allegedly require frequent adjustment, that really isn't the case if you adjust the valves correctly and just check the lash periodically, say, with every oil change. Gen V big-blocks also use the same cam design as the Mark IV, although they were only available with hydraulic lifters.

Most Gen VI engines were equipped with hydraulic roller lifters and camshafts. The primary reason that General Motors went with the much more costly roller tappet design was to prevent cam and lifter wear, and subsequent failure when used with modern motor oils that have greatly reduced zinc (ZDDP) content. The zinc additive is needed to prevent scuffing for the highly stressed cam and flat-tappet junction, but emission and hazardous waste concerns have forced car manufacturers to delete it from their oil specifications. This has actually been a benefit to those who still want to "hot rod" the Rat motor, because roller lifter cams can have more aggressive lift curves with the same lift and duration. The added "area under the curve" also offers more airflow and, consequently, more power, but without the increased valve overlap and loss of low-speed power that are characteristic of traditional high-performance cams.

The use of hydraulic roller lifter cams in Gen VI big-blocks requires two additional changes to the engine: the addition of a thrust plate to the front of the block, and the use of melonized distributor gears for compatibility with the steel camshaft core. Big-block racers have also had to address these concerns when they use a mechanical roller lifter cam, but Mark IV engine builders have to resort to thrust buttons that butt against the inside of the front timing cover, and using bronze distributor gears to mate with the steel camshaft.

Recently, some manufacturers have introduced composite distributor gears that are also compatible with steel billet roller cams. They claim to have a much longer service life, making them a good choice for street-driven big-blocks with roller cams. Note that OEM distributors have a .491-inch shaft diameter, and most aftermarket distributors use a larger .500-inch shaft, so be sure that the replacement gear you use has the correct hole diameter for your distributor. Also note that hydraulic roller lifters require shorter pushrods than conventional flat tappets.

Because a camshaft thrust plate is used on Gen VI engines, the bolt circle and the nose of the cams are reduced, and a different cam sprocket is required. The original equipment timing set uses a single roller timing chain and there is not enough clearance between the block and the front cover for a traditional high-performance double-roller chain. Fortunately, aftermarket aluminum front covers for the Gen VI are available from Comp Cams (PN 217) and IMCO (PN 04-1325), and probably will be offered by other companies as the popularity of the Gen VI engines grows. There are several companies now making double roller timing chain sets for the Gen VI big-block. Cloyes PN 9-3670X3 and Rollmaster PN CS2095 are both high-quality billet steel timing sets with true rolling chains, and more choices are bound to follow as the Gen VI gains popularity with the gearhead community. GM Performance Parts does offer a high-performance version of the Gen VI single-roller timing set, PN 12371053, which includes the chain, both sprockets, cam bolts, a thrust plate and thrust plate bolts. It is used in the 620- and 720-hp 572-ci crate engines, so it is more than adequate for most high-performance street Gen VI engines.

Lifters

As previously mentioned, there are four types of lifters for the big-block Chevy engine: so-called flat-tappet lifters (they're not really flat on the bottom; they are convex) in both mechanical (solid lifters) and hydraulic (self-adjusting); and roller lifters that feature a roller bearing where they contact the cam lobe, also in mechanical and hydraulic versions. All four types of lifters are .842 inch diameter, and interchange among Mark IV, Gen V, and Gen VI engines when used with the correct matching camshaft and lifter alignment hardware. Many aftermarket engine blocks come with taller-than-stock lifter bores that better stabilize the lifter with high-lift cams, and they usually require lifters that are .300 inch longer than stock. Only Gen VI engines came from GM with roller lifters, and they use lifters with two flats machined into the lifter body, which match the lifter guides and guide retainers used with those engines.

There are plenty of aftermarket roller lifter cams, in both mechanical and hydraulic lifter versions, for the Mark IV and Gen V engines, but they require "retro-fit" tie-bar lifters to keep their rollers aligned with the cam lobes.

Mechanical lifters are frequently referred to as "solid" lifters because they have no moving internal parts. But they are not really solid because that makes them unnecessarily heavy. They have a hardened-steel hollow lifter body and a separate pushrod seat that is retained by a spring clip, and they are virtually impossible to distinguish from hydraulic lifters with the naked eye. If you place the lifter

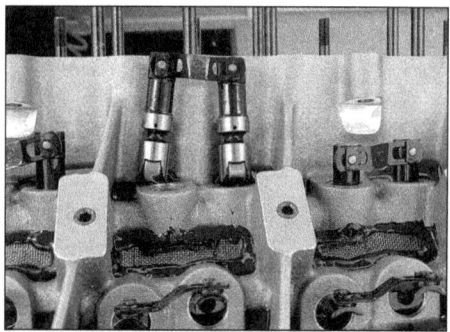

Self-aligning mechanical roller lifters feature a tie bar between each pair of lifters to align the lifter's roller with the camshaft lobe. Note that the tie bar is slotted where it connects to the lifter body to allow each lifter to move independently.

GMPP hydraulic roller lifters for Gen VI engines have flats at the top of the lifter body that fit into lifter guides. Gen VI blocks have machined lifter bosses in the valley of the block for those guides, so these lifters do not work in Mark IV or Gen V engines. (Photo Courtesy GMPP)

In hydraulic flat-tappet lifters, the pushrod seat is retained by a spring clip, and the oil feed orifice in the side of the lifter is supplied pressurized oil from the lifter oil gallery in the engine block. (Photo Courtesy GMPP)

upright on your workbench and use a pushrod to push down firmly on the seat, you can get a hydraulic lifter plunger to move down in the lifter body, and it will probably spit some oil out of the oil feed orifice. Solid lifters are, well... solid.

Hydraulic lifters are self-adjusting, using a hydraulic plunger inside the lifter body with a controlled oil metering device (usually a thin steel piddle valve). When set to the proper preload, usually around .030 inch or 1/2 turn of the adjuster nut, the plunger is pushed down, away from the retainer ring in the lifter body. When the engine is running, oil under pressure fills up the cavity to eliminate all clearance. After the cavity is full and the lifter is pushed up the lifter bore by the camshaft, the trapped oil under the plunger/pushrod seat becomes "solid," just like a hydraulic jack or the brakes in your car. As the engine temperature changes and/or small amounts of valvetrain wear and run-in occur, the hydraulic plunger takes up the clearance, which is what makes it self-adjusting.

Currently, hydraulic lifters are RPM limited to around 6,000 or 6,500. If the engine is over-revved to the point that valvetrain instability occurs (valve float), the self-adjusting lifter does its job of taking up excessive clearance, which then doesn't allow the valve to return to its seat.

Now the engine is popping and misfiring due to the "pumped-up" lifters and attending dead cylinders. How do you fix it? Shut the engine off and wait a few minutes. The lifters bleed down through the very small (less than .001 inch) clearance passages, and you'll be back in business in no time.

Recent interest in hydraulic roller lifters for mild racing applications have led to the development of "short travel" hydraulic rollers, which have a reduced amount of adjustability. They are designed to operate with as little as .002 to .004 inch of preload (hot), and the reduced plunger travel and tighter tolerances make them less affected by high-RPM engine speeds. I expect to see more development in this aspect of racing engine development in the future, because opening the valves by hitting them on the head with a hammer doesn't seem like a good idea. Zero lash valvetrains are used in Formula 1 engines turning 18,000 rpm, although they use pneumatic valvesprings to accomplish that feat. Just some food for thought.

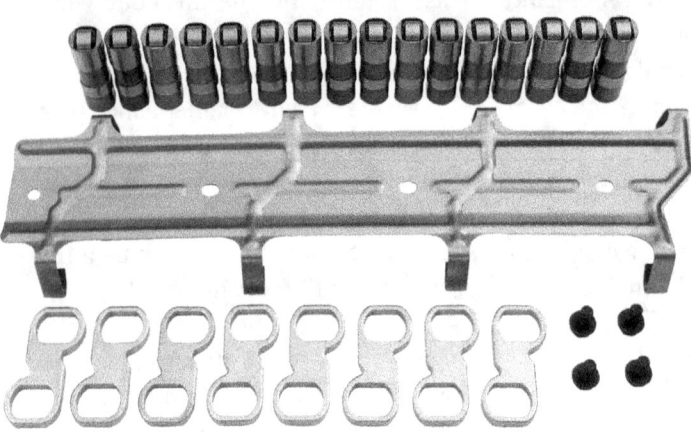

GMPP PN 12371056 is a complete set of 16 hydraulic roller lifters plus lifter guides and guide retainer for Gen VI engines. These lifters allow more oil to the rocker arms than production truck engine lifters. (Photo Courtesy GMPP)

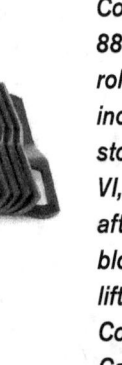

Comp Cams' PN 883-16 mechanical roller lifters are .300 inch taller than stock to fit Gen V/VI, Bowtie, and most aftermarket engine blocks with raised lifter bosses. (Photo Courtesy Comp Cams)

Oversized Lifters

The stock lifter diameter of .842 inch is adequate for all street performance and

Comp Cams makes these lightweight M-2 grade tool steel solid lifters with DLC (diamond-like carbon). This multi-layer coating provides the lifters with extremely slick and hard surface properties, making them resistant to abrasive wear in extreme contact-pressure environments and compatible with almost any camshaft material. (Photo Courtesy Comp Cams)

To improve lubrication to the critical cam/lifter junction, some manufacturers offer flat-tappet lifters with a small oiling hole EDM machined in the lifter face. These Comp Cams solid lifters feature a .012-inch oil orifice. (Photo Courtesy Comp Cams)

CAMSHAFTS, LIFTERS AND VALVETRAIN COMPONENTS

Valve Adjustment

Valve adjustment requires that the engine's camshaft is rotated to a position where the lifter of the valve being adjusted is on the base circle of the cam, which is the point when the lifter is all the down in its bore and the valve itself is closed. At that point, adjust the clearance between the tip of the valvestem and the rocker arm to the manufacturer's specs using a feeler gage for mechanical (or "solid") lifters, or by tightening the rocker adjustment nut to preload the lifters if you are using hydraulic (or "self adjusting") lifters.

Mechanical

One method you can use to determine if the cam is at the right position for valve adjustment is this: when the exhaust valve starts to open, adjust the intake; when the intake starts to close, adjust the exhaust. It's best to use a 1/2-inch-drive ratchet and socket that fits the harmonic dampener bolt on the front of your crank, but you can also just "bump the starter" until the engine stops in the correct position. (You may have to try several times to get the engine to stop in just the right place.) Many racers rig up a starter button in the engine compartment just for this purpose, and you can buy hand-held starter buttons that clip onto the starter terminals for the same purpose. If you use a 1/2-inch-drive ratchet to turn the engine by hand, remove the spark plugs from high-compression engines to make turning the crankshaft easier.

Hydraulic

The adjustment procedures described above are for mechanical (solid) lifter cams, whether flat-tappet or roller lifter, which require clearance in the valvetrain (valve lash) so that the valves can close tightly against their seats. Hydraulic lifters, whether flat-tappet or roller, require lifter preload, and they self-adjust to zero lash while the engine is running. That is why hydraulic lifter engines are quieter in operation, and solid lifter engines have a characteristic mechanical noise that is music to a gearhead's ears.

With hydraulic lifters, adjust lifter preload before the intake manifold is installed so that you have a clear view of the lifters. Rotate the crankshaft to the proper checking position (same as for mechanical lifters), and run the rocker adjusting nut down with just your fingers until all clearance is gone. This is zero lash, and a visual check of the lifter verifies that the pushrod seat is still all the way up against the spring clip that retains it in the lifter body. Using a wrench on the adjuster nut, tighten the nut 1/2 turn, which should depress the pushrod seat in the lifter by .025 inch (the 7/16-20 rocker stud threads move .050 inch per revolution).

If the lifter was previously "pumped up" and is full of oil, the pushrod seat does not move down and away from the retaining clip; instead, the valve is opened against the tension from the valvespring. After a short time, the valvespring tension eventually forces the excess oil from the lifter cavity, allowing the valve to close and the pushrod seat in the lifter to move away from the retaining clip. This is why most cam manufacturers do not recommend pumping up hydraulic lifters before installation. If you install the lifters as delivered (with proper assembly lube for your application, of course) and adjust them "dry," the lifters are filled with oil when you prime the oil pump. Just be sure to rotate the crankshaft to several positions while priming the oil pump; the lifters do not receive oil when the cam raises the oil-feed orifice above the oil gallery in the block.

If you have to adjust hydraulic lifters with the intake manifold already installed, an old mechanic's trick is to twirl the pushrod with your fingers as you slowly tighten the rocker adjuster nuts. As soon as all clearance is gone, the pushrod is pinched tight, and that is your zero lash point. Then tighten the rocker nut with your wrench 1/2 turn for proper lifter preload and move on to the next one. With hydraulic lifters, I recommend adjusting each pair of valves starting on the compression stroke of the number-1 cylinder (engine timing marks at 0 degrees), then rotate the engine 90 degrees, and adjust the next pair following the firing order (1-8-4-3-6-5-7-2).

Cold Valve Lash Compensation

With iron block and iron heads, add .002 inch to hot lash settings. Example: .024/.028-inch hot becomes .026/.030-inch cold.

With iron block and aluminum heads, subtract .006 inch from hot lash settings. Example: .024/.028-inch hot becomes .018/.022-inch cold.

With aluminum block and aluminum heads, subtract .012 inch from hot lash settings. Example: .024/.028-inch hot becomes .012/.016-inch cold.

All high-performance big-blocks should be equipped with rocker adjuster nuts with internal setscrews, sometimes called polylocks, because the factory-crimped adjuster nuts either work loose or deform the threads on the rocker stud after repeated adjustments.

most bracket racing big-blocks, but high-level racing engines benefit from larger diameter lifters. Most common diameter sizes are .875 inch (stock Ford), .903 inch (stock Chrysler), .937 inch, and 1.062 inches. If you have to use a flat-tappet camshaft, the larger face of the "fat" lifters accept a more aggressive lobe profile before the edge of the lifter digs into the cam lobe, which of course leads to nearly instant camshaft failure. Most engines of this type use a roller lifter, so a larger, more durable roller can be fitted within the lifter bore.

With the current trend of using spread port cylinder heads, which have severe rocker arm offsets, oversized lifters can better accommodate offset pushrod seats for better pushrod clearance and less angular deflection. At the highest levels of competition, top manufacturers like Jesel offer keyway lifters that require a precisely machined keyway groove in the lifter bores to align the lifter's roller with the camshaft lobe.

Obviously, the stock lifter bosses must be machined for oversized lifters, and most engine shops that have the capability of doing this type of work bore the lifter bosses large enough for pressed-in bronze-wall lifter sleeves, taking care to locate the lifter bores more accurately than production-line machining operations. This is not cheap; yet another reason to consider using an aftermarket engine block, many of which offer this option right out of the box.

Replacement Big-Block Camshafts

GM Performance Parts currently offers camshafts only for Gen VI big-blocks; however, there are many OEM replacement cams available from aftermarket cam manufacturers if you are looking to duplicate the original-equipment sound and feel of a vintage high-performance Rat motor. The chart on page 61 lists some popular grinds, but these are just a small sampling of the hundreds of cams available, so I encourage you to contact the manufacturer of your choice for a recommendation.

There are many more modern designs available today that offer better overall performance than the factory grinds developed in the 1960s, most of which were single-pattern designs that use the same specs for both the intake and exhaust lobes. The GMPP hydraulic roller lifter cams could be used in a Mark IV or Gen V engine if the Gen VI thrust plate and single-roller timing set is used, but you can buy similar cams specifically for the Mark IV using retro-fit tie-bar hydraulic roller lifters and Mark IV-style double-roller timing sets.

Note that all the GMPP Gen VI cams are steel billet roller lifter cams, so a distributor with a melonized steel gear must be used. Use distributor PN 93440806 or distributor gear PN 10456413 with all GMPP steel core roller lifter camshafts.

Oversized Cam Journals

It is not unusual in large-cubic-inch racing big-blocks to see roller lifter cams with very high valve lifts of .900 inch to more than 1.000 inch, which translates to .588-inch lobe lift. Remember that high-lift cams don't actually raise the lifter any higher in the block than a stock cam; they simply reduce the base circle, allowing the lifter to sink deeper into the lifter bore. This is another reason that nearly all dedicated racing-only big-blocks must be equipped with custom-length longer-than-stock pushrods or taller-than-stock lifters. There is a limit to how far you can reduce the base circle because the cam core becomes less rigid and starts to suffer from torsional twist when the engine is running. Additionally, the lifter may drop in its bore so much that the oil feed passages are blocked off. Last, the severe opening and closing ramp shapes of a high-lift cam impart a heavy side load to the lifter, increasing lifter bore wear and wasting power.

While the stock 1.949-inch-diameter cam journals are adequate for any street performance and modest racing engine builds, the trend for high-end racing big-blocks is to use larger-than-stock cam cores with 2.125-inch (460 Ford spec), 55-mm (2.165 inches), or 60-mm (2.362 inches) roller cam bearings. Of course this requires machining the cam tunnel in the block for the oversized bearings, but any good high-performance machine shop should be able to handle this relatively simple operation.

There are several advantages to using oversized cam cores. First, the larger cam bearings distribute the load of very high-pressure valvesprings over a larger area, reducing the load on the bearings,

The roller cam on the left is ground for use with stock-dimension cam bearings and the cam on the right uses 60-mm cam journals. Both racing cams have similar lift and duration specs, but notice that the 60-mm cam lobes appear to be much "softer" to the naked eye with a less radical change in shape. The nose of the 60-mm cam is reduced to the stock 1.949-inch dimension for compatibility with stock-specification cam drives. This step is not generally used for thrust control in racing engines, even though it resembles the stepped nose on a Gen VI big-block cam, which is designed for use with a thrust plate on Gen VI blocks.

especially if roller cam bearings are used. The real advantage however, is that the base circle of the cam lobes can be increased, which not only strengthens the cam, but pays dividends in terms of reduced side loading of the lifters. If you look at two roller lifter cams with similar lift and duration, one ground on a stock core and the other ground for use with 55- or 60-mm cam bearings, it is obvious that the oversized cam lobe appears "softer" in terms of the shape of the lobe.

Of course there is a limit to how far you can take this concept. Not only must the oversized cam still fit into the original block location, but also the larger perimeter of the new lobes means increased lifter bearing speeds as the roller travels more distance per revolution of the cam.

As for the cam location, most big-blocks using oversized cams are built with aftermarket blocks featuring a raised cam location (anywhere from .400 to 1 inch higher than stock), which provides additional cam-to-connecting-rod clearance for long-stroke crankshafts. One last benefit to the larger cam base circle is that the pushrods can now be shorter (due to the higher lifter height at full lift), which makes them lighter and stiffer.

Alternative Firing Orders: 4-7 Swap

The traditional Chevrolet firing order of 1-8-4-3-6-5-7-2 has been with us since the small-block was introduced in 1955, and it works pretty well. However, in the search for every last bit of power for their competition Rat motors, racers have discovered that a change in the firing order usually produces a bit more power, though not as much as some want you to believe. On professional level racing engines, simply changing the cam to one with a firing order of 1-8-7-3-6-5-4-2 has shown power gains of 1 to 2 percent on average, which is really not enough to justify the purchase of another cam for most performance enthusiasts. The reason for the gain is subject to speculation. Some claim better fuel distribution because cylinders number-5 and -7 no longer fire sequentially, but they ignore the fact that you simply move the sequentially firing cylinders to numbers-4 and -2, so why does the engine care?

Popular Performance Camshaft Choices

Manufacturer and Part Number	Description	Duration @ .050-inch Lift (degrees)	Lift @ Valve (inches)	Lobe Centerline	Technical Notes
GMPP PN 12366543	Steel hydraulic roller Gen VI	Int: 224, Exh: 234	Int: .527, Exh: .544	110	For 502/502 special engine
GMPP PN 24502611	Steel hydraulic roller Gen VI	Int: 211, Exh: 230	Int: .510, Exh: .540	112	For 454 and 502 HO engines
GMPP PN 88961557	Steel hydraulic roller Gen VI	Int: 254, Exh: 264	Int: .632, Exh: .632	112	For ZZ572/620 engine
GMPP PN 88962216	Steel mechanical roller Gen VI	Int: 278, Exh: 282	Int: .714, Exh: .714	112	For ZZ572/720 engine
Crane Blueprinted Series PN 969391	Hydraulic flat-tappet Mark IV	Int: 214, Exh: 218	Int: .461, Exh: .480	115	Replacement for GM 3883986 for 396/350 engine
Iskenderian 270-HL PN 396270	Hydraulic flat-tappet Mark IV	Int: 216, Exh: 216	Int: .510, Exh: .510	114	Replacement for 454/360 LS5 engine
Comp Cams Nostalgia Plus PN 11-670-4	Hydraulic flat-tappet Mark IV	Int: 229, Exh: 236	Int: .530, Exh: .524	112	Replacement for 454/460 LS6 engine
Lunati Cams Factory Perf PN 20202	Solid flat-tappet Mark IV	Int: 242, Exh: 242	Int: .530, Exh: .530	114	Replacement for 396/375, 427/425 engines; .024/.028 lash (hot)
Lunati Cams Factory Perf PN 20203	Solid flat-tappet Mark IV	Int: 264, Exh: 270	Int: .560, Exh: .580	112	Replacement for GM 3925535 for 427/400 (1st design L88), engine; .024/.026 lash (hot)
Crane Blueprinted Series PN 968561	Solid flat-tappet Mark IV	Int: 264, Exh: 269	Int: .560, Exh: .580	112	Replacement for GM 3925535 for 427/400 (1st design L88), engine; .024/.026 lash (hot)
Crane Blueprinted Series PN 131141	Solid flat-tappet Mark IV	Int: 262, Exh: 272	Int: .575, Exh: .615	110	Replacement for GM 3959180 for 427/430 (2nd design L88, ZL1 427, LS7 454 engines; .024/.026 lash (hot)

It could be that the heat build-up from the sequentially firing cylinders is cooled better at the front of the engine, which is where the water pump is located. Most likely, the alternative firing order changes the dynamics of the power impulses on the crankshaft as each cylinder fires, but why the engine prefers one firing order over the other is still unclear. The bottom line is that a cam with the 4-7 swap firing order should help your racing engine, but don't expect to reduce your quarter-mile times by two tenths of a second from the change. If you're ordering a new roller cam anyway, it wouldn't hurt to give it a try. Just don't expect miracles. And don't forget to re-route your spark plug wires to cylinders-4 and -7.

Cam Drives: Chains, Gears and Belts

All production big-blocks for automotive and truck applications were equipped with timing chains, and chains are still the most popular choice for driving your camshaft. Original equipment timing chain sets are adequate for stock engines, but high RPM, increased valvespring loads, and high-volume or high-pressure oil pumps put a strain on the cam drive so it's always a good idea to strengthen this weak link in the valvetrain.

The most common upgrade is to use a true-rolling double roller timing chain set, and there are dozens of good sets offered by aftermarket manufacturers at a reasonable price. Many low-budget timing sets come with a double roller chain, but some are "split roller" sets, not true-rolling sets, which have solid rollers between each link of the chain. If the timing chain set you're considering cost $25, you may want to keep looking—good sets typically cost around $100 to $150, but it's money well spent.

High-quality timing chain sets have many other desirable features such as multiple keyways for advancing or retarding your camshaft (three is normal, some have as many as nine positions); a thrust bearing behind the cam sprocket to prevent the sprocket from wearing into the block; and some even

Grade-8 bolts and a locking plate keep your cam sprocket from coming loose. You should always use a thread-locking compound like Loctite 242 as well. (Photo Courtesy Comp Cams)

have fully machined steel-billet cam and crank sprockets for added strength. The stock big-block crank-center-to-cam-center distance is 5.152 inches. Your new timing chain set should have less than 1/4 inch of lateral movement if you grab the chain between the two sprockets and move it left and right with your fingers. If there is more movement than that, you need a timing set with a different reduced center-to-center distance, such as in the following chart:

Movement	Reduced Center-to-Center Distance
1/4 inch	.002 to .004 inch
5/16 inch	.004 to .006 inch
3/8 inch	.006 to .008 inch
1/2 inch	.008 to .010 inch

Gear drives substitute one or two idler gears for the chain so that both the crank and camshaft rotate in the same direction. Some marine engines came from General Motors with reverse rotation camshafts using a simple gear-to-gear

GMPP timing set PN 12371053 contains a single-roller timing chain, cam sprocket, crank sprocket, thrust plate, and bolts for Gen VI engines. (Photo Courtesy GMPP)

Rollmaster in Australia makes a high-quality double-roller timing chain for Gen V and Gen VI big-blocks (PN CS2095). It features nitrided billet steel crank and cam sprockets, a Torrington thrust bearing, and nine keyways for cam timing adjustment. (Photo Courtesy Rollmaster)

Dual-idler gear drives use a floating pair of gears between the crank and cam gears, and usually require no modifications to the block. They offer rock-solid timing and less chance of breakage than timing chains, but they transmit crankshaft harmonics to the cam and valvetrain, and tend to wear the upper portion of Babbitt-type camshaft bearings. It's a good idea to switch to roller cam bearings if you use one of these gear drives. (Photo Courtesy Comp Cams)

setup to enable the engine to run in a counter-clockwise direction for twin-engine boats, but avoid these unless that is what your big-block is to be used for. The main virtue of gear drives is brute strength and reliability, and they are a good choice for marine engines and supercharged drag race engines, which typically drive a front cover-mounted fuel pump with the camshaft. Single idler-gear drives feature a special front cover, usually cast aluminum, which mounts the idler gear in the correct position between the crank and cam gears. Dual-idler sets use a "floating" idler gear assembly sandwiched between the crank and cam gears, and are usually designed to fit under a stock front cover.

This Jesel belt drive fits big-blocks with a .400-inch raised cam location, but Jesel also offers drives for standard cam locations, as well as other non-stock variations. Note the timing marks on the top of the cam pulley. The cam may be quickly advanced or retarded by simply loosening the four nuts securing the pulley to the cam hub and rotating the crank and pulley to the new timing location. Advancing or retarding the cam changes the valve-to-piston clearances, but you checked all of that during the test-assembly phase of your engine build, right?

Gear drives make a lot of mechanical noise, and some manufacturers even offer "noisy" gear drives that mimic the sound of a supercharger whine. You won't find those units on any professional level racing engines. The main drawback of gear drives is that they directly transmit harmonic vibrations from the crankshaft to the camshaft, which can have detrimental effects on your valvetrain. Another problem with dual-idler gear drives is that the vector forces generated by the gears tend to push the camshaft upward so much that cam bearings exhibit heavy wear on the upper side of the bearings.

The best method of turning your camshaft is a belt drive, which uses cogged pulleys and a heavy-duty cogged timing belt. Although it defies logic, the belt drive has proven to be much more durable than metal timing chains, but the real pay-off is that belt drives free-up power—as much as 10 to 20 hp according to most professional engine builders. The reason is that the belt absorbs harmonic vibrations from the crankshaft, imparting a smoother rotational force to the camshaft. Jesel belt drives use a cogged belt that is precisely fitted to the crank and cam pulleys, similar to a timing chain, while Comp Cams offers a belt drive with an idler roller to take up slack and dampen vibration on the unloaded side of the belt between the two main pulleys.

Another feature of belt drives is that the camshaft can be quickly advanced or retarded without engine disassembly; usually all that is required is to loosen four nuts, rotate the crankshaft the desired amount, and re-tighten the nuts. So why doesn't everyone use a belt drive? They are expensive, tearing up the better portion of a $1,000 bill (some are even more expensive). That's a lot of cash for a 10-hp gain, and not really worth it until you reach the professional competition level of engine madness. Every competitive NHRA Pro Stock car uses a belt drive.

Pushrods

It is the pushrod's job to transfer the linear motion from the lifter to the pushrod cup in the rocker arms, which travels in an arc from the rocker's resting position to full lift at the valve. In the big-block Chevy, the pushrod's job is further complicated by the Rat motor's compound valve angles, meaning that the pushrods are never actually in line with the axis of the lifter. This puts extremely high lateral and bending loads on the pushrods, so they must be much stronger than would be required for a simple inline valve engine like the small-block Chevy.

OEM big-block pushrods were available in diameters of 5/16, 3/8, and 7/16 inch, and the nominal stock lengths for short-deck big-blocks (9.800-inch deck height) are 8.280 inches for the intake pushrods and 9.250 inches for exhaust pushrods. All OEM and most aftermarket big-block pushrods have 5/16-inch ball ends that nest in the lifter seats and rocker arm's pushrod cups.

From a performance standpoint, bigger is better when it comes to pushrods, with the only negative effect of larger diameter pushrods being their increased weight. Still, the benefit of more precise valve motion is well worth the small weight penalty if you are using valvesprings of adequate pressure in a high-RPM engine.

The OEM 5/16-inch pushrods are found on late-model truck engines that have low-pressure valvesprings and a low RPM range. Most big-block pushrods used in passenger car applications from the 1960s and early 1970s were 3/8-inch diameter, while the high-performance versions of those engines received 7/16-inch pushrods. All production big-blocks use pushrod guideplates between the rocker arm studs and the cylinder heads, and these guideplates must match the pushrod diameter in order to keep the

CHAPTER 4

Big-block Chevys use two different pushrod lengths. Stock intake pushrods are 8.280 inches, and exhaust pushrods are 9.250 inches long. Comp Cams PN 7954 is a set of stock-length .080-inch-wall 3/8-inch-diameter chrome-moly pushrods for the Rat motor. (Photo Courtesy Comp Cams)

rocker arm aligned with the tip of the valvestem.

There are many sources of good competition quality pushrods—nearly all cam manufacturers offer pushrods that are compatible with their cam and valvetrain components, and companies like Manley, Manton, Smith Brothers, and Trend specialize in competition pushrods. Most specialty pushrod manufacturers offer pushrods of various wall thicknesses (usually .080, .120, and .165 inch) to suit the most demanding applications. For a typical high-performance street or mild racing big-block, the .080-inch-wall pushrods are adequate.

Top-of-the-line competition pushrods are usually tapered, offering the benefit of high strength in the mid-section with reduced diameters for component clearance where the pushrod comes closest to the lifter body and the cylinder head. Of course, tapered pushrods are not compatible with guideplates, so they should only be used with shaft-mounted rocker arms. Some competition pushrods offer undercut ball ends with a 210-degree radius that provides more pushrod cup clearance at the rocker arm for use with extremely high lift cams. Speaking of clearance, some experts recommend that minimum pushrod-to-cylinder head clearances be kept to .010 inch and no more, so that the slight contact with the head while the engine is running helps to dampen pushrod vibration and deflection. Just be sure to check for adequate clearance (.010 inch) throughout the entire lift cycle for all 16 pushrods.

Pushrod Length

Selecting pushrods of the correct length is one of the most critical steps in building a high-performance big-block. Stock-length pushrods (8.280-inch intake, 9.250-inch exhaust) may be right for mild engines using a stock block, cylinder heads, valve lengths, and a modest cam (up to .600-inch lift at the valve), but there are so many variables that affect pushrod length that it's always a good idea to check for the correct rocker-arm-to-valvestem-tip contact pattern.

You need adjustable checking pushrods for this, but they are not too expensive—a lot less expensive than replacing the broken parts you end up with if you don't get the pushrod lengths right! You

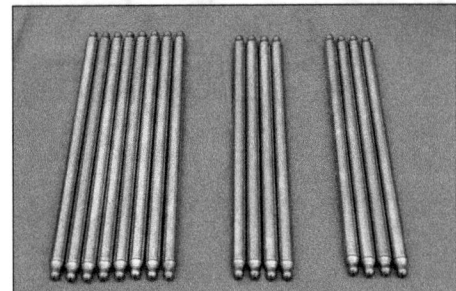

Most spread port heads like the Dart Big Chief and Brodix Big Duke require three pushrod lengths: eight long ones for the exhaust rockers and two different intake lengths for the offset intake rocker arms.

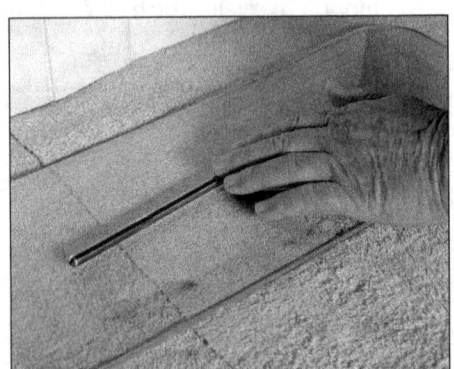

Pushrods must be checked for straightness. You can use V-blocks and a dial indicator, but this old mechanic's trick works just as well. Roll the pushrod on a plate of flat glass, and you can see and hear any bend or run-out.

Using adjustable checking pushrods and a dial indicator, you can see that the roller tip is nearly centered over the valvestem tip at mid-lift. Notice that the outer valvespring has been removed for this check, as full-tension racing springs bend the flimsy checking pushrods. You don't have to use the dial indicator; just paint the valvestem tip with machinist's dye or a felt-tip marker and check the roller contact pattern on the valvestem tip. Adjust the pushrod length in .050-inch increments until the pattern is centered over the tip. This is also a good time to check for adequate rocker-arm-to-retainer clearance. A slight increase in pushrod length might be needed to provide clearance in that area, instead of removing material from the rocker arm body.

CAMSHAFTS, LIFTERS AND VALVETRAIN COMPONENTS

Since stock big-block pushrods are 8.280 inches (intake) and 9.250 inches (exhaust), you need two adjustable pushrods for your big-block engine project: an 8- to 9-incher, and a 9- to 10-incher. If you're building a very-tall-deck aftermarket motor (over 10.500 inches), you may need a 10- to 11-inch adjustable pushrod too.

also need a dial or digital caliper long enough to measure the pushrods, but there are 12-inch calipers on the market now that fit even modest gearhead budgets. Use machinist's dye or a black felt-tip marker to paint the valvestem tip, then rotate the engine through several revolutions to get a contact pattern where the rocker's roller rubs on the valvestem. If the pattern is offset toward the inside (intake manifold side), the pushrod length is too short. If the pattern is offset toward the outside (exhaust side), the pushrod length is too long.

Rocker Arms

The rocker arms are merely the fulcrums that transfer the upward motion from the camshaft, lifters, and pushrods to a downward push on the valvestems. Because the dimension from the pivot point of the rocker to the valvestem tip is longer than the dimension to the pushrod cup, the rocker arms multiply the movement of the pushrod to yield more lift at the valve. This is the rocker arm's ratio, and all factory big-block rocker arms had a 1.7:1 ratio. The stock rocker arms pivot on hardened steel rocker balls that mount over rocker studs in the head, and rocker alignment with the valvestem is controlled by pushrod guideplates. The original equipment stamped-steel rocker arm and rocker ball design is a miracle of lightweight, mass production engineering, but it quickly loses favor to the more specialized and, yes, more expensive aftermarket roller bearing rockers when power levels and attending increases in valve motion and engine speed escalate.

Standard OEM rockers for trucks and passenger car engines have a slot in the bottom of the rocker ball area for the rocker stud, and the rocker arm binds against the stud if cams with more than about .600-inch lift at the valve are used. Traditional gearhead lore states that you should be able to insert the end of a paper clip (about .030-inch diameter) between the rocker stud and the end of the slot in the rocker arm with the cam at full lift to verify adequate clearance.

High-performance big-blocks from the muscle car era used long-slot stamped-steel rocker arms that can be identified with a raised "H" or "L" on the rocker. These long-slot rocker arms are still available from GMPP (PN 12368085 is for a set of 16 rockers, balls, and adjuster nuts), although I strongly recommend a set of true-roller bearing rocker arms from the aftermarket if you are upgrading your valvetrain to accommodate a high-lift camshaft.

Even General Motors seems to agree with this logic; its king-of-the-hill 572-ci crate engines come with aluminum-bodied roller rocker arms, private-labeled from aftermarket manufacturers. These are available from GMPP as PN 19210726 for a set of 16 with "polylocks," with the caveat that they do not fit stock-height valve covers, which is true of all roller rocker arms with their tall locking adjuster nuts. Now you have a perfect excuse to get those cool-looking tall valve covers that you've been wanting. Just be sure to check for adequate clearance in the engine compartment first, as taller-than-stock valve covers may hit the power brake booster, A/C compressor, or other engine accessories.

All Mark IV big-block cylinder heads are tapped with 7/16-14 threads on the bottom of the rocker studs, and pushrod guideplates for 5/16-, 3/8-, or 7/16-inch pushrods are clamped between each pair of rocker studs and the head. The rocker studs feature 7/16-20 threads for the adjuster nuts. Production Gen V and Gen IV engines were changed to non-adjustable valvetrains, which rely on precision manufacturing tolerances and

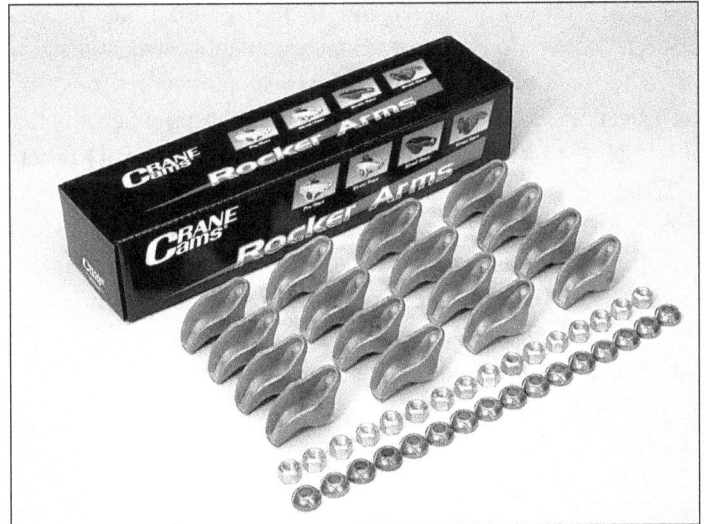

Crane Cams offers an economical stamped-steel replacement rocker arm set complete with grooved rocker balls and crimped adjuster nuts. These rockers are nitrocarburized for improved wear resistance. (Photo Courtesy Crane Cams)

CHAPTER 4

Gen V and Gen VI heads came with a non-adjustable valvetrain. They can be converted to adjustable Mark IV–type valvetrains by using special rocker studs with a 3/8-16 threaded lower section. All Mark IV and aftermarket heads use rocker studs that are 7/16-14 where they screw into the head. (Photo Courtesy Comp Cams)

Roller bearing stud-mount rocker arms with a roller tip, like this Crane extruded aluminum-bodied rocker, are an excellent choice for any big-block with conventional heads and valve lifts up to .850 inch. (Photo Courtesy Crane Cams)

A stud girdle clamps around the rocker adjuster nuts to prevent stud flexing and should be used with stud-mount rocker arms any time valve lift exceeds .700 inch, especially with high-pressure roller lifter valvesprings. This CNC-machined aluminum Edelbrock stud girdle precisely matches the non-stock valve locations of the Edelbrock Victor 24-degree heads. The fit is so precise that the girdle cannot be installed with all eight rocker nuts in place; you should install all four intake or exhaust adjuster nuts, then slide the girdle over them and install the remaining four adjuster nuts through the holes in the girdle. One of the complaints about stud girdles is that the valve lash can change after you tighten the girdle bolts. If that happens, either the girdle does not match your cylinder head, or you don't have it positioned correctly. It takes time to get everything just right when adjusting valves with a stud girdle. You can make just about as much power with stud-mount rockers and a good girdle, but shaft rockers are much easier to adjust or replace quickly, which is a major consideration for engine thrashing between rounds at the track.

Roller rocker arms, polylocks, and stud girdles all require tall valve covers for clearance. What more excuse do you need to buy those nice aluminum valve covers you've been wanting? (Photo Courtesy GMPP)

self-adjusting hydraulic lifters to maintain the correct lifter preload. They use a shouldered 3/8-16 rocker bolt, which is simply torqued to 50 ft-lbs for installation. If you are using production Gen V or Gen VI cylinder heads for your engine and want to change to a more aggressive camshaft, you need to convert to an adjustable valvetrain. Special conversion rocker studs with a 3/8-16 bottom thread and a 7/16-20 adjuster thread are available from Comp Cams (PN 4514-KIT), GMPP (P/N12495518), and other sources.

Any time that maximum valve lift exceeds .600 inch, you should consider using aftermarket roller rocker arms. They do not bind against the stud, they are much stronger than the stock stamped steel rockers, and they offer more precise control over the valve throughout the lift cycle because they only rotate about one axis. Yes, they also reduce friction, but that is not why they make more power—it is because they offer better control of the valve motion.

Most aftermarket roller rocker bodies are manufactured from aluminum extrusions, but there are also roller rockers made from chrome-moly steel and stainless steel. Just like connecting rods, the steel rocker bodies can be much smaller in physical size so that the weight difference between steel and aluminum rockers is not that great, and steel-bodied roller rockers are very popular in endurance applications such as offshore boat racing.

The stock 1.7:1 rocker ratio is most popular, although many manufacturers offer high-ratio 1.8:1 rockers. 1.6:1 rockers are also available if you want to reduce your valve lift, although they have largely fallen out of favor with most modern engine builders. One advantage of high-ratio rocker arms is that the rocker tip swings through less of an arc at the same valve lift, which reduces side loading on the valvestem tip.

At the top of the heap in the competition rocker arm world are shaft-mounted rocker arms. Stud-mounted rocker arms simply cannot offer the rock-solid valve motion control of shaft rockers, which pivot on a shaft bolted solidly to the head (via rocker stands) with bolts on each side of the rocker arm shaft. In order to be adjusted, stud-mount rockers must have some amount of clearance where the stud passes through the trunion and this clearance also allows the rocker to shift around during the lift cycle, wasting some of the cam's motion. Additionally,

CAMSHAFTS, LIFTERS AND VALVETRAIN COMPONENTS

Shaft mount rocker arms like these T&D units offer the ultimate in precise valvetrain control. The rocker shaft is secured directly to the head (via rocker stands) by bolts or studs on each end of the shaft, eliminating all lateral movement of the rocker arm. Another major benefit of shaft rockers is that they accommodate severe pushrod seat offsets with no negative effects. This allows cylinder head manufacturers to put the valves where they need to be for best power instead of trying to fit within the big-block's stock valvetrain configuration. All current spread port heads, like these Brodix Big Duke heads, require shaft rockers.

Some manufacturers offer Sportsman-level shaft rockers like these from Crane Camshafts. They offer the benefits of a shaft rocker system without the expensive custom features that pro racers desire, and are a good choice for most street performance and racing big-blocks. They are mounted on the original rocker stud bolt bosses and use an adjustable link for proper alignment with the valvestems. (Photo Courtesy Crane Cams)

Comp Cams' shaft rocker arms are available for popular big-block cylinder heads. The 1.7:1 rocker bodies are made from 2024 aluminum and the stand is 8620 hardened steel. (Photo Courtesy Comp Cams)

a single 7/16-inch stud flexes much more than a solid-steel shaft secured by bolts at both ends.

Stud girdles have been used for years with stud-mount rockers to prevent stud flex, but they are time-consuming to adjust properly and require extremely tall valve covers for adequate clearance. Because shaft rockers pivot on a fixed shaft, valve lash adjustment is accomplished with adjustable pushrod seats and locknuts, so adjusting or checking valve lash is quick and easy. Furthermore, if the rocker arms must be removed for quick engine disassembly (for instance, while changing valvesprings), they may be re-installed without losing the previously adjusted valve lash dimension.

Most shaft rocker manufacturers make the rockers in any ratio you want from 1.7:1 to 2.0:1, and these specialty components are pretty much custom-made to your specifications from a list of dozens of options. As you can imagine, shaft rockers are not cheap; top-of-the-line sets can cost four or five times as much as a set of stud-mount roller rockers. To bridge that gap, manufacturers such as Jesel, T&D, Comp Cams, and Crane are starting to offer less expensive "Sportsman" shaft rockers without some of the bells and whistles that the pros demand. When you factor in the cost of a good stud girdle with the cost of premium stud-mount roller rockers, the cost differential between shaft rockers and stud-mount rockers is not that much.

Valvesprings, Retainers and Keepers

If the camshaft is the boss of the valvetrain gang, the valvesprings are the muscle. To say that the valvesprings must match the camshaft is like saying that you need two legs to run a marathon. In reality, the camshaft, lifters, pushrods, and rocker arms are only responsible for opening the valves; the valvesprings have to make sure they get closed on time.

One of the endearing features of the big-block's canted valve design is that there is plenty of room for large-diameter valvesprings, and increasing the physical size of the springs is the easiest way to get more pressure and longer life from them. Even stock big-block valvesprings measure about 1.550 inches in diameter, the same size as typical racing springs for small-block engines. However, don't be complacent—the OEM valvesprings found on most truck and passenger car big-blocks are not suitable for use with anything other than the most mild camshaft grinds. Also, valvesprings cannot be expected to last the entire lifespan of your engine between rebuilds, and should be checked and replaced as needed on high-performance street or racing engines.

Most new aftermarket cylinder heads include valvesprings that are compatible with performance camshafts, but you must verify this yourself. Installing heads equipped with roller cam springs on an engine with a flat-tappet camshaft wipes out the cam and lifters in short order. Check with the cylinder head and camshaft manufacturers to see if the parts are theoretically a match, then check the springs for proper installed height and tension yourself.

The Rat motor has a huge appetite for valvesprings, due to its larger and heavier valves compared to small-block V-8s. As the weight and displacement of the valvetrain increases, it takes bigger and stronger springs to prevent valve float, which is the point when the spring can no longer keep the parts in constant contact. When that happens, the parts eventually slam back together with very destructive results. Valvesprings must be strong enough to achieve the desired peak RPM level for top horsepower, but not so much that they damage the cam and lifter interface. For this reason, roller lifters, which can handle much higher spring pressures, are even more desirable in the big-block than they are in smaller engines.

Valvesprings suitable for use in the Rat motor can have one, two, or three springs per assembly, and some double-spring sets have a dampener between the inner and outer valvesprings to control harmonic vibrations that are present at different engine speeds. Previously, only dual or triple valvesprings were considered adequate for controlling the heavy valvetrain of a Rat motor, but new valvespring technology has made the installation of single "Beehive" valvesprings a possibility for street big-blocks operating up to 6,000 or 6,500 rpm.

The Beehive design features a single spring that is wound on a decreasing radius, so that the base of the spring is larger than the top where the spring retainer fits. There are two benefits to this approach: first, the weight of the small diameter retainer and the spring itself is reduced so that less pressure is required at elevated engine speeds. Second, Beehive springs do a better job of dampening harmonic vibration than traditional cylindrical valvesprings, so that no additional spring dampeners or interference fit between multiple springs is required to control vibration damping. Consequently, there is no additional heat build-up generated from the friction of springs rubbing against each other, which leads to longer valvespring life.

At this time, Beehive valvesprings are only strong enough for use with moderate cam profiles typically used on street-driven big-blocks, and higher RPM levels require the use of true double or triple valvesprings, especially with roller lifter camshafts. Maximum valvespring pressure for flat-tappet cams is generally between 150 and 170 pounds on the seat

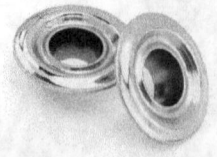

Beehive valvesprings (left) are single springs that are wound on a decreasing radius, so that the base of the spring is larger than the top where the retainer fits. Special reduced-diameter retainers, like these tool steel retainers (right) from Comp Cams, must be used. (Photos Courtesy Comp Cams)

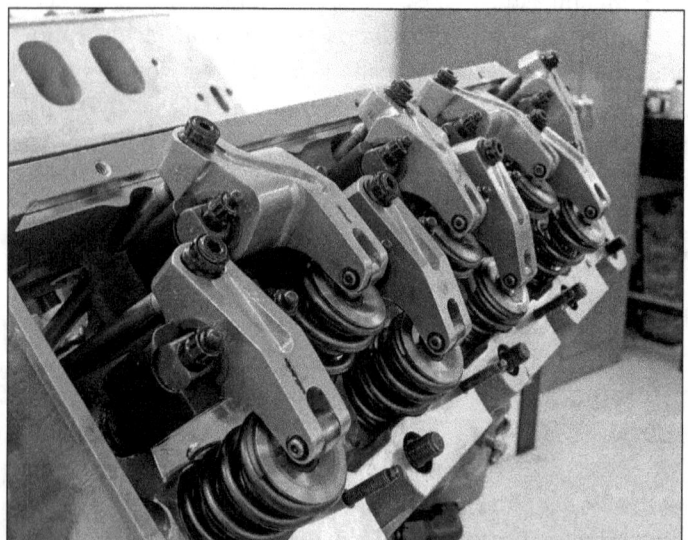

Competition big-blocks need serious valvetrain pieces: fat pushrods, shaft rocker arms, long valves (these are titanium), triple valvesprings, titanium retainers and matching keepers, valvespring locators, and good valvestem seals are standard fare for 1,000-plus-hp Rat motors with over .900-inch lift at the valves.

Triple valvesprings are the norm for high-lift, high-RPM roller cam big-blocks. They are tightly fitted to each other to dampen harmonic vibrations and create a lot of frictional heat in a high-RPM racing engine. Spring oilers are a very good idea with triple springs. (Photo Courtesy Crane Cams)

CAMSHAFTS, LIFTERS AND VALVETRAIN COMPONENTS

with a spring rate of about 400 pounds per inch, and even that's on the high side in terms of lifter and cam lobe longevity. With roller lifters, spring pressures typically start at around 200 pounds on the seat and go up—way up—from there. Competition roller lifter springs can have 300-plus-pounds of pressure on the seat and eclipse 1,000 pounds of pressure at maximum lift.

The only way to get these kinds of pressures is to use physically larger springs, and most competition big-block valvesprings are 1.625 inches or more in diameter. The springs must be physically taller as well, and typical installed height for competition roller springs starts at 2.000 inches (compared to 1.880 inches at stock installed height) and goes up from there; installed heights of 2.100 inches are generally considered standard in racing big-block engines.

Increased spring installed height is one of the main reasons that most aftermarket valves for competition engines are offered in longer-than-stock lengths. It's simple math: if your springs coil bind at 1.150 inches and your valve lift is .850 inch, you're already at 2.000 inches with no safety margin. Add at least .050-inch clearance to prevent coil bind, and the minimum installed height becomes 2.050 inches. These numbers are just generalizations, but you could summarize the situation like this: if you are looking at a set of heads with stock-length valves and a stock-installed spring height of 1.880 inches, here's the formula for the calculation:

Maximum Valve Lift = Installed Height − (Coil Bind + .050-inch Clearance)

1.880 inches − (1.150 inches + .050 inch) = .680 inch

If you want more than .680-inch lift, you have to upgrade to better springs and longer valves.

There are "Band-Aid" approaches to getting more installed spring height, such as offset spring retainers and keepers, which usually offer around .050-inch more spring height, but now your retainers are getting close to hitting the bottom of the rocker arms. Lash caps on top of your valvestems, combined with longer pushrods, help provide clearance in that area, but you really should use parts that are designed for the job at hand. Big-block racing engines need longer-than-stock valves and larger-than-stock valvesprings—period.

Valvespring retainers are available in either steel or titanium and must match your valvesprings perfectly so that the springs cannot move around laterally while the engine is running. The correct size varies, so you should always use the

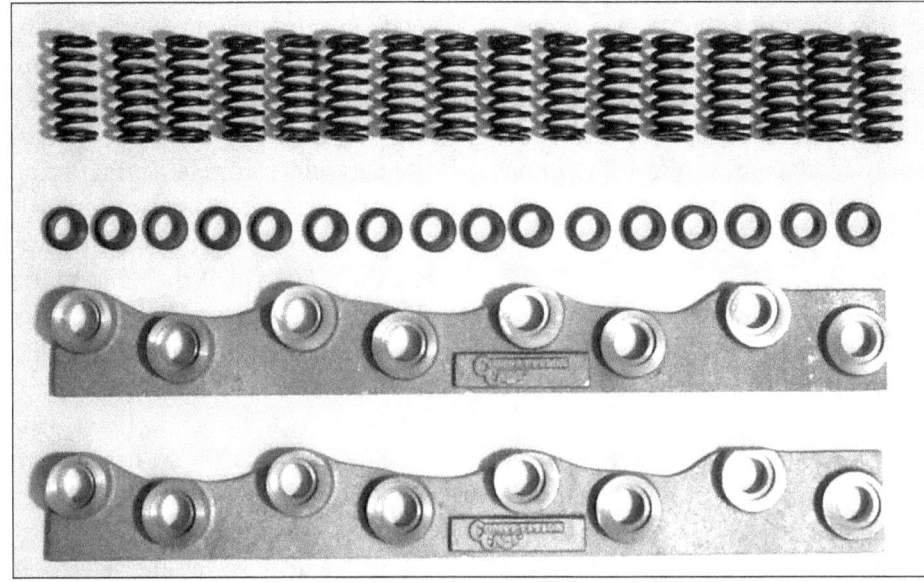

Rev kits like this Comp Cams PN 4003 feature an aluminum plate that registers against the bottom of the cylinder head. The plate has pockets to position springs that apply additional pressure directly to the tops of roller lifters. They have largely fallen out of favor in most professionally built big-blocks used for drag racing, because the relatively soft springs don't add much pressure compared to the excellent double or triple valvesprings available today. They are still a good idea for offshore and other endurance racing applications, because the rev kit retains the lifter in its bore in the event of pushrod or rocker arm failure. If the lifter is ejected from its bore following valvetrain failure, it causes a massive internal oil leak in the lifter oil gallery and could lead to engine failure. Some companies also advocate the use of rev kits with hydraulic roller lifter engines to extend the RPM range, since the added spring pressure bears directly against the lifter body, not the hydraulic plunger—an interesting concept. (Photo Courtesy Comp Cams)

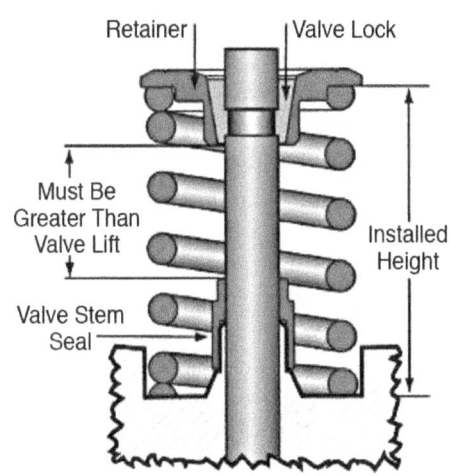

This cutaway view shows the relationship between the valvespring, retainer, and spring pocket in the head. (Illustration Courtesy Comp Cams)

retainers specified by your valvespring manufacturer.

Original equipment big-block retainers are made from steel, and steel retainers are the economical choice for most street-driven Rat motors, but titanium retainers are relatively inexpensive compared to other titanium engine parts, and you should consider them when selecting your cam and spring combo. Some aftermarket manufacturers offer lightweight tool steel retainers that are only a few grams heavier than titanium, and they are certainly a viable option for any street or street/strip big-block.

Retainers must be used with matching valve locks (also known as keepers) for the valvestem diameter in your Rat motor, and they are not all the same. While all OEM big-blocks use 3/8-inch-diameter valvestems, most aftermarket big-block heads are fitted with 11/32-inch valvestems. There are even 5/16-inch-stem valves, which some engine builders use for very-high-RPM drag race engines.

Also, various manufacturers have developed their own version of the correct retainer-to-keeper angles and dimensions. There are standard 7-degree keepers, 10-degree keepers, "Super 7-degree" keepers, and others. Some racing valves come with a radius cut for the keeper groove and must be used with matching radiused valvestem locks. Unless you really know what you are getting into, just order your springs, retainers, and keepers from the same manufacturer for a proper fit.

Valvespring Oiling

The big-block's stock valvetrain oiling system starts with oil delivery from the lifter gallery to supply the lifters with oil, then the pressurized oil travels up the hollow pushrods to the rocker arms, which have a small orifice to dribble oil onto the rocker pivot ball and the valvesprings. The primary purpose is to lubricate the highly stressed valvetrain components, but a very important secondary benefit is to remove heat from the valvesprings as the multiple coils rub against each other.

It's common practice in drag racing engines to reduce the oil delivery to the lifters by installing restrictors in the lifter oil gallery, because roller lifters and roller rocker arms don't need as much lubrication as the OEM parts, but the cooling effect of oiling the valvesprings is disregarded. High-end racing engines usually incorporate valvespring oilers into their design, and many shaft rocker arm manufacturers offer the option of a small oil-squirter hole drilled into the body of the rocker arm to oil the valvesprings.

Some endurance racing engine builders opt to have pressurized oiling tubes built into the valve covers to direct oil onto the springs. Of course, the valvestem seals must be very good to prevent oil contamination in the combustion chamber if you're going to bathe the springs with oil, and most competition engines using spring oilers benefit from

Lash caps are necessary to protect titanium valvestems from wear at the tip, but they can also be used to gain rocker-arm-to-retainer clearance. They must be used with relieved keepers for clearance. (Photo Courtesy Comp Cams)

either a dry sump oil pump or external vacuum pump. The negative crankcase pressure from a vacuum pump lessens the pressure differential between the intake port and the top of the valveguide, which reduces the chances of oil being pulled into the engine past the stem seals.

Valvespring Locators

Stock cast-iron big-block heads do not need spring locators, because the valveguide positively locates the inner spring and the step from the seat machining operation locates the outer spring of a dual spring assembly. With aluminum cylinder heads, spring locators or spring cups must be used to prevent the spring from digging into the soft aluminum. Although spring cups do a good job of holding the spring in position, they require machining the spring seat to a diameter larger than the spring, which may interfere with adjacent headbolt holes and hardware. Spring inside diameter locators are just large enough to support the outer spring, but they feature a shoulder to pilot the inner spring and prevent spring "walking" or any unwanted movement while the engine is running.

Some 1973 through 1981 454-ci engines with cast-iron heads were equipped with exhaust valve rotators to prevent "hot spots" with unleaded gasoline. Modern valve and valve seat materials have made this unnecessary, and I recommend that these valve rotators be removed when upgrading to a performance cam and valvespring combination. To take up the space left by the rotators, you could stack valvespring shims until you achieve the necessary .300-inch thickness, but a better solution is to purchase exhaust rotator eliminators, available from most aftermarket cam companies.

CAMSHAFTS, LIFTERS AND VALVETRAIN COMPONENTS

New Camshaft Break-In

Since the camshaft and lifter interface represents the highest metal-to-metal friction point in your engine, it is imperative that proper break-in procedures are followed to prevent scuffing and wear that can lead to premature parts failure. There are several methods of accomplishing this, but here are the basics:

1. Use the appropriate assembly lube during engine assembly.
2. Use motor oils with the correct anti-scuff additives.
3. Pre-lube the engine prior to start-up.
4. Carefully adjust valve lash (solid lifters) or preload (hydraulic lifters).
5. Be sure the distributor is installed correctly and "static timed" to prevent excessive cranking of the starter before the engine starts.
6. Fill the cooling system completely to eliminate air pockets.
7. Fill the carburetor with fuel to prevent excessive cranking of the starter before the engine starts.

   It is necessary to reduce excessive cranking of the starter because the assembly lube (usually some form of moly disulfide) can be wiped off by too much "dry cranking" before the engine starts and builds oil pressure. Your new engine should start within one or two seconds after turning the key, or pushing the starter button if it's a racecar. If it doesn't start, stop and figure out why.

8. Once the engine starts, immediately bring the engine speed up to 2,000 to 2,500 rpm and run the engine for 30 to 40 minutes before shut-down (flat-tappet cams only).

   You need to bring the engine speed up to 2,000 or 2,500 rpm because the cam and lifters are only lubricated by oil thrown off of the spinning crankshaft, and that engine speed ensures that they are bathed in a flood of oil. That oil not only lubricates the lifters, it also carries away excessive heat from the friction of the lifters rubbing on the cam lobes. Many mechanics like to vary the engine speed within that RPM range to throw the oil at different areas within the engine, and I'm one of those. If you are using roller lifters, either mechanical or hydraulic, this step is not necessary—another advantage of roller lifter camshafts.

   Keep a sharp eye on the oil pressure gage. Depending on your oil pump, you should have at least 30 to 40 psi at that RPM, usually even higher. If the pressure drops too much (it goes down a little as the oil heats up), the filter may be getting plugged up with the moly lube. If that happens, shut off the engine, replace the filter (filled with fresh oil, of course), then continue the break-in.

   After the engine starts, you need to make sure it doesn't overheat, so eliminating all the air trapped in the cooling system ensures a good supply of water throughout the engine to carry away heat. Yes, I said water, not coolant. Water is a better conductor of heat than antifreeze, so use straight water for the initial cam break-in. If the car has a belt-driven water pump, you should be running a thermostat. But before you install the water neck and thermostat, fill the engine with water through the water neck opening in the intake manifold so that air is not trapped in the engine by the closed thermostat. It's also a good idea to have a large fan set in front of your radiator since there is no airflow while the car is stationary. If the ignition timing is retarded, that also builds excessive heat, so too much timing is better than too little, at least while the engine is not under load.

9. Change the oil and filter while it is still warm to remove all contamination (small pieces of metal, dirt, lint from shop towels, etc.).

   After the initial cam break-in is performed, you can change the oil and filter, add antifreeze (street-driven cars only; racetracks frown on antifreeze getting dumped on their racing surface), lower the idle speed, and set the final timing with your timing light. If you are running a hot solid-lifter cam that requires high-pressure dual valvesprings, it's a good idea to remove the inner springs before cam break-in, then re-install them afterward. Just be sure not to rev the engine to more than 3,000 rpm with the "lightened" springs, or you run the risk of hitting the piston tops with the valves. If you have an oil filter cutter, it's a good idea to cut apart the filter and inspect for any metal chips, bearing flakes, or other stuff that shouldn't be there. If you find them, figure out where they came from and do something about it now, before a small problem becomes a big one.

CHAPTER 5

OIL AND LUBRICATION SYSTEMS

If oil is the lifeblood of your engine, then the oil pump and lubrication system are indeed the heart and circulation system of your big-block Chevy. For power levels up to about 500 hp, there's really not much that needs changing, other than to ensure that your parts are up to spec, and that the lubricant you are using is the right choice for your parts combination.

For the high-performance and racing markets, there are two choices in oiling system designs: wet sump and dry sump. All original equipment big-blocks were wet sump systems, so-called because the reservoir of oil is contained in the sump portion of the oil pan, and the oil pump pickup is submerged in this (hopefully) continuous supply of life-giving lubricant. Dry sump systems are the high end of the performance spectrum and they utilize a belt-driven external oil pump with multiple scavenge sections, which pull oil from several points in the engine and pump the evacuated oil to a holding tank. In addition to providing a much larger oil capacity, the tank allows any air in the oil to separate, delivering an uninterrupted supply of non-aerated oil to the pressure section of the pump.

The benefits of a dry sump system are many—first and foremost, the engine receives a continuous delivery of oil under all conditions, whether accelerating, braking, cornering, or whatever. Second, the scavenge sections pull excess oil away from the turbulence of the rotating assembly, freeing up some horsepower by reducing the drag of engine parts "swimming" through a pool of excess liquid. Third, the scavenge sections are so efficient that they can pull a vacuum in the crankcase. This helps free up more

Dry sump oil systems use a cogged, belt-driven pump with multiple scavenge sections and one pressure section. This Barnes four-stage pump has three scavenge sections that pull oil from the pan and pump it into the oil tank. The main oil supply line from the bottom of the tank feeds the pressure section at the rear of the pump, which supplies pressurized oil to an adapter bolted between the block and the oil filter. The drive belt and filter have not yet been installed in this photo.

OIL AND LUBRICATION SYSTEMS

horsepower and prevents oil contamination from getting past the piston rings and into the combustion chamber, where it could cause detonation, oil-fouled spark plugs, and other problems. Finally, because there is no need for a deep sump in the oil pan, dry sump oil pans can be much shallower that wet sump pans, giving car builders the option of positioning the engine lower in the chassis for a lower center of gravity and a lower hood scoop height for reduced aerodynamic drag.

So what's the downside to dry sump systems? Instead of spending hundreds of dollars for an upgrade in performance, you'll be looking at a bill for thousands of dollars, making dry sump systems the choice of all professional racers (when legal), but not a very cost-effective item when you calculate power gained per dollar spent.

Oil Pumps

Stock big-block Chevy oil pumps have been available in two configurations: standard volume or high volume. The difference is merely the length of the spur gears inside the pump housing; standard-volume gears are 1.135 inches long, and high-volume gears are 1.300 inches. Either design fits any standard big-block rear main cap. Note that Mark IV and Gen V/VI oil pumps are slightly different, so be sure to specify which version you want. Mark IV pumps do not clear the inner rear main cap bolt of a Gen V/VI engine, but Gen V/VI pumps can be used on Mark IV engines. The GM Performance Parts pump (PN 19131250) is standard on their 572 crate engines and is a good choice for any high-performance Mark IV or Gen V/VI big-block, when used with a pickup that matches your oil pan.

So why does everyone seem to think that all high-performance engines need a high-pressure, high-volume oil pump? It used to be standard practice to open up the main and rod bearing clearances in a high-performance Rat motor beyond the stock .0025- to .003-inch clearance, and to use a high-viscosity oil the belief that it gives more protection to the crank. Such practices increase the amount of internal hemorrhaging (leakage) in the lubrication system, and do indeed require an increase in oil pump volume.

Today, we can enjoy the benefits of better lubricants, especially with synthetic oils, and tighter bearing clearances actually provide better bearing life because the hydrodynamic wedge of oil, which supports the crankshaft when the engine is running, is stronger when the clearance is only .0025 to .003 inch. The general rule for high-performance engine oil pressure is 10 pounds per square inch for every 1,000 rpm.

Stock Chevy oil pumps have the pickup tube pressed into the pump body, and they have been known to fall out when subjected to the vibration of a high-RPM engine. All high-performance Chevy pumps should have the pickup tube secured by tack-welding the pickup to the pump body, or by a tab from the pickup tube that is bolted to one of the pump cover bolts. Using both methods is a very good idea, and most aftermarket pan manufacturers offer pickup tubes with mounting tabs to match their oil

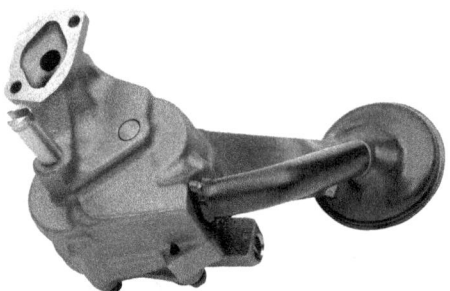

GM Performance Parts pump PN 19131250 is a good choice for any high-performance Mark IV or Gen V/VI big-block, when used with a pickup that matches your oil pan. (Photo Courtesy GMPP)

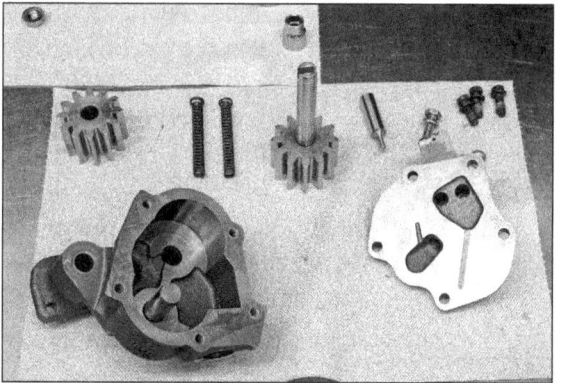

The main components of a stock Chevy oil pump are the pump body and cover, two spur gears (a drive gear and a driven gear), a pressure relief valve, and spring. This pump came with two springs; one high-pressure and one standard-pressure. You can use small washers or even a small nut to shim the spring for more pressure, but be careful not to shim so much that the valve can't open or you'll blow the filter apart. It's best to simply buy the right pump to begin with, rather than try to jury-rig something that may or may not work properly. The most important thing to check is the clearance between the gears and the pump cover; it should be between .0025 and .0035 inch. If it is too loose, you can carefully dress the pump body with some 400-grit wet-or-dry sandpaper on a flat surface. If it is too tight (this is rare), you could dress the bottom of both gears to get the clearance just right. Before installing the pump on your engine, pour a generous amount of STP, assembly lube, or GM EOS into the pump body between the two gears and rotate the gears to coat all inside surfaces for easy priming. If you ever put a dry pump into an engine, you'll only do it once. It's practically impossible to prime a dry pump. You have to jack-up the front of the car about 4 or 5 feet in the air, over-fill the pan with oil, and then drain out the excess oil. Not recommended.

  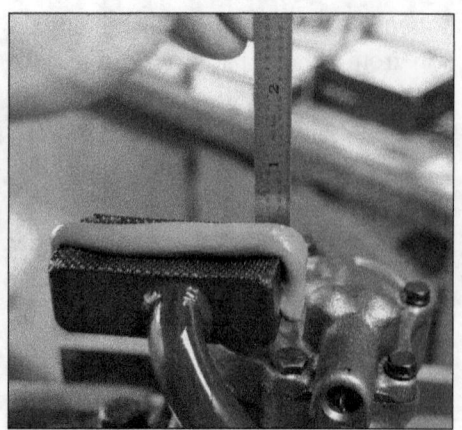

Measure your oil pump pickup height and pan depth to ensure that you have adequate clearance. After measuring, it's still a good idea to physically check the clearance with modeling clay, and don't forget to add gasket thickness if you checked this without the gasket in place. Normal clearance is 1/4 to 3/8 inch, but check with your oil pan manufacturer to be sure.

pans. Be sure to remove the relief valve spring before welding the pickup to prevent damage to the spring. Chilling the pickup tube in your freezer and heating the pump body by setting it out in the sun before pickup installation also helps the job along. Be sure to test fit the pan and pickup clearance before tack welding everything together. Recommended pickup-to-pan clearance is usually 1/4 inch, and don't forget to add the thickness of the pan gasket.

Some pump manufacturers machine anti-cavitation slots and pressure balance slots into the pump body and cover to lessen the chance of cavitation at high engine speeds. Cavitation is a vacuum that occurs in a fluid when it cannot flow fast enough fill in the void behind the rapidly moving gears. This is not needed for street high-performance engines, and is not recommended for street use by most pump makers.

Fluids, such as motor oil, prefer to be pushed under pressure than sucked through a lengthy section of tubing, so keeping the pump pickup as short as possible is a good thing. Taking that concept to extremes, some aftermarket oil pumps for big-block Chevys use spacers between the oil pump and the rear main cap to submerge the pump into the sump portion of the pan. This may require a longer pump driveshaft, and the pump must be carefully matched to the oil pan depth to maintain the correct pickup-to-pan clearance. These extended pumps don't fit most stock oil pans and must be used with aftermarket competition pans designed for the job.

Many of these extended pumps are machined from billet aluminum, and some use gerotor gears instead of common spur gears. Gerotor gears deliver a smoother supply of oil pressure without the pulsing that is characteristic of spur gear pumps, and the gerotor design greatly reduces the chance of cavitation at high engine speeds. Many dry sump oil pumps also feature gerotor pressure sections for the same reasons.

The stock Chevy pump driveshaft is a simple mild steel shaft that is driven by the camshaft via the bottom of the distributor, so that the oil pump rotates at 1/2 crankshaft speed. It uses a plastic bushing

Oil pump primers fit into the distributor hole and engage the pump drive. Drive the shaft with your 3/8- or 1/2-inch-drill motor until you have full pressure for 20 or 30 seconds, then rotate the crank to a different position and repeat. Oil pump primers are available from many sources, and this one is from GMPP (PN 12368084). (Photo Courtesy GMPP)

This competition pump features anti-cavitation slots for high-RPM oil pressure stability. It is mounted with a stud and nut, and has a copper gasket between the pump body and the rear main cap. The gasket is not original equipment, but helps to seal the pump-to-cap junction, especially if either part has been roughed up or scored. Always inspect the cap-to-pump mating surfaces for irregularities, which cause a loss of oil pressure and volume.

OIL AND LUBRICATION SYSTEMS

Titan Speed makes billet aluminum pumps with gerotors instead of traditional spur gears. The dual-feed gerotor design produces less cavitation and delivers a much smoother oil delivery without the pulsing that is characteristic of spur-gear pumps. The adjustable pressure relief valve eliminates the need to "shim and guess" when setting maximum oil pressure. This type of pump won't fit stock pans and must be used with a dedicated racing oil pan. (Photo Courtesy Titan Speed)

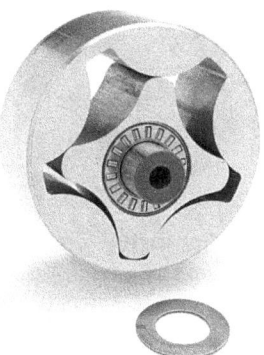

Gerotor gear design produces oil chambers that progressively expand and contract in volume to draw in oil and push it out without the "chopping" characteristic of spur gears. (Photo Courtesy Titan Speed)

A heavy-duty all-metal pump driveshaft, like this one from GMPP (PN 3865886), should be used in every high-performance big-block. (Photo Courtesy GMPP)

to hold it in place on the oil pump during assembly and to keep it inside the engine block when the distributor is removed. Heavy-duty all-metal driveshafts are available from the aftermarket and GMPP (PN 3865886) and should be in every high-performance Rat motor.

Oil Pans

Until your power expectations exceed 500 hp, it's quite likely that your original oil pan works just fine, as long as the pump is right for the engine. Remember that the first rule of oil pan selection is that it must fit on your car, and many large-capacity oil pans do not clear stock crossmembers, steering and suspension components, or other obstacles on the dark side of your ride. If you have the room, the Corvette 5-quart pan (PN 14091356) is a good first step up from the standard Mark IV passenger car 4-quart pan. It includes a windage tray and requires four main cap studs (PN 3902885) for mounting the tray.

Remember that oil pan capacity is listed without regard to the extra quart of oil in the filter: if you have to add 5 quarts of oil after an oil change, you have a 4-quart pan. Gen V and Gen VI engines were never offered in the Corvette, but there are plenty of large-capacity pans available for those engines, such as the 6-quart pan (PN 10240721), but it does not fit an early Chevelle or Camaro without modifications.

Fortunately, there are many excellent aftermarket pans available for Mark IV and Gen V/VI big-blocks from Hamburger's Performance Products, Milodon, and Moroso for any application from street to all-out racing, and specialty oil pan manufacturers such as Dan Olson Racing Products, Jeff Johnston's Billet Fabrication, and Stef's Fabrication Specialties.

Competition pans include such features as crank scrapers to shear excess oil off of the spinning crank and rod assembly, built-in windage trays to shield oil in the sump from the turbulence of the spinning crank, and kick-outs on the right side of the pan. A kick-out provides an "escape route" for the oil thrown off the spinning crankshaft and channels the oil back to the sump more efficiently than a straight-wall oil pan.

Choose a pan that fits your car with as much capacity as possible to keep the oil cool. The number-one priority of your oiling system should be to keep the engine supplied with oil, and big boxy pans make it harder to control oil slosh

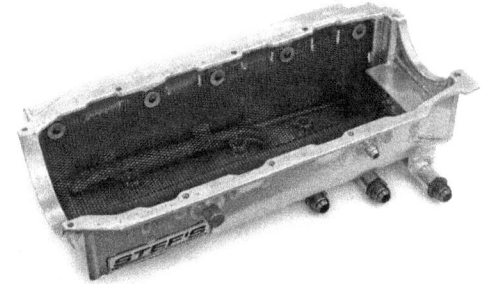

This dry sump aluminum oil pan has three scavenge pickups, integral windage screen/separator, a rear anti-slosh baffle, and right-side kick-out. The pan rail surface is notched to clear the 4.5-inch-stroke crank and rods it is used with.

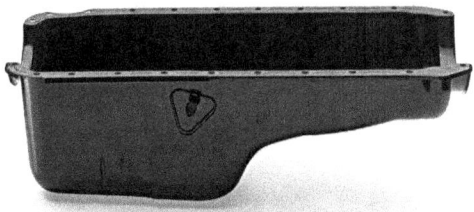
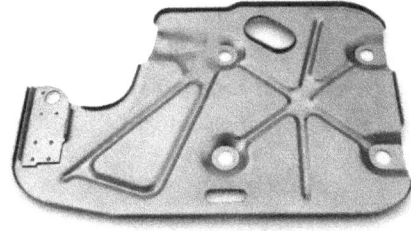

The 1965–1974 Corvette 5-quart pan (GM PN 14091356) fits most big-block full-size cars. It includes a windage tray (PN 3967854), but requires the purchase of four mounting studs (PN 3902885). (Photos Courtesy of GMPP)

CHAPTER 5

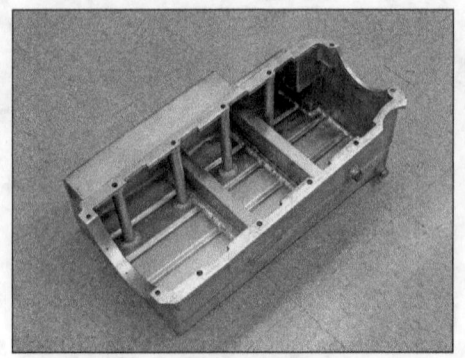

Jeff Johnston's Billet Fabrication Specialties created this aluminum wet sump pan for dragster and altered drag race vehicles. Features include notched pan rails for stroker crank clearance, large kick-out, and anti-slosh baffles. There is no dipstick provision; you're expected to know how much oil you put in your race car, and change it before it leaks out enough to cause concern. This is the kind of wet sump pan you find on a 1,000-hp Rat motor, but it is not the best choice for a street-driven car. It won't fit any stock chassis, and the large flat floor makes oil control difficult for anything other than drag racing.

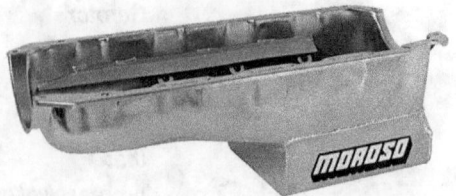

This Moroso oil pan (PN 20408) is a 6.5-quart Mark IV pan designed to fit most stock chassis cars (except 1962–1967 Chevy II, V8 Monza/Vega, and 1955–1957 Chevy). It offers power-producing features like a crank scraper and uni-directional windage tray, trap door baffling, and clearance for long-stroke crankshaft/rod assemblies. (Photo Courtesy Moroso)

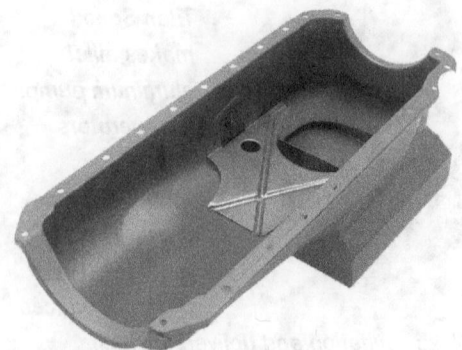

Hamburger Oil Pans' PN 0428 is a 6-quart pan with an expanded 8-inch-deep sump for Mark IV engines in early Camaros and Chevelles. (Photo Courtesy Hedman Performance Group)

K&N oil filters have a 1-inch nut welded to the bottom of the filter for easy removal. Spin-on filters should be installed hand-tight only.

Original equipment oil filter adapter (left) includes a bypass valve to ensure continuous oil supply even if the oil filter becomes clogged or is unable to deliver adequate oil supply during cold starts. Some racers prefer a non-bypassing adapter like this one from Jegs (right).

during braking and cornering. Consult with the oil pan manufacturer for application guidance; they'd rather sell you the pan you'll be happy with than some exotic pan that's wrong for your street car.

Oil Filters and Adapters

1965 through 1967 big-blocks used a metal canister and pleated filter element, and all 1968 and later Mark IV engines have an oil filter adapter with an integral bypass valve for use with spin-on oil filters. Gen V and Gen VI engines use a spin-on filter with the bypass valve installed in the block, and these bypass valves are a source of much misinformation. Their function is to bypass the filter when there is a pressure differential caused by a clogged oil filter. It's possible that the valve also bypasses the filter dur-

The oil filter adapter bolts to Mark IV blocks with two 5/16-18 bolts. Stock bolts are 1 3/8 inches long, but most aftermarket blocks require shorter 1 1/4-inch-long bolts. OEM bolts have very short hex heads to clear the oil filter, so if you are using replacement bolts it is usually necessary to shorten the bolt heads for clearance. You can use a bench grinder, belt sander, or even a file—just make sure the bolt heads do not protrude higher than the gasket surface of the block. You could use cheap grade-5 bolts, but why not spend the extra buck and use grade-8 or stainless steel bolts? Also, the lower left 3/8-16 bellhousing bolt-hole is drilled and tapped all the way through into the oil filter recess. If you use a transmission bolt that is too long, it punctures the oil filter. Don't ask me how I know. Total bolt length depends on the boss thickness of your transmission or bellhousing, but the bolt should not extend more than 5/8 inch into the block.

ing cold start-up when the oil is thickest, so some racing engine builders remove the bypass valve and plug the hole with a pipe plug. This positively ensures full filtration all the time, but may blow out the filter if you rev the engine before it is fully warmed-up. I prefer to leave the bypass valve in place and use a filter, such

76   HOW TO BUILD KILLER BIG-BLOCK CHEVY ENGINES

OIL AND LUBRICATION SYSTEMS

Gen V/VI oil filter pad contains two bypass valves, one for the oil filter (A) and one for the oil cooler (B). The filter adapter, which is nothing more than a threaded fitting to mount the filter, has been removed in this photo to show the recessed oil cooler bypass valve. Oil cooler fittings thread into the cooler outlets (C) to the oil cooler and the return (D) from the cooler. If you are not using an oil cooler, you should remove the cooler bypass valve (B) and plug the cooler line holes (C and D) with 1/4-inch NPT pipe plugs. The bypass valves are a light press fit in the block and may be removed by threading a long 3/8-16 bolt into the valve and wiggling it free, which usually damages the valve. That's okay, because replacement valves are inexpensive and you want to replace the old one with a new bypass valve (GMPP PN 25013759). Note that Gen V/VI rear main caps require an O-ring that fits in a recess in the block (E) to seal oil delivery from the pump.

as the excellent K&N (PN HP-3002) that is large enough to keep up with the oil flow demands of the engine.

There are single and dual remote oil-filter adapters on the market, which can be very handy for plumbing custom vehicles, boats, etc., that have interference issues with the stock oil filter location. Very-high-end racing motors, such as the GM DRCE, have the starter on the left side so that an oil pan with a full-length kick-out can be used, and these require remote oil filters.

Pan Evacuation Systems and Vacuum Pumps

Production big-blocks relieve crankcase pressure and blow-by through breathers and a positive crankcase ventilation (PCV) valve in the valve covers. The PCV valve is connected by a rubber hose to a port under the carburetor, which draws the crankcase gases back into the engine where they are burned off. Racers discovered years ago that reducing the crankcase pressure produced power gains. The first systems to capitalize on this effect were pan evacuation systems that use a probe in the exhaust headers connected to the valve cover breathers to create low pressure at high engine speeds. This was a step in the right direction but it was not nearly as effective as a dry sump pump, which could create a much stronger crankcase vacuum.

Several decades ago, Competition Eliminator drag racers, who could not use dry sump systems because of class rules, started adapting the OEM belt-driven smog (Air Injection Reactor, or A.I.R.) pump to pull a vacuum in the crankcase and were rewarded with gains of up to 20 hp. That doesn't sound like much, but on a competition engine with every possible modification already done, another 20 hp was like finding gold in a coal mine. In addition to freeing-up some horsepower, vacuum pumps do a good job of "housekeeping" by reducing oil buildup in the combustion chambers from leakage past the piston rings and valveguides, plus they reduce any small external oil leaks from pan gaskets, valve covers, etc.

For proper vacuum pump operation, the engine must be well sealed, and a vacuum relief valve is necessary to prevent excessive vacuum. If crankcase vacuum makes more power, how can you have too much? In a wet sump engine, there must be some pressure in the oil pan to push the oil into the oil pump pickup, and excessive crankcase vacuum lowers the oil pressure. Also, too much vacuum tends to rob the piston pin of splash lubrication; so many engine builders increase wrist-pin-to-pin-bore clearance slightly with a vacuum pump. Since vacuum pumps do such a good job of controlling the oil on the cylinder walls, low-tension oil rings can be used for reduced drag and even more horsepower. Wet sump engines should be limited to 18 to 20 inches of Mercury, while dry sump engines can get by with 24 to 26 inches because the pressure section in a dry sump pump is ventilated with normal atmospheric pressure through the oil tank breather.

There are companies that still modify the GM smog pump for racing engines, but most modern vacuum pump producers whittle their pumps out of billet aluminum, which gives them greater latitude for improving the design and features of the pump. Modern vacuum pumps are available in a variety of sizes suitable for different applications; you don't need the massive flow capacity of a

Pan evacuation systems like this Moroso example (PN 25900) come with two probes that must be welded into the exhaust header collectors and two sealed valve cover breathers with tubes to connect to the probes with 5/8-inch hoses. The anti-backfire valves prevent possible ignition of flammable crankcase vapors. These are for competition use with open headers and should never be used on street cars with a full exhaust system. (Photo Courtesy Moroso)

CHAPTER 5

There are a lot of "bits and pieces" required to assemble a vacuum pump system for your Rat motor, and Reher-Morrison Racing Engines has simplified the process by offering a vacuum pump kit with everything you need to put together a pump for a typical Super class or bracket racing big-block. Kit includes a Moroso vacuum pump plus drive pulleys, brackets, relief valve, plumbing lines and fittings, and a breather tank to catch oil drawn out of the engine. (Photo Courtesy Don Cooper/Reher-Morrison Racing Engines)

A Star Machine four-vane vacuum pump mounted on an all-aluminum 598-ci big-block. Aluminum block engines typically need a vacuum pump even more than a cast-iron motor, because aluminum is not as rigid as iron so there is more shifting of the cylinder liners and an increase in blow-by past the piston rings. The pump inlet hose was not yet attached to the fitting in the valve cover during engine break-in, since the dry sump oil pump is sufficient for handling initial crankcase ventilation.

pump designed for an 800-cube Pro Mod motor on your bracket-racing 454. Most common are the three-vane pumps, while four-vane pumps pull more vacuum at lower engine speeds. Vacuum pumps are available from Aerospace Components, GZ Motorsports, Moroso Performance Products, Star Machine, and others.

Accumulators, Coolers and Accessories

Oil Accumulators are simple cylinders with a floating piston that store oil under pressure, providing a reserve supply that is automatically released when oil pressure drops below a safe level. If oil pressure suddenly drops because of hard acceleration, severe cornering, or hard braking, the air pressure immediately pushes oil into the engine's oiling system to prevent damage to the main bearings and other engine components. Most accumulators have a manual valve between the supply line and the storage cylinder, so that you can close the valve before shutting off the engine and store oil under pressure for pre-lubing the engine prior to the next startup.

Oil coolers should be used any time your oil temperature nears 240 degrees F; conventional motor oil can start to break down at that temperature. Most high-performance street and drag race big-blocks don't need an oil cooler; the engine is not operated at full throttle for more than 10 or 12 seconds at a time, and if your oil pan has increased capacity, as recommended, your temp should remain below that level. Road race cars need them, but not too many big-blocks are forced to turn left and right with regularity.

There are exceptions, of course: you might want to build a killer Rat motor for the Silver State Classic, in which "sorta-street" cars are driven at high speeds for hundreds of miles, and trucks absolutely need oil coolers. There are plenty of Rat motor powered trucks used to haul your favorite toys to and from the playground. As mentioned in Chapter 2, late-1960s and early-1970s high-performance blocks with four-bolt main caps are already drilled and tapped for oil cooler lines just above the oil filter pad. If you want to plumb a cooler into one of these blocks, order a bypass valve (GM PN 5575416) and install it in the rear hole. If your Mark IV block doesn't have the factory oil cooler provisions, it's no problem; there are plenty of aftermarket adapters that can be sandwiched between the block and the oil filter to accommodate cooler plumbing.

All Gen V and Gen VI blocks are drilled and tapped for the factory oil cooler lines in the oil pan rail just ahead of the oil filter. All production Gen V/VI engines come with oil cooler bypass valves already installed. If you are not using a cooler, you need to plug the two threaded holes in the pan rail surface, and remove the bypass valve directly underneath the filter fitting. If you want to plumb an aftermarket oil cooler, replace the bypass valve in the oil filter pad's offset hole with GM PN 25161284, which has the higher pressure differential necessary for the added restriction of the add-on cooler.

So what are oiling system accessories? The first thing that comes to mind is a magnetic drain plug, the best under-10-dollar part you can buy for your

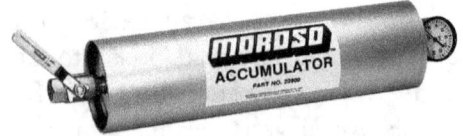

Accumulators hold a reserve supply of oil under pressure that is instantly released when oil pressure drops below a safe level. This Moroso (PN 23900) holds 3 quarts of oil. (Photo Courtesy Moroso)

OIL AND LUBRICATION SYSTEMS

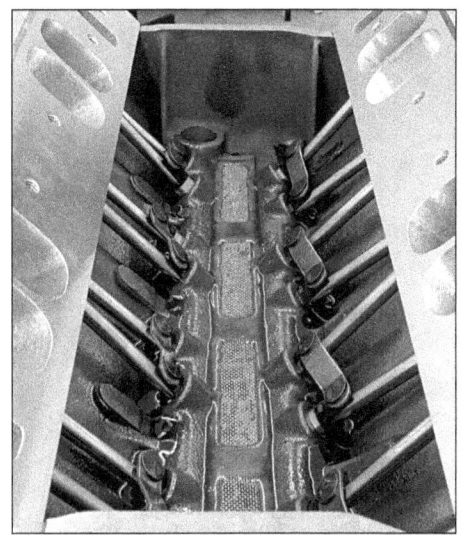

Big-blocks have four generous casting cavities in the lifter valley that can let small pieces of broken valvetrain parts fall into the spinning camshaft and crank. Screens epoxied over these openings, plus the 1.5-inch hole in the front of the lifter valley, keep a little problem from becoming a big problem.

Rat motor. If you see "fuzz" on the magnet while changing oil, don't bother putting fresh oil back in; you need to drop the pan and find out what's going wrong. Similarly, Moroso makes a magnet and epoxy kit for cylinder-head oil drain-back passages that catch broken valvetrain parts, such as valvesprings and roller bearings, before they find their way deeper into the engine and cause real damage. Many companies also offer screen kits that can be epoxied over the large openings in the lifter valley for the same purpose.

A FilterMag is a strong magnet that clamps tightly around the oil filter to trap small ferrous particles inside the oil filter, which seems like an incredibly smart thing to do. To really take advantage of that feature, you should cut apart the used oil filter from any new or freshly rebuilt big-block to check for debris, and a good oil filter cutter makes that job much more palatable.

Motor Oil

Motor oils can be divided into two categories: conventional mineral-based oils and synthetics. Conventional oils have been used for decades with good results, and their attributes include good performance under normal conditions, ready availablility, and relatively low cost, which can be important if you plan to change oil frequently (for instance, if you are using alcohol for competition and change the oil after every weekend of racing). Conventional oils are recommended to break-in a new or rebuilt engine, since synthetics are too slippery to allow some parts, such as piston rings and cam/lifters, to properly seat-in.

Synthetics are superior to mineral-based oils in every other aspect, providing better protection under severe conditions. They free-up more power in your big-block in two ways: first, they reduce the friction of metal-to-metal contact, such as with rocker arm to rocker pivots, timing chain to sprockets, etc. Second, because they offer better protection at full-floating junctions, like the main and rod bearings, a lower viscosity may be used, and that reduces parasitic pumping losses and windage losses.

Is there a downside to synthetics? Yes. They cost as much as three or four times as much as conventional oils, and they are good at finding little leaks and turning them into big leaks. If your old two-piece rear main seal is dripping a little bit now, it's going to become a real problem with synthetic oil. That's another reason that Chevrolet switched to a one-piece rear main seal on Gen V/VI engines.

Standard automotive motor oils have severely reduced or eliminated zinc (ZDDP) from their formula due to environmental concerns, and it is the zinc that provides the high-shear lubrication necessary for the overstressed junction between the cam lobe and flat tappets. These new-age lubricants have been responsible for a rash of cam/lifter failures in older vehicles as well as in high-performance engines using conventional lifters. High-performance big-blocks need motor oils that have been specially formulated with zinc and/or other wear-reducing additives, especially if you are using a flat-tappet cam and lifters. Many cam companies, such as Comp Cams, offer their own brand of high-performance and break-in oils, which are highly recommended for use with flat-tappet camshafts.

Brad Penn break-in oil and Penn-Grade 1 Partial Synthetic oils are formulated with a high level of detergency for protection against bearing corrosion and piston deposits in both turbocharged and non-turbocharged engines. They are a favorite of many top engine builders. It's always good practice to fill your filter with oil before installing it on the engine, and don't forget to lubricate the rubber sealing gasket.

Many cam companies, such as Comp Cams, offer their own brand of high-performance and break-in oils, which are highly recommended for use with flat-tappet camshafts. (Photo Courtesy Comp Cams)

HOW TO BUILD KILLER BIG-BLOCK CHEVY ENGINES

CHAPTER 6

CYLINDER HEADS

The big-block Chevy's canted valve heads are largely responsible for the tremendous power capability of the Rat motor and its continued popularity. The original head design is often referred to as having a 26-degree valve angle, although this intake valve angle of inclination is only one of four angles needed to numerically describe the big-block's valve angles. The exhaust is tilted 17 degrees relative to the deck surface, and both are inclined 4 degrees laterally. This compound arrangement of valve angles gives the big-block head its characteristic "valves pointing everywhere" appearance when the valve covers are removed and is responsible for the early "porcupine head" nickname when the big-block made its debut in the mid 1960s.

Big-block Chevy factory heads are offered in aluminum and cast iron, with either open or closed combustion chambers, and with oval or rectangular intake ports. In the aftermarket, most performance heads are aluminum rectangular port, open-chamber designs reminiscent of the original LS6 casting, although you can also buy aftermarket oval port and cast-iron heads.

Factory heads are classified as either high-performance (rectangular port) or standard passenger car (oval ports). Late-model trucks feature an even smaller oval intake port, frequently referred to as the "peanut" port, on heads that appear to be nearly round at the port entrance. Rat motor heads feature a unique combination of siamesed intake ports mated with symmetrical combustion chambers and equally spaced exhaust ports.

As a result of this arrangement, each siamesed pair of intake runners features non-symmetrical left-hand and right-hand ports. The port on the right side of each pair (as you face the intake flange surface) is longer and directs the inlet charge more to the center of the chamber, and is referred to as the "good" port; the one of the left, obviously referred to as the "bad" port, dumps the air/fuel mix toward the cylinder wall and usually doesn't flow as well as the right port. This minor idiosyncrasy of the big-block's

Aluminum aftermarket cylinder heads offer tremendous airflow potential to maximize power potential.

CYLINDER HEADS

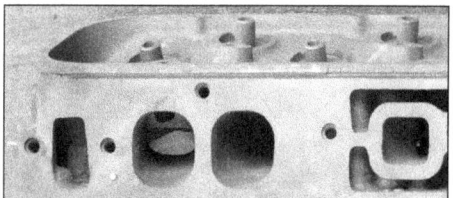

Stock iron oval ports from a "206" casting head. Note distance from the ports to the center bolt-hole above the pair of runners.

Stock iron rectangular ports from a "990" casting head. Note that the tops of the ports are almost even with the bottom of the center bolt-hole.

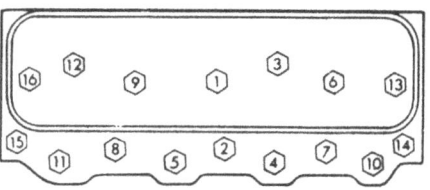

Big-block head bolt torque pattern. Stock head bolts get torqued to 70 ft-lbs in three steps of 40, 55, and 70 ft-lbs. Use thread sealer on all bolts that go into the water jacket, which means all blocks except Bowtie and aftermarket. Aftermarket studs usually get torqued to 60 ft-lbs, but check with the fastener manufacturer for specific torque recommendations.

design has never been a real problem in terms of limiting the engine's power potential, until extremely high airflow levels are reached on large-displacement or very-high-RPM engines. On engines approaching or exceeding the 1,000-hp mark (normally aspirated), the use of race-only spread port or Big Chief–style heads serves to even out the port volume, shape, and airflow in all eight intake ports.

Why didn't the Chevrolet engineers just make it a mirror-image design like the small-block V-8? Because the big-block has six head bolts around each bore (if you count the hidden bolt bosses on the bottom of two of the intake ports), and that dictates where the intake ports must be placed. Also, it's possible that the resulting siamesed exhaust ports might run too hot for long-term reliability with the big-block's higher power levels and resulting increased exhaust flow.

Oval or Rectangular Intake Ports

Much has been said about the differences between rectangular ports and oval ports, and the only fact that everyone agrees with is that each design has its own strengths and weaknesses. All factory high-performance engines featured the larger rectangular port heads, which have higher airflow rates than production oval port heads. However, the larger volume of the rectangular ports produces rather sluggish flow velocities at low speeds, and smaller oval port heads are often a better choice for a daily driver or street and strip car.

When reworked by someone who really knows what to do, oval port heads are capable of providing very good performance up to 600 or more horsepower. However, most high-performance street and full-race big-blocks can still take advantage of larger rectangular port heads. When I refer to the port size as larger or smaller, I'd like to think in terms of port cross-sectional area, but that dimension changes constantly throughout the length of the port, so the most common way to measure port size is to determine the volume in cubic centimeters, just as with the combustion chamber.

While intake port volumes are a valuable guide in cylinder head selection, remember that port volume is not necessarily proportional to port flow, and that just because one design has 340-cc runners and another has 320s, that doesn't mean that the larger head flows more air or makes more power, although that is usually the case.

In fact, if two heads with different-size runners have the same flowbench numbers, you are generally better off with the smaller runner head, especially if low-RPM throttle response and drivability are important. Also, when comparing port volume of spread port cylinder heads, remember that because these heads have

The GMPP head (PN 12363400) with 300-cc rectangular intake ports (left) performs very similarly to the oval port head (PN 12363392) with 290-cc intake ports (right), if both have the same compression ratios. The oval port head has 110-cc chambers, and the rectangular port head comes with 118-cc chambers.

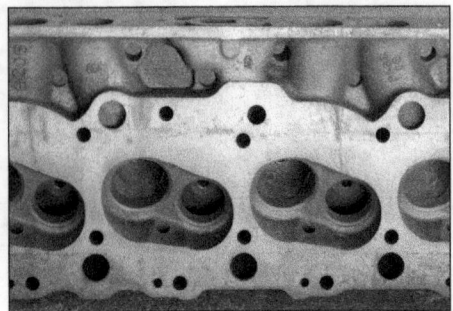
Cast-iron late-1960s "206" head with bathtub-shaped 98-cc closed combustion chambers.

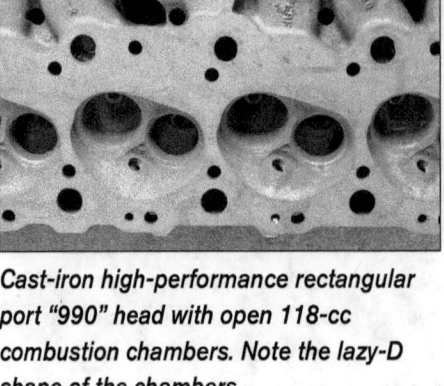
Cast-iron high-performance rectangular port "990" head with open 118-cc combustion chambers. Note the lazy-D shape of the chambers.

Cast-iron oval port "215" head with 109-cc semi-open combustion chambers.

raised runner locations, they are longer than conventional cylinder head intake ports, and the port volume is greater due to the extra length. A 400-cc raised-runner intake port may actually be smaller in cross-sectional area than a 380-cc conventional intake port. Be careful when comparing apples to oranges.

There are aftermarket oval port heads with about 290-cc intake runners, and small rectangular port heads with around 300-cc ports. I'll bet you a year's supply of donuts that the power difference on the dyno is minimal, and you could never tell the difference from the driver's seat.

Open or Closed Combustion Chambers

Big-block heads all had closed combustion chambers, or bathtub-shaped chambers, when the engine was introduced in the mid 1960s. In 1969 the open combustion chamber was introduced and it offered better air/fuel flow and a better combustion burn in the chamber. The only drawback to the new chamber design was that it was large, around 118 cc compared to closed chamber heads, which had about 101 to 109 cc, so high-dome pistons were needed to achieve the same compression ratios as the closed chamber heads. Note that domed pistons designed for open chamber cylinder heads do not work with closed chamber heads due to insufficient clearance. While introduced on high-performance rectangular port heads, the open combustion chamber was soon being used in common oval port heads to lower the compression ratio for use with unleaded gasoline, and the reduced quench area was found to be helpful in reducing exhaust emissions.

Mark IV, Gen V and Gen VI Heads

All production big-block heads have similar characteristics, including 7/16-inch rocker studs (except Gen V and Gen VI) and the same seven-bolt valve cover pattern. Early cast-iron and all-aluminum heads used 3/4-inch-reach gasketed spark plugs, while most 1970-and-later iron heads switched to the smaller taper seat "peanut" plugs. Aluminum heads have two additional threaded bosses under the intake runners for additional clamping and better head gasket retention when used with engine blocks equipped with corresponding bosses in the lifter valley. The only OEM blocks with these bosses were the rare ZL1 aluminum blocks, but many modern aftermarket blocks have this added feature. Mark IV, Gen V and Gen VI heads all have the same head bolt pattern, but they are not interchangeable

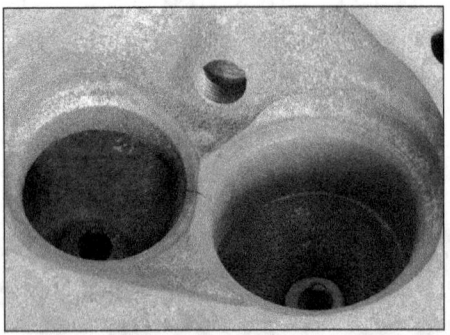
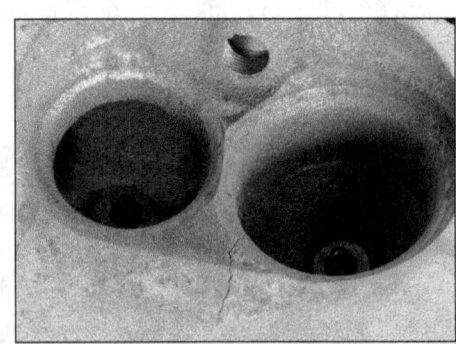
Inspect used cast-iron heads carefully for cracks, which are common with high-performance heads that have been used hard. Cracks in the valve seat area (left) might be repaired with new seats, but cracks in the chamber/deck surface (right) make the head unusable.

Gen V and Gen VI heads have different water jacket passages than Mark IV heads, and do not work on Mark IV blocks. (Photo Courtesy GMPP)

due to different water jacket cooling passages. Most aftermarket aluminum heads feature a universal water passage design allowing their use on Mark IV or Gen V/VI blocks, but you need to check with the manufacturer to verify this feature.

All production big-block heads have stamped steel pushrod guideplates under the rocker arm studs for either 5/16-, 3/8-, or 7/16-inch pushrods, but Gen V/VI heads switched to a non-adjustable valvetrain. Although Gen V/VI heads retained the original valve cover bolt pattern, their matching cast aluminum valve covers were equipped with a durable rubber O-ring in place of the traditional valve cover gasket. All production heads use the same intake and exhaust bolt patterns, which include a bolt-hole between each pair of intake ports. The boss required for this additional bolt-hole intrudes on the port entrance, so it is deleted on most aftermarket heads because it is not necessary for a good gasket seal.

All OEM big-block heads had an exhaust crossover passage for intake manifold heat and automatic choke operation, as well as supplying exhaust gas for EGR-equipped (exhaust gas recirculation) vehicles from the early 1970s on. High-performance engine builders try to keep the intake manifold as cool as possible for maximum intake charge density, so performance intake gasket sets usually include metal plates to block off this exhaust crossover passage, and most aftermarket heads delete the exhaust crossover provision entirely.

All OEM Rat motor heads were equipped with steel valves that have 3/8-inch diameter valvestems, and the overall length of the intake valves is 5.218 inches while the exhaust valves measure 5.350 inches. Aftermarket heads typically come with 11/32-inch-diameter valvestems, and frequently use longer than stock valve lengths that allow installation of taller valvesprings that are better suited for use with high-lift camshafts. The smaller-diameter stems not only lighten the valves for better high-RPM performance, but also offer a slight improvement in airflow. OEM intake valve head diameters were either 2.06 or 2.19 inches, and exhaust valve heads measured either 1.72, 1.84, or 1.88 inches. All production heads and most aftermarket heads come with traditional 45-degree valve seats; however, some high-end aftermarket heads are available with 55-degree seats, which offer improved high-lift flow at the expense of some low-lift flow.

Aftermarket Cylinder Heads

The vast majority of aftermarket heads are rectangular port aluminum with open combustion chambers, similar to the fabled LS6/LS7 production heads. However, they are much more than mere copies of the Chevy part, and many offer such advanced features as non-stock valve angles, larger valve head diameters for more flow, more robust valvesprings for high-RPM operation, and your choice of various intake port sizes to match your requirements. Some offer raised ports, usually by .100 inch on the intake ports and as much as 3/4 inch on the exhaust ports.

Note that if you plan to use exhaust headers designed for stock heads in a stock engine compartment, you need to check for possible header interference with raised port heads, or have custom headers made. Typical material specs call for the use of either A355 or A356 aluminum alloy, usually hardened to T-6 specs, and most offer beefier construction with thicker-than-stock deck surfaces and port walls, allowing additional modifications by knowledgeable cylinder head specialists.

In addition to GMPP, there are an abundance of manufacturers offering high-performance heads for the big-block Chevy including Air Flow Research (AFR), Brodix, Carl Foltz Engineering (CFE), Dart, Edelbrock, Pro-Filer, Racing Head Service (RHS), Raptor (Reher-Morrison Racing Engines), Sonny's Racing Engines (SRE), Trick Flow Specialties (TFS), World Products, and probably more by the time you read this. See "Aftermarket Cylinder Head Manufacturers" on page 88 for a

All production big-block heads had an exhaust crossover passage between the two pairs of siamesed intake ports. The casting cavities above and below the center exhaust crossover are blind cavities that don't connect to anything. Some aftermarket intake manifolds don't cover the upper opening, which does not cause any problems.

Many aftermarket heads, such as this Edelbrock Performer RPM 454-R, are rectangular port aluminum with open combustion chambers, similar to the fabled LS6/LS7 production heads. (Photo Courtesy Edelbrock)

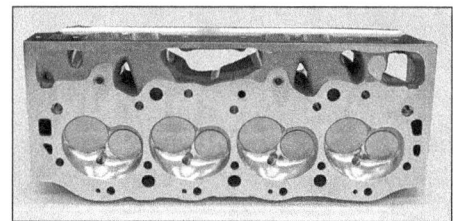

Modern competition heads usually have heart-shaped combustion chambers to minimize chamber volume and increase the quench area.

brief review of these heads. Contact the manufacturer of your choice for more specific information before making your final head selection.

Spread Port Heads

As good as the original Chevy head design was, things really started to heat up when GM engineers got involved in the Pro Stock wars in the 1980s. Because of the Corporate Engine policy, GM competitors were allowed to use any GM family engine in their race cars and the big-block Chevy was obviously better suited to all-out racing than any other GM big-block engine. Pontiac engineers took advantage of this break to create a head for the Rat motor with a superior port design, shallower valve angles, and smaller, more efficient combustion chambers.

The Pontiac Super Duty Pro Stock cylinder head (PN 10045427) featured intake ports that were spread apart to even out the flow differential inherent in the original Chevrolet siamesed port design, and the shallow valve angles required substantially raised intake ports to straighten the airflow path from the port entrance to the valve seat.

From there, Oldsmobile engineers took their shot at creating the best possible drag race head, and introduced the Oldsmobile Pro Stock head (PN 24502585). The Olds Pro Stock head evolved into the GM DRCE, the development of which was spearheaded by a young Warren Johnson, soon to be the dominant NHRA Pro Stock racer of the 1980s and 1990s.

Not to be forgotten, Chevrolet engineers also developed a spread port head, the Chevy Symmetrical Port Head (PN 10051128), with similar design parameters: evenly spaced intake ports and shallow valve angles with miniscule combustion chambers.

Today, the latest version of the Olds DRCE is the spec cylinder head for all GM-powered vehicles in NHRA Pro Stock competition, while the Pontiac Pro Stock head has been widely copied by aftermarket manufacturers, resulting in the Dart Big Chief head (paying tribute to the Pontiac Indian tribe), the Brodix Big Duke head, and Edelbrock's Big Victor head, with more development sure to follow. If you want to make 1,000 hp or more without power adders, "Big" heads are the way to go.

Even though these "Big" heads all share some common design parameters, they are not identical and most require specific matching components such as pistons, intake manifolds, and shaft rocker arm assemblies. All spread port big-block Chevy heads require shaft rocker arms because the pushrods must be relocated around the revised intake port location, and the large amount of rocker arm offset eliminates the use of traditional stud-mount rockers. Most accept the original Pontiac-designed eight-bolt valve covers, although the Edelbrock Big Victor head features a unique valve cover bolt pattern to relocate the bolt-hole bosses for improved rocker arm clearance and valvetrain geometry. This is one of the reasons that fabricated aluminum sheet-metal valve covers are so popular these days—they can be quickly produced one at a time or in relatively small batches to fit whatever bolt pattern you want. Besides, they look racy!

What's Your (Valve) Angle?

Production big-block Chevy heads all came with 26-degree intake valve angles, and that dimension was standard throughout the first two decades of competition cylinder head development, both by Chevrolet and the performance aftermarket. Savvy racers soon realized that a smaller combustion chamber, combined with less dome on the piston, resulted in a more efficient burn

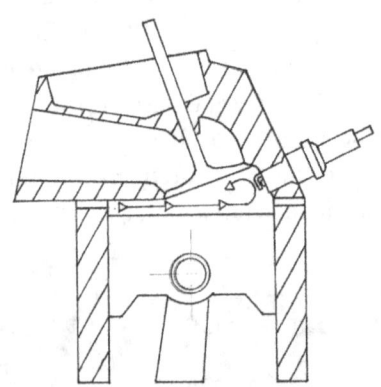

The quench or squish area of the cylinder head is the flat surface that hangs over the bore. As the piston comes to TDC the air/fuel mixture is rapidly expelled, creating turbulence in the chamber, which greatly increases combustion efficiency.

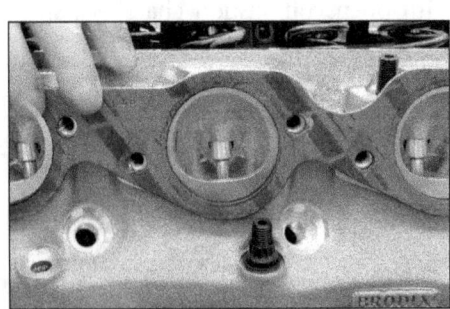

D-shaped exhaust ports decrease the flow differential between the floor and the roof of the exhaust ports, and they help to combat reversion.

The Pontiac Super Duty Pro Stock head was the predecessor to today's crop of spread port heads like these Brodix Big Duke cylinder heads with reduced intake valve angles and raised runners. You'll find spread port heads on most 1,000-plus-hp big-blocks.

and made more horsepower than a large chamber/large dome combination. However, the 26-degree intake valve angle placed the valve seat precariously close to the deck surface of the head and was the limiting factor in how far the head could be flat milled to reduce chamber volume.

The process of angle milling was developed, in which more material was removed from the exhaust side of the deck surface to produce a smaller chamber than was possible with a flat milled head. Angle milling reduced the intake valve angle slightly, usually by about one degree, and it required that the rest of the head be re-machined to correct the intake flange and head-bolt holes, as well as re-facing the tops of the head-bolt holes to present a parallel surface for the head bolt or stud hardware to register against.

Progressive aftermarket companies began offering their Rat motor heads "rolled over," essentially rotating the raw casting before any machining was done to produce an angle milled, small-chamber head while maintaining the original fitment of the part. Today, most conventional design (siamesed intake ports) competition heads are engineered with an intake valve angle around 24 degrees, which is about the minimum valve angle with the stock port locations. Why? Because as the intake valve angle is reduced, the intake port is "bent" more if you start with the stock port entrance. To really take advantage of shallow valve angles, the ports must necessarily be raised to straighten out the flow path, and that is precisely what was done with all of the spread port heads.

Current trends among spread port big-block heads are to have intake valve angles of 18, 14, 12, and occasionally even fewer degrees. While it seems that each new generation of spread port head design offers reduced valve angles, there is a limit to what the engine actually "likes." A prime example of this phenomenon is that modern competition heads for nitrous or boosted applications typically have an 18-degree valve angle, perhaps because the additional volume of air/fuel requires a larger combustion chamber to contain the intake charge before ignition. Nitrous racers say that the 18-degree heads offer a wider tuning "window" compared to the 14- or 12-degree heads, meaning that if the exact nitrous/fuel/timing combination is off just a little, the bigger chamber heads are less likely to result in catastrophic failure, usually in the form of burned or collapsed pistons.

Modifications

With the selection of excellent cylinder heads already available for the big-block, you really don't need to know anything about porting, CNC-finished combustion chambers, titanium valves, and all that other nasty technical stuff if you don't want to. Just pay the man and bolt on a set of fully prepped, ready-to-rumble cylinder heads and go have fun. On the other hand, I can think of two good reasons to keep up with cylinder head mods: first, if the family budget is already stretched thin with your passion for collecting big-block parts as economically as possible and you want to "tune up" that old pair of heads you just scored at the swap meet. Second, if you can afford to pay the man, you might want to be sure of what you're getting.

Intake Port

Let's start at the beginning, the intake port, or runner. The runner entrance is nearly perpendicular to the intake flange face, and goes several inches into the head before making a rather abrupt turn into the valve bowl. Since the intake port is merely an extension of the intake tract, which started in the intake manifold, it is important that port opening in the head closely aligns with the port in the intake manifold. So it is common practice to port match the two parts to the intake gasket being used.

The port exit in the manifold is usually left about .050 inch smaller than the gasket, in order to combat reversion and to account for any slight mismatch when the manifold and heads are assembled. Normally, lay-out dye is painted around the port entrances and a sharp scribe is used to trace the shape of the gasket around the openings. Using a 1/4-inch die grinder and some stones (for cast iron) or cutters (for aluminum), open up the port to a depth of about 1 inch. You can trim a little metal off of the rocker arm stud boss that hangs down from the port roof, but don't shorten it or remove so much material that its strength is compromised.

Valve Bowl

With the poppet valves currently used in all automotive four-stroke engines, it has been shown that the valve bowl, or area of the port directly under the valve seat (viewed from the combustion chamber), is critical in setting up the flow around the perimeter of the valve as it opens. As a result, there is a bend in the port as it makes the transition from the entry corridor to the valve bowl, and that bend must be carefully shaped to reduce the air/fuel flow as little as possible while maintaining a homogenous air/fuel mixture. If the turn is too abrupt, the fuel tends to separate from the mixture and pool into large droplets that do not burn completely in the combustion chamber. The port floor at this bend is referred to as the short turn radius, while the roof is called the long turn radius. Because the airflow path is shorter at the short turn radius, flow velocity tends to increase, just as it does over the curved surface of an airplane wing, and many cylinder head specialists widen the port floor at that point to equalize the flow along the short and long turns.

CHAPTER 6

Chevrolet Big-Block Cylinder Head Casting Numbers

Note that all casting numbers are located under the valve cover.

RECTANGULAR PORT
Valve size 2.19 intake, 1.88 exhaust

Casting No.	Years	CI	Chamber	CC	HP, RPO, Comments
3856208	1965	396	Closed	109	375/425 Z-16 Chevelle
3873858	1966–1967	396/427	Closed	109	375 L-78
3904391	1967	396/427	Closed	107	L-71/L-72, (1.72 ex. valve)
3904392	1967	427	Closed	106.8	430, 435 L-88/L-89, (1.72 ex. valve)
3919840	1967–1969	396/427	Closed	107	375 L-78 425, 435 L-71/L-72, 425 COPO
3919842	1968–1969	396/427	Closed	106.8	375 L-89 430, 435 L-88/L-89, (1.84 ex. valve)
3946074	1969–1971	396/402/427/454	Open	118	375 L-89 430 L-88/ZL-1 425, 465 LS6/LS7
3964291	1969–1970	396/402/427/454	Closed	109	Large or small spark plug
3964292	1970	454	Closed	109	450 LS6
3994025	1971	454	Open	118	425 LS6
3994026	1971	454	Open	118	LS6
6258723	1971	454	Open		
6272990	1970	454	Open	118	Service replacement Mk IV, 318 int. ports, 125 ex. ports
10045427		454+			Pontiac/Chevy aluminum small port/race
10051128	1990–1994	454	Semi-Open	72	IP 400, Bowtie, symmetrical port
12363401	1996-up		Open	118	Bowtie aluminum Mk IV Gen V/VI, 322 int. ports, 120 ex. ports
12562934	2000-up	502	Open		Gen VI 502 marine
14011077	1989–1994	454	Open	118	IP 295, replacement, C port
14044861	1989–1994	454	Open	115	425, 105.0, IP 380, Bowtie, W port
14096188	1970–1971	454	Open	118	Service replacement LS6 Mark IV, 317 int. ports, 125 ex. ports
14097088	1991-up	454/502	Open	118	
24502585	1997				Olds/Chevy aluminum

OVAL PORT

Casting No.	Years	CI	Chamber	CC	HP, RPO, Comments
330864	1970–1981	366/427/454	Open		
330865	1970–1984	366/427/454	Open		
330866	1968–1978	366/427	Open		
330867	1968–1973	427t	Open		
336765	1973–1984	427/454	Open		
336768	1973–1976	427t	Open		
336781	1973–1985	454	Open	119	258 int. ports, 116 ex. ports
343771	1968–1985	366/427/454	Open		
343772	1976–1984	366/427/454	Open		
343783	1975–1978	454	Open		Car and truck
346236	1975–1987	454	Open	120	208 "peanut" ports, 112 ex. ports
346238	1975–1987	454	Open	120	
352625	1970–1976	454	Open		Truck
353049	1970–1973	402/454	Open	122	253 int. ports, 115 ex. ports
366725	1974–1978	427			
473328	1968–1985	366	Open		

CYLINDER HEADS

Casting No.	Years	CI	Chamber	CC	HP, RPO, Comments
3856206	1965–1966	396	Closed	98	325
3856213	1966–1970	366	Closed		Truck
3856260	1968	396	Closed		Truck
3872702	1966	396/427	Closed	101	325, 360 L-34/L-35 390, L-36, 253 intake ports
3876875	1966–1970	427	Closed		Truck
3904390	1966–1967	396/427	Closed	98.4	325, 350 L-34/L-35 390, 400, L-36/L-68
3904393	1966–1968	366	Closed		Truck
3908952	1967	427	Open		Truck, marine
3909802	1966–1967	396/427	Closed	101	L-34/L-35, L-36/L-68
3917215	1967–1969	396/427	Semi-Open	109	325, 350, 335, 385, 390, 400 L-34/L-35
3917219	1966–1970	366/427	Closed		Truck
3931063	1968–1969	396/427	Closed	101	325, 350, 335, 385, 390, 400L-34/L-35
3933148	1969	366/396	Open	122	2V/427, 265 car & truck
3933149	1969–1970	427	Open	122	Truck
3935401	1968–1976	427	Open		
3964280	1966–1970	427/454	Closed		335, 385, 390, 400 LS5
3964290	1969–1970	396/402/427/454	Closed	101	325, 330, 350 400 LS -5
3965198	1969	396			Truck
3975950	1968–1970	366/427	Closed		Truck
3986133	1970–1985	366/427	Closed		Truck
3986135	1969–1973	366/427	Open		
3986136	1970–1984	366/427	Closed		Truck
3993820	1971	402/454	Open	113	300, 330 LS3, 365 LS5, 253 int. ports, 114 ex. ports
3999241	1972	402/454	Open	113	240, 300, 330 LS3 365 LS5
6272292	1971	402/454	Open		240, LS3 270, LS5
10052902		427	Open		Mk IV
10101136	1991–1994	454	Open		Truck
10114140	1991–up	366/427	Closed		Gen V
10114156	1991–up	454	Open	115	Gen V, 195 int. ports
10121033	1978–1988	454	Open		Truck
10141279	1996–up		Open	100	Vortec 7400
10487052	1977–1990	366	Open		
12352783	1979–1993	454	Open		Truck
12363391	1996–up		Open	110	Aluminum Mk IV, Gen V, Gen VI
12558162	2001–up	496 (8.1L)	Closed		VII Vortec 8100 truck
12560241	1998 –up		Closed	100	Vortec 7400
14025175	1983–1993	454	Open		Truck
14081044	1986–1990	454	Open		Truck
14081045	1978–1987	454	Open		
14081052	1985–1987	366/427/454	Open		Truck marked HIPERF
14092359	1986–1989	427	Open		Truck
14092360	1985–1989	454	Open	119	Truck "peanut" port
14101398	1986–1990	454	Open		Truck

CHAPTER 6

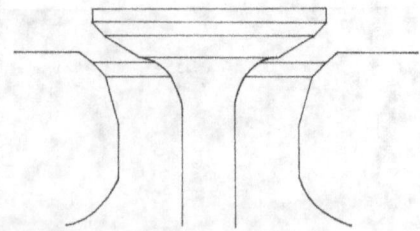

Three-angle valve job narrows the 45-degree valve seat in the head with a 30 degree top cut and a 60-degree bottom cut. Valve seat width should be a minimum of .040 to .060 inch for the intake seat, and .080 to .100 inch for the exhaust. The valve has a matching 45-degree seat and should be narrowed with a 30-degree back-cut to match the seat in the head. These angles are standard, but many cylinder head specialists have their own pet angles that work for them. Note that valve seats of 55 degrees are used in some racing heads to improve high-lift flow, with a trade-off in low-lift flow numbers.

Valve Seat

After the port bowl, the inlet charge flows through the valve seat, another critical area in a performance engine and the source of improved performance when done correctly. Obviously, the first job of the valve seat is to provide a gas-tight seal against the valve face to maximize the push against the piston from the combustion process. That is accomplished with a 45-degree angle on both the seat and the valve face. You can improve the airflow through the valve seat as the valve begins to open by narrowing the seat with top and bottom cuts, typically with a 30-degree top cut (the side closest to the chamber) and a 60-degree bottom cut. This is known as a three-angle valve job. The narrowing cuts un-shroud the seat and produce better flow, especially at low valve lifts. More flow means more air/fuel in the chamber, which equates to more power. To complement the narrowed valve seat, the valves are also narrowed with a back-cut of around 30 degrees.

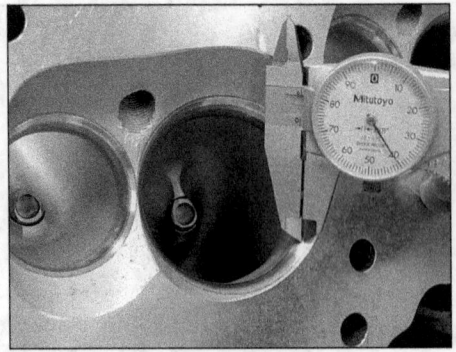

Intake valve seat width on this Brodix competition head measures .040 inch. Note copper-beryllium seats, compatible with the titanium valves used in this engine.

Combustion Chamber

Moving on to the combustion chamber, there is little that needs to be done by the do-it-yourself head modifier; any material removed lowers the compression ratio and usually results in less power. Certainly professional head porters spend lots of time on the combustion chamber and may make radical alterations to improve airflow or combustion efficiency, but that type of work demands evaluation on a flow bench and plenty of experience in shaping the chamber for the most performance.

High-end aftermarket heads frequently feature CNC-machined chambers that are uniform from cylinder to cylinder, and have a smooth finish to lessen the mechanical bond between the chamber and carbon deposits that occur in every engine. Lightly polishing the chambers on your junkyard refugee iron heads may indeed help to reduce the carbon build-up which can cause pre-ignition, but don't get carried away; removing more metal than necessary just lowers the compression ratio.

Naturally, if the chambers are re-shaped, compression can be restored by milling the deck surface of the heads, and milling the heads for more power is one of the oldest tricks in the book; hot rodders have doing that since the days of

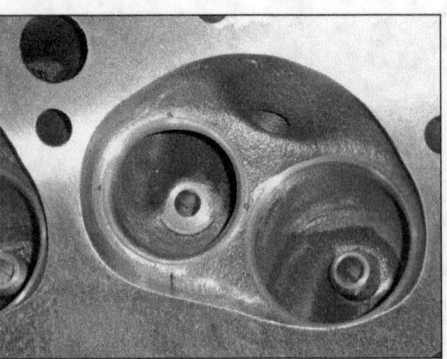

Mark Jones in Colorado Springs, Colorado, preps a lot of cast-iron oval port heads for his crate engines. Note the clean-up of the valve bowls, the area just under the seats. Very little metal is removed from the chambers; just enough to improve exhaust flow. He routinely gets more than 600 hp from his 496- to 505-ci big-blocks with a modest flat-tappet cam and Performer RPM dual-plane intake manifold. He generally chooses either "049" or "781" castings, which are commonly available.

the flathead Ford, and it is still a good idea anytime you're "tuning up" a set of stock heads.

Exhaust Seat

The exhaust valve seat should get the same three-angle narrowing treatment as the intake seat, but it should not be narrowed as much as the intake seat because the wider seat also transfers heat from the valve to the head. Typical widths are .100 inch for the exhaust seat and .040 to .060 inch for the intake. Remember that these specifications are minimums, and the cylinder head specialist of your choice may have his own pet set of dimensions that he has found to work best with his combination.

Aftermarket Cylinder Head Manufacturers

There's no way to list every big-block Chevy head offered by the after-

CYLINDER HEADS

Milling Heads to Increase Compression

Machining the deck surface of cylinder heads to make them perfectly flat not only ensures a good sealing surface for the head gasket, it also reduces the combustion chamber volume, which raises the compression ratio. As long as you are using fuel with the correct octane rating for your compression, this is as close to free horsepower as you can get for your big-block Chevy.

So how much metal can you mill off the heads? Even though there are several different combustion chamber shapes, the average open chamber head requires .004 inch to reduce the chamber volume by 1 cc, and each 1-cc change typically raises the compression by 1/10 point (on a 454-ci engine). So milling .040 inch off the deck surface usually increases compression one full point; for instance, from 8.5:1 to 9.5:1. The limiting factor in flat milling big-block heads is the intake valve seat: you must not cut the deck so much that it intersects the valve seat. If you do, the valve seat can be re-machined, but you then sink the valve deeper into the bowl, which impairs flow and reduces the power potential of the heads.

This is a general guide that you can use for low-compression street engines; very-high-performance and racing big-blocks mandate that you use precise chamber volume measurements and mathematical formulas to calculate the exact compression ratio of your engine. (See "Calculating Compression Ratio," page 94.)

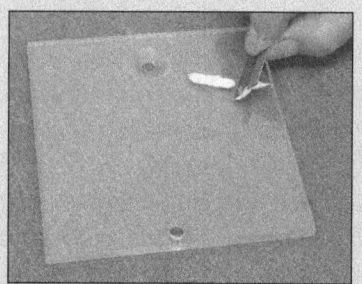

Many big-block heads have the valve seat so close to the deck that part of the valve sticks up higher than the deck. Here's a nifty fix for that problem, courtesy of K&N's John Reedy. He grinds a relief slot in the plexiglass plate, then packs it with white grease and scrapes off the excess with a razor blade. The edge of the valve can protrude into the slot so that the plate lays flat against the head, and the displaced white grease exactly equals the volume of the protruding valve head. Smart.

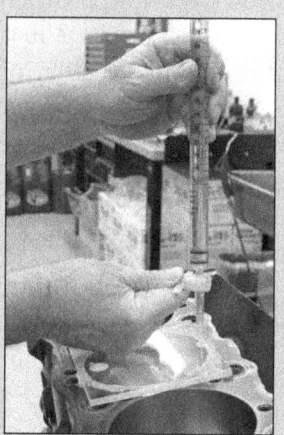

With the piston exactly .500 inch down the bore and sealed with white grease, measure the volume required to fill the top of the bore. Many forged pistons have .006 inch or more of bore clearance, so use masking tape on the piston skirts to square it up if necessary. Calculate the theoretical volume using the formula: (3.14159 x bore x bore x .500-inch) ÷ 4 ci. Multiply by 16.387 to convert to cubic centimeters. If you are using domed pistons, this number is greater than your measured volume, and the difference is your dome volume. With dished or flat-top pistons with valve reliefs, the measured volume is greater, and the difference is added to the total chamber volume, not subtracted.

market performance industry, but here is a brief review of what's currently available. Remember that numerical specifications tell you something about a particular head, but trying to compare one head against another based on nothing but specs is often misleading. It's like trying to describe your spouse by telling weight, height, and eye color. It may get you close, but there's a lot more to it than just the numbers. Call the manufacturers, and talk to other racers or performance enthusiasts who have real-world experience with the products you are considering.

And don't sweat the small stuff. The fact that head A made 5 hp more than head B in a magazine shoot-out does not mean that head A is necessarily the best choice for your engine. It just means that it made more power on that engine with that particular combination of parts. Your engine should be a total system of compatible parts designed to work together to produce the power you want under the conditions you experience.

AirFlow Research (AFR)

AFR offers a tremendous selection of traditional big-block replacement aluminum heads designed to fit within the stock architecture—siamesed ports with traditional valve locations and open combustion chambers. Their eminently logical approach to marketing big-block heads consists of offering all of their heads with either as-cast ports and chambers, or CNC machine ported for a slight increase in port volume plus consistency in port-to-port and chamber-to-chamber dimensions. All AFR big-block heads feature "rolled-over" valve angles, which are listed as 24/4 degrees (intake) and 15/4 degrees (exhaust); 3/4-inch-thick deck surfaces for brute strength; and 3/8-inch-raised exhaust ports.

Most exhaust headers still fit, but you need to check for adequate clearance in your engine bay to be sure. All AFR heads delete the stock exhaust crossover port to reduce intake charge temperature, so they do not work with EGR or hot-air carburetor chokes, and they are not street legal for applications that require those provisions. All AFR big-block Chevy heads have water jackets that are compatible with Mark IV, Gen V, or Gen VI blocks when used with the appropriate head gaskets.

AFR offers two versions of oval port heads: 265-cc as-cast intake runners or CNC ported with 290-cc runners. These oval port heads come with slightly smaller combustion chambers (107-cc as-cast, 112-cc CNC'd) than the rectangular port heads, and the smaller chamber sizes work well with the stock low-compression pistons used in typical 396/454 engines, yielding more compression and more power. Remember that aluminum heads tolerate more compression, without engine-damaging detonation, than their cast-iron counterparts, due to aluminum's superior heat transfer characteristics.

AFR has four rectangular port head castings with runner volumes that could be classified as small, medium, large, and oh-my-god! As-cast runner volumes are 305, 325, and 345 cc; CNC ported volumes are 315, 335, 357, 375, and 385 cc. Remember that intake port size, like every other component in your Rat motor, must match the intended RPM range and usage. Don't select the largest head you can carry out of the store unless you're building a 600-inch stroker motor that is turning 8,000 rpm at the dragstrip. There is an AFR cylinder head that is the perfect match for your engine combo whether it's a stock short-block engine for your tow-truck, a 600-cube race-only dragstrip warrior, or anything in between.

Brodix Cylinder Heads

Brodix is one of the oldest and most respected names in the business of manufacturing aluminum cylinder heads for the big-block Chevy, and the company offers an almost bewildering assortment of Rat motor heads from mild to wild. Just the conventional siamesed port heads are available in 27 different models, with options available including roller or flat-tappet valvesprings, steel or titanium spring retainers, flat milling or angle milling, and as-cast or CNC-machined ports and chambers.

At the modest end of the scale, the Race-Rite heads are designed as straight bolt-on replacements for stock Chevy heads with 26/4-degree intake angles and 17/4-degree exhaust angles, even down to the inclusion of the center bolt-hole between each pair of intake runners. Exhaust port exits are in the stock location for compatibility with standard headers or exhaust manifolds, but all Brodix heads delete the stock exhaust crossover port to reduce intake charge temperature, so they do not work with EGR or hot-air carburetor chokes, and they are not street legal for applications that require those provisions. Brodix Race-Rite heads are available with 270-cc oval intake ports or rectangular ports from 294 to 320 cc, and there are even Jesse James signature-series heads featuring a black hard-anodized finish and embossed Jesse James logos on the ends of the heads. Although aimed at the street performance crowd, the black hard-anodized finish is an especially good idea on any marine engine.

AFR oval port 24-degree head features 100-percent CNC machined 290-cc intake ports and 112-cc combustion chambers with 2.250/1.880-inch valves. (Photo Courtesy AFR)

AFR rectangular port 24-degree head with 100-percent CNC machined ports and chambers. Intake port volumes range from 315 to 385 cc, and the optional black anodized finish resists corrosion in marine applications. (Photo Courtesy AFR)

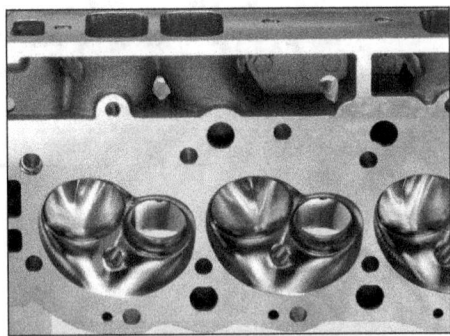

CNC machined 121-cc combustion chambers on AFR rectangular port heads feature a heart-shaped design for superior flow and combustion efficiency. This shape may require hand fitting of the dome on high-compression pistons based on the original LS6 Chevy. (Photo Courtesy AFR)

The BB-1, BB-2, and BB-3 series rectangular port heads retain the 26-degree intake valve angle but offer more power potential via .600-inch raised exhaust port exits and intake port sizes from 280 to 370 cc. The BB-3 Xtra series heads change the intake valve angle to 24 degrees, and are available with rectangular ports from 363 to 380 cc, or large oval ports from 332 to 365 cc. Don't confuse these oval ports with stock Chevy oval ports: they are a large oval shape with about the same width and height as rectangular intake ports, intended for serious racers who desire a high-velocity port with good flow potential.

Taking the large oval intake ports to the next level, the Head Hunter series is available with 383- or 395-cc large oval intake ports with an improved exhaust port design, and they retain the 24-degree valve angle. Brodix BB-4 and BB-5 series 24-degree heads feature traditional rectangular intake ports from 340 to 390 cc, but they are raised approximately .400 inch for a better intake flow path and improved short turn radius from the ports into the valve bowls.

For really serious drag racing or other high-horsepower applications, Brodix Big Duke PB 1800, PB 1600, PB 2005, and Man Eater PB 1200 series heads are based on the popular Pontiac Pro Stock head design with raised runners, spread intake ports, and shallow valve angles for reduced combustion chamber volumes. Those heads are offered in 13 different model numbers with intake valve angles of 18, 16, 14.5, and 12 degrees, and intake port volumes ranging from 375 to 510 cc. If you want to live on the cutting edge of big-block racing engine design, Brodix even offers three versions of the PB 5000 series 15-degree heads for use on 5.0-inch-bore-spacing blocks. And yes, Brodix also makes 5.0-inch-bore-spacing blocks so you have a nice home for those new heads. Of course, 5.0-inch-bore-spacing engines require custom everything—sheet-metal intake manifold, custom headers, special cam, crank, oil pan, valve covers, rocker arms, etc., but you knew that when you committed to building an 800-ci Rat motor, didn't you?

Carl Foltz Engineering (CFE)

If you're looking for the perfect head for your mild street-driven big-block, keep looking: CFE specializes in no-compromise, hard-core competition cylinder heads and custom sheet-metal and billet aluminum intake manifolds. The extensive line of big-block competition heads runs from conventional siamesed port BMF (Beat More Fords?) heads that accept traditional Chevy pattern intake manifolds and stud-mount rocker arms, to symmetrical port heads for 5.000-, 5.200-, and 5.300-inch-bore-space mountain motors. If you want to dive into NHRA Pro Stock racing, CFE-prepared DRCE cylinder heads have won multiple Pro Stock national events and championships. All CFE heads are fully CNC ported for consistency in runner shape and volume, and to produce the port shapes that extensive flow bench and dyno testing has revealed to produce more flow for a given application.

BMF heads are available with intake runner volumes of 310, 330, 350, 385, and 405 cc, the last requiring modifications of most cast aluminum intakes to work with the very large intake ports. All BMF heads feature 24.5-degree intake valve angles and intake valve sizes from 2.250 to 2.325 inches, with chamber volumes of 114 to 124 cc. Exhaust valves are 1.880 inches and they accommodate standard Rat motor exhaust headers.

BMF II heads have additional aluminum added in the rocker arm support area to accommodate CFE's one-piece intake rocker bar and double-bolted exhaust stands for shaft-mount rockers, which must be used with these heads. The use of .180-inch offset lifters is required to provide adequate pushrod-to-head clearance.

CFE spread port heads are available for standard 4.840-inch-bore-space engines with 11-, 14-, and 18-degree intake valve angles, and they accept industry-standard Big Chief–style shaft rockers, valve covers, etc. A dedicated 18-degree Nitrous Special version can be had in either 4.840- or 4.900-inch-bore-space versions. For 5.000-inch-bore-space motors, they offer 14- and 18-degree heads with valve sizes so large they only fit motors with a minimum of 4.600-inch bores.

Symmetrical port heads are available for 5.000-, 5.200-, and 5.300-inch-bore-space engines in either cast or billet aluminum with whatever combination of valve angles, port shapes, and chamber volumes are needed for ultra-high-horsepower Pro Mod, truck pulling, and mountain motor Pro Stock racing. Symmetrical

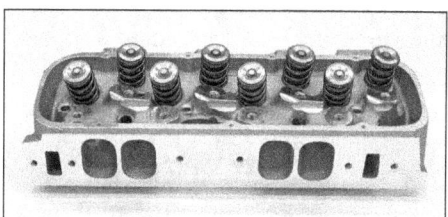

Brodix 383 Head Hunter head with large oval intake ports.

Brodix Big Duke PB 1200 spread port head with 12-degree intake valve angles is fully CNC ported. It features raised oval intake ports, 55-degree seat angles, copper/beryllium valve seats, and 483-cc intake ports with 68-cc combustion chambers.

ports differ from spread port heads in that every intake runner is evenly spaced, producing eight identical flow paths throughout the engine. This puts every intake port directly on top of one of the head-bolt holes, requiring special head attachment hardware and installation procedures. If you want to make more than 2,000 hp, you have to work at it!

Dart Machinery

When Dart's founder, Richard Maskin, cut his teeth in NHRA Pro Stock racing in the 1970s, Pro Stockers had to use real production cylinder heads but you could do just about anything to them. Since the AMC V-8 he was using (he was always a bit of a "Rebel") didn't have much to offer in the form of competitive cylinder heads compared to the big-name marquees, he sectioned two pairs of AMC heads horizontally and grafted then together to create a pair of very tall port, very competitive cylinder heads that kept his team in the thick of competition. This innovative approach to racing engine development led to the creation of Dart Machinery. When the Pontiac Super Duty Pro Stock head was introduced, he refined that design and came up with the Dart Big Chief spread port head that held several NHRA Pro Stock records until it was outlawed.

Thankfully, most Sportsman class big-block racers don't have to comply with restrictive rules and regulations governing cylinder head selection, and Dart's Big Chief heads have become the standard spread port heads by which all others are judged. In the arena of conventional siamesed port heads, Dart also continues to innovate, offering very competitive 24- and 18-degree heads.

Dart Iron Eagles are budget-priced cast-iron rectangular port heads offered in two runner sizes: 308 cc for small displacement big-blocks and 345 cc for big-inch, high-RPM engines. With 2-degree rolled valve angles and standard spacing, they are a direct bolt-on replacement for stock Chevy heads and offer a great bang-for-the-buck option to junkyard stock castings. Like all Dart aluminum heads, PRO 1 24-degree heads are cast from virgin 355-T6 aluminum for its greater strength than standard A356 alloys. They are available with as-cast 310-, 325-, and 345-cc intake ports. PRO 1 CNC heads are fully CNC machined throughout, with 335- or 355-cc intake ports. Heart-shaped 121-cc combustion chambers hold 2.300-inch intake and 1.880-inch exhaust valves.

Dart Race Series 24-degree heads are offered with rectangular 320-, 360-, or 410-cc intake ports and 119- or 139-cc combustion chambers. The 360-cc versions are available as a solid casting for alcohol-fueled drag racing engines. Oval port Race Series heads with 340- or 370-cc intakes come with 119-cc chambers fitted with 2.250- or 2.300-inch intake valves and 1.880-inch exhausts. The 18-degree oval port heads feature a raised intake port floor and small 102-cc chambers with 330- or 383-cc intake port options.

Dart's acclaimed Big Chief spread port heads are offered in many configurations including valve angles of 18, 14, or 11 degrees and with oval or rectangular intake ports measuring 402, 421, 433, 440, and 512 cc. Intake valves are 2.400 or 2.470 inches, and exhausts are 1.800 or 1.900 inches.

Edelbrock Corporation

One of the oldest and most respected names in the high-performance and racing parts business, Edelbrock offers big-block cylinder heads in a variety of configurations specifically designed for the application, whether it is a modest street performance vehicle, a street and strip/weekend warrior, or all-out competition car. Most are traditional siamesed port heads, but the Big Victor is an 18-degree spread port design with several unique features not found in similar heads.

Performer and Performer RPM heads are clearly aimed at the street market, offering bolt-on convenience with solid performance improvements over stock castings. Performer big-block heads even retain the exhaust crossover passage for emissions compliance, and work with EGR and/or exhaust heated chokes. Their 290-cc version of the oval intake port is actually a small rectangular port that fits within the stock oval port window, and is compatible with traditional oval port intake manifolds. Port matching the manifold to this new shape is not necessary, and in fact the mismatch helps to combat reversion.

They retain traditional valve angles and sizes of 2.19/1.88 inches (intake/exhaust) and are available with 110-cc chambers similar to the semi-open chamber Chevy heads. The Performer High-Compression 454-O has been rolled 1½ degrees to produce a 100-cc chamber that gives a compression ratio of 9.2:1 with 454 flat-top pistons.

Dart PRO 1 CNC head is available with 335- or 355-cc fully CNC machined intake ports. (Photo Courtesy Dart)

Dart Big Chief spread port head has D-shaped exhaust ports to equalize flow along the short turn in the ports and help to combat reversion. (Photo Courtesy Dart)

CYLINDER HEADS

Edelbrock Performer 454-O oval port head has a small rectangular port that fits within the stock oval port window, and is compatible with traditional oval port intake manifolds. Performer heads retain the exhaust crossover passage in the center of the intake flange for emissions compliance. (Photo Courtesy Edelbrock)

Performer RPM 454-R heads have rectangular 315/300-cc (long/short) intake ports and 118-cc open chambers. A revised spark plug location promotes better combustion, but they do not clear high-dome pistons based on the LS6 Chevy chamber.

Edelbrock E-CNC 355 rectangular port cylinder heads are designed for very large street Rats and mild race applications. They feature fully CNC machined ports and 110- or 118-cc combustion chambers. They have a 24.5-degree intake valve angle and intake port volumes of 348/356 or 344/352 cc. Stock exhaust port locations provide a no-hassle fit with any big-block header designed for stock applications.

The Victor 24-degree head is competition oriented with revised valve angles and locations specifically for large-bore (4.470 inches or more) big-blocks. Their 340-cc intake ports feed 119-cc combustion chambers via 2.300/1.900-inch

Edelbrock/Musi Victor 24-degree CNC large oval port head is fully CNC machined and assembled for 950-plus-hp potential right out of the box. (Photo Courtesy Edelbrock)

Edelbrock Performer High-Compression 454-O oval port head has 100-cc semi-open combustion chambers that produce a 9.2:1 compression ratio with flat-top pistons in a 454. (Photo Courtesy Edelbrock)

stainless steel valves, and exhaust port exits are raised 3/4-inch.

The Victor Jr. 24-degree head is a similar design for smaller bore engines (4.310 inches minimum) with 300-cc runners, 118-cc chambers, and 2.250/1.900-inch valves.

The Edelbrock/Musi Victor 24-degree CNC head is a large oval port member of the Victor 24-degree family, designed in cooperation with noted Pro/street racer Pat Musi. With fully CNC machined 377/367-cc intake ports and 114-cc chambers, it has 950-plus-hp potential right out of the box on current 555- to 582-ci normally aspirated racing engines.

The Big Victor Spread Port 18-degree CNC is Edelbrock's version of the latest spread port cylinder heads. It has an 18-degree intake valve angle, is fully CNC ported, and assembled with 2.500/1.960-inch stainless steel valves in 92-cc combustion chambers. Intake port volume is 405 cc, and it is treated to a special Hot Isostatic Pressing process which compacts the casting, yielding a much denser and stronger part. The valvetrain configuration was re-engineered in cooperation with Jesel Valvetrain Components to address several problematic areas with other spread port heads. The Big Victor head requires dedicated Jesel shaft rocker arms and unique valve covers, since one of the valve cover bolt bosses in traditional spread port heads interferes with the ideal rocker arm placement.

General Motor Performance Parts (GMPP)

GMPP offers a large number of high-performance heads suitable for your Rat motor recipe. Of particular interest to owners of Gen V/VI engines are the cast-iron rectangular port heads (PN 12562920, casting number 12562934) as used on the 502 HO crate engine. They have 325-cc intake ports and 118-cc combustion chambers with 2.180/1.880-inch valves. Some came with 7/16-inch rocker stud bolt-holes, while most have 3/8-inch stud holes that require special studs to convert to adjustable valvetrain. Aluminum oval-port Bowtie street heads are available in several configurations with 290-cc intake runners, 110-cc semi-open combustion chambers, and either 2.19/1.88- or 2.25/1.88-inch valves. It also uses a small rectangular port shape that fits oval port intake manifolds. PN 12363408 is an NHRA-legal replacement for the L88 aluminum head used on 1968–1971 Corvettes and 1969 Camaros (original PN 14011076).

The same heads used on the 572 crate engines can be yours by ordering PN 12499255 (hydraulic roller lifter valvesprings) or PN 88961160 (mechanical

The same GMPP heads used on the 572 crate engines can be yours by ordering PN 12499255 (hydraulic roller lifter valvesprings) or PN 88961160 (mechanical roller lifter valvesprings). They come with modest 310-cc intake ports that produce outstanding low-end power on the street, 118-cc chambers, and 5/8-inch raised exhaust port exits. (Photo Courtesy GMPP)

Calculating Compression Ratio

Here is the basic formula you can use for calculating compression ratio:

(Swept Volume + Total Chamber Volume) ÷ Total Chamber Volume

Where:
Swept Volume = (3.14159 x bore x bore x stroke) ÷ 4
Total Chamber Volume = combustion chamber volume − piston dome volume + head gasket volume + deck clearance volume

Since the combustion chamber, piston dome, and gasket volumes are measured in cubic centimeters, you have to multiply the swept volume by 16.387 to convert all numbers to the same unit of measurement–cubic centimeters.

Here's where these numbers come from:
Combustion chamber volume: Must be measured with a 100-cc burette and flat plexiglass sealing plate.
Head gasket volume: Listed by the manufacturer. If not, use the area of the gasket bore multiplied by the gasket thickness, then multiply by 16.387 to convert to cc.
Deck clearance volume: Deck clearance must be measured with a depth micrometer or dial indicator with the piston at TDC. Use the same formula as for swept volume, but substitute the clearance in place of the stroke: (3.14159 x bore x bore x deck clearance) ÷ 4. This gives the volume in cubic inches. Multiply by 16.387 to convert to cubic centimeters.
Piston dome volume: Listed by manufacturer, or must be measured with a burette and flat plexiglass sealing plate. Locate the piston exactly .500 inch down the bore then seal the piston ring to the cylinder with white grease. Now measure the amount of fluid from the burette it takes to fill that chamber. By calculating the theoretical volume of the cylinder and subtracting the measured volume, you have the actual dome volume. If you use dished pistons or flat-top pistons with valve reliefs, then the measured volume is larger than the theoretical volume so you have to add that number to the Total Chamber Volume.

Here's an example:
Combustion chamber volume: 115 cc
Dome volume: 43 cc
Head gasket volume: 10.3 cc
Bore: 4.560 inches
Stroke: 4.250 inches
Deck clearance: .010 inch

Swept Volume = (3.14159 x 4.56 x 4.56 x 4.25) ÷ 4
= 69.407772 ci
69.407772 x 16.387 = 1137.38 cc
Round off to 1137.4 cc

Deck Clearance Volume = (3.14159 x 4.56 x 4.56 x .01) ÷ 4
= 0.1633124 ci
0.1633124 x 16.387 = 2.67 cc
Round off to 2.7 cc

Now you have all measurements in cubic centimeters, so you just plug them into the formulas and do the math:

Total Chamber Volume = Combustion Chamber Volume − Dome Volume + Gasket Volume + Deck Clearance Volume
115 − 43 + 10.3 + 2.67 = 84.97 cc; round off to 85 cc

Compression Ratio = (Swept Volume + Total Chamber Volume) ÷ Total Chamber Volume
(1137.4 + 85) ÷ 85 = 14.38

So, the compression ratio for this engine is 14.38:1.

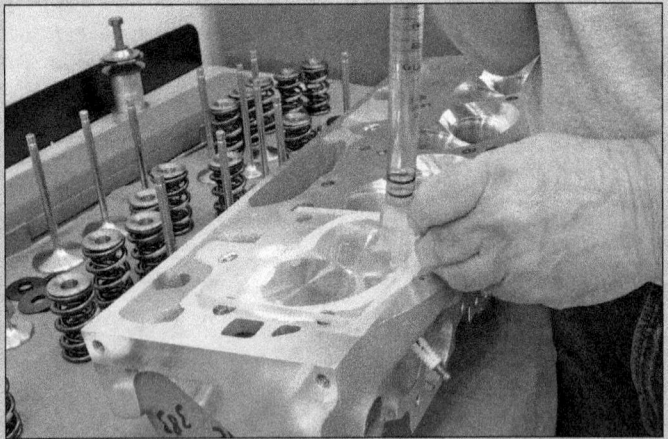

Use a 100-cc burette and flat plexiglass plate sealed to the deck of the head with white grease to measure chamber volume.

CYLINDER HEADS

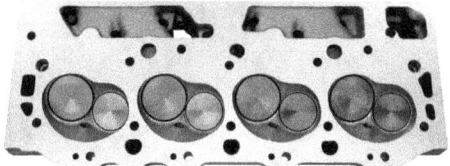

PN 12363400 is an aluminum 300-cc rectangular port head with 118-cc open chambers and 2.25/1.88-inch valves. (Photo Courtesy GMPP)

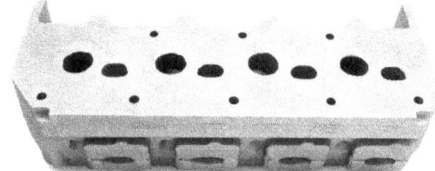 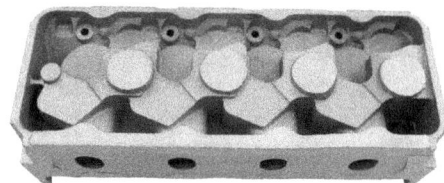

GMPP's DRCE 2 head (PN 24502585) on the left and DRCE 3 head (PN 25534404) on the right are raw castings designed for the 4.900-inch-bore-space DRCE block specified for use in NHRA Pro Stock competition. Most Pro Stock teams have developed their own port and chamber shapes, valve angles, and all other machining operations required to transform these chunks of aluminum into world-class cylinder heads. (Photos Courtesy GMPP)

roller lifter valvesprings). They come with modest 310-cc intake ports that produce outstanding low-end power on the street, 118-cc chambers, and 5/8-inch raised exhaust port exits. Valve sizes are 2.250/1.880 inches.

The current "bad-boy" Bowtie race head is PN 12363425 (casting number 14044861), a bare head with 380-cc intakes and valve seats for 2.19/1.88-inch valves. Exhaust port exits are raised 3/4 inch and feature a distinctive vane, giving rise to the poplar nickname of the "W" port head. The vane improved the flow numbers by filling in an area of low-flow activity on the exhaust side, but contemporary gearheads have found other ways around that problem; most head specialists remove the vane when preparing a set of these heads.

Pro-Filer Performance Products

Pro-Filer offers its Sniper cylinder heads in siamesed port as-cast or CNC machined versions, plus the Hitman 12-degree spread port head for standard 4.840-inch bore space engines and symmetrical port heads for 4.900-inch and 5.000-inch-bore-space big-blocks. The conventional Sniper heads feature 24-degree intake valve angles and 290- or 320-cc oval intake runners (as-cast), or 365-cc and 385-cc CNC machined rectangular ports with 2.300- or 2.350-inch intake valves and 1.880- or 1.900-inch exhaust valves. The Hitman 12-degree spread port head come with 415- or 470-cc large oval intake ports and 2.400/1.880-inch valves. The 12-degree valve angles allow very small 60-cc combustion chambers for maximum compression with flat-top or small-dome pistons.

Reher-Morrison Racing Engines (RMRE)

Raptor heads were developed and are marketed by Reher-Morrison Racing Engines. If you know anything at all about big-block Chevys, RMRE should need no introduction. Founder David Reher is one of the pioneers of modern Pro Stock drag racing, and RMRE is one of the most respected builders of big-block competition and street engines in the nation. The fact that they build and dyno test hundreds of racing Rat motors each year has given them plenty of experience in cylinder head selection, and they sell crate engines with Brodix and Dart conventional heads, as well as Big Chief and Big Duke spread port heads. So when they announce that they have something better for a particular engine combination, you know it's not just speculation.

Like all spread port heads, the Raptor is not for everybody, or every big-block engine. It is for competition engines with a very high airflow requirement: big cubic inches, high RPM, or both. It is used on the RMRE Super Series 12-degree 565, 588, 622, and 665 engines making as much as 1,340 hp with racing gasoline.

The Raptor's rap sheet looks like this: 12-degree intake valve angles, 465-cc intake ports, 65-cc combustion chambers, and your choice of titanium valve sizes to fit a particular engine size (2.450/1.850 inches is standard). Since many of RMRE's customers race in NHRA Super classes with set indexes, the head has to deliver not only good peak power numbers, it also exhibits strong and repeatable throttle response when used with a throttle stop. It is versatile enough to work well with a single carb, multiple carbs, or with nitrous and supercharged induction systems. It was engineered to be compatible with other traditional spread port components such as intake manifolds and shaft rocker assemblies, making the cost of conversion less for racers already running those parts.

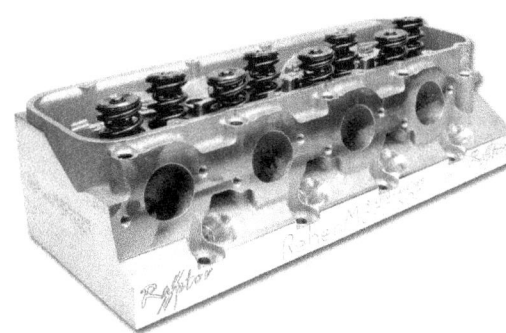

Developed by RMRE, the spread port Raptor features 12-degree intake valve angles, 465-cc intake ports, 65-cc combustion chambers, and a choice of titanium valve sizes. (Photo Courtesy Don Cooper/RMRE)

CHAPTER 6

Racing Head Service (RHS)

RHS Pro Action 24-degree heads are aimed at 496-ci and larger big-blocks and are available in either cast iron or aluminum with 320- or 360-cc intake ports. Traditional open combustion chambers measure 119 cc, and intake valves are either 2.250 or 2.300 inches, while exhaust valves are 1.880 inches.

Pro Elite 24-degree CNC-Ported aluminum heads are recommended for drag racing and powerboat racing big-blocks from 496 cubes on up, and they feature either 339- or 376-cc intake ports and fully CNC machined 121-cc chambers. Valve sizes remain 2.250/1.880 inches or 2.300/1.880 inches.

Sonny's Racing Components

It's hard to say "mountain motor" without mentioning Sonny's Racing Components in the same sentence. Owner Sonny Leonard has made a specialty of building really big big-block Chevys, up to 932 ci, and produces his own cylinder heads to feed them. Sonny's hemispherical Chevy heads and symmetrical port wedge heads are legendary, setting records in nearly every form of drag racing competition using monster motors—ADRL Extreme Pro Stock and Pro Nitrous Extreme, NHRA Top Sportsman and Top Dragster, truck pulling, offshore boat racing, NHRA Pro Modified, and more. For "mundane" stock-bore-space engines, Sonny's offers completely CNC machined and ported cylinder heads from Brodix and Dart, but for the 5.000- and 5.300-inch-bore-spaced big-blocks, his heads are the ones used by the big dogs. His 5.300 symmetrical port heads fit 5.000-inch bores and have 16-degree intake valves measuring up to 2.750 inches and exhaust valves up to 2.000 inches. Intake ports are up to 650 cc—these are big big-block heads!

Trick Flow Specialties (TFS)

TFS offers PowerOval 280 oval port big-block aluminum cylinder heads for street and strip applications featuring 280-cc intake ports, 113-cc chambers, and 2.190/1.880-inch stainless steel valves. Exhaust port exits are .300-inch raised to improve exhaust flow.

PowerPort 320 and 360 aluminum heads have rectangular intake ports with 2.250/1.880- or 2.300/1.880-inch valves, both with 122-cc chambers.

World Products (Merlin)

Merlin cast-iron big-block cylinder heads offer a tremendous bang-for-the-buck with affordable 269-cc oval port and 320- or 345-cc rectangular port heads. They feature 2.300/1.880-inch stainless steel valves and 119-cc combustion chambers. Marine versions are available with Inconel exhaust valves for use on MerCruiser and other marine applications.

Merlin III 355-T6 aluminum rectangular port heads are available with as-cast runners of 310 or 350 cc, and with 345- or 380-cc CNC ported runners. Chambers are 119-cc open design, and exhaust port exits are standard location for use with production big-block headers.

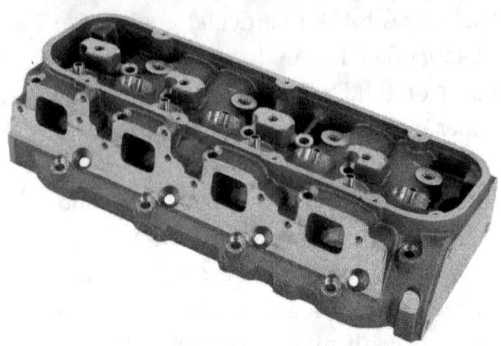

RHS Pro Action 24-degree cast-iron heads are designed for 496 and larger big-blocks with 320- or 360-cc intake ports. Traditional open combustion chambers measure 119 cc, and valve sizes are either 2.250/1.880 or 2.300/1.880 inches. (Photo Courtesy RHS)

RHS Pro Elite 24-degree CNC ported aluminum heads feature either 339- or 376-cc intake ports and fully CNC machined 121-cc chambers. Valve sizes are 2.250/1.880 or 2.300/1.880 inches. (Photo Courtesy RHS)

Merlin III aluminum rectangular port heads with 310- or 350-cc as-cast runners and 119-cc open combustion chambers. (Photo Courtesy World Products)

CNC ported Merlin III 355-T6 aluminum rectangular port heads are available with 345-cc or 380c runners. Chambers are 119-cc open design, and exhaust port exits are standard location for use with production big-block headers. (Photo Courtesy World Products)

CHAPTER 7

INDUCTION SYSTEMS

There are a variety of induction system options for the big-block Chevy including carburetion, fuel injection, superchargers and turbochargers (which must include either carburetors or fuel injection to mix the air and fuel), plus induction system power adders such as nitrous oxide injection. The vast majority of OEM big-blocks came with traditional carburetors and intake manifolds, and that is still the most popular and cost-effective choice for feeding your pet Rat motor both on the street and the racetrack, so I'll start there.

Intake Manifolds

Intake manifolds generally fall into one of two categories, either dual-plane or single-plane design. All big-block Chevy factory intake manifolds were of the dual-plane design, in which the manifold is divided into two separate plenum chambers, each feeding four cylinders. The layout of a dual-plane manifold is such that each intake event alternates drawing air/fuel from the two separate planes following the firing order (1-8-4-3-6-5-7-2), so cylinders 1, 4, 6, and 7 feed from one plane, and cylinders 8, 3, 5, and 2 are supplied by the other plane. Because the volume of each plane is half as big as with a single-plane manifold, this design is much more responsive to the vacuum signal as each intake valve opens, and dual-plane manifolds provide excellent power and throttle response at low to medium engine speeds.

Original equipment intake manifolds are certainly capable of supplying adequate power-producing flow rates for many engines (NHRA Stock class big-block racers routinely run 10-second quarter-mile times with them) but there are so many better choices available from the aftermarket that there's little reason to use that old cast-iron intake unless you have to comply with restrictive rules.

Even Chevrolet went to aluminum intake manifolds for all of the high-performance rectangular port engines,

While there are many good induction system options for the big-block Chevy, on the street it's hard to beat a good single 4-barrel setup like this Edelbrock RPM Air-Gap intake manifold topped with the right carb and a high-flow K&N air cleaner.

CHAPTER 7

Dual-plane intake manifolds are a good choice for any street-driven big-block. The Edelbrock Performer 2-O (left) for oval port heads is sized to work well with stock cylinder heads in the idle to 5,500-rpm range, and the Performer RPM (center) is available for oval port or rectangular port Rat motors. It has larger runners and plenum chamber for an operating range of 1,500 to 6,500 rpm. The RPM Air-Gap (right) for oval port heads is similar to the Performer RPM, but with elevated runners to let air circulate underneath and cool the intake charge. (Photos Courtesy Edelbrock)

and those manifolds are certainly good performers and make an excellent choice for street and modest racing engines, but there are better choices readily available from the aftermarket, and the OEM manifolds usually command a price premium due to their scarcity and desirability to the restoration enthusiast market. Maybe you already have a vintage L88 intake manifold and it works well on your 11-second street car, but why not sell it to someone who needs it to win some concours d'elegance car show, and use the money to purchase a modern manifold that makes more power?

If you are building an oval port motor, most of the factory intakes were cast iron, and there are far better choices from the aftermarket, whether you want to make more low-end torque or more high-RPM horsepower.

When it comes to high-RPM horsepower, the single-plane manifold really starts to become the standard choice, whether for high-end street performance or the racetrack. The single-plane design consists of a simple common chamber, called the plenum chamber, connected to all eight intake ports, not unlike a spider with its eight legs (anyone remember the appropriately named Edelbrock Tarantula series?).

The larger plenum chamber serves two purposes: first, it acts as a kind of reservoir, storing the air/fuel mix delivered by the carburetor and reducing the velocity of the mix so that it can more easily make the turn into the individual intake runners. The flip side of this coin, however, is that the large plenum also reduces the signal strength to the carb's metering circuits and usually requires re-calibration of those circuits. Low-speed throttle response is reduced, and a larger accelerator pump shot is needed to cover up the bog, which can occur when the throttle is suddenly opened.

The second effect of larger plenums is that they do a better job of dampening the reversion pulses from each of the intake port runners. As the intake valve closes, the inertia of the air/fuel mixture causes it to slam into the "closed door" and a reversion pulse travels back up the runner. A properly designed plenum chamber absorbs that pulse before it reaches the carb, where it would obviously have detrimental effects on the metering circuits.

There are a host of good manifold choices available for the venerable Rat motor including cast aluminum manifolds from Brodix, Dart, Edelbrock,

Although discontinued, the Edelbrock C-454, later called the Torker 4500, was a very large dual-plane manifold for use with 4500 series carbs. If you just have to run a Dominator carb on the street, this one made it work. Most street Rats are better off with something like the modern RPM Air-Gap and an 850- to 950-cfm standard flange carb. It does look impressive, however, and ran pretty well!

Edelbrock's Torker II 2-O is a low-rise single-plane manifold with an operating range of 2,500 to 6,500 rpm. It was engineered low enough to fit under big-block Corvette hoods. (Photo Courtesy Edelbrock)

INDUCTION SYSTEMS

Holley/Weiand, Profiler, and some offshore brands, which, at this point in time, are usually copies of the more popular domestic intake manifolds. Upper echelon racers can have custom manifolds hand-crafted from billet or sheet aluminum, but

This Edelbrock Big Victor 2 Spread Port manifold has been ported and blended with a special carb spacer by Reher-Morrison Racing Engines for use with their Raptor 12-degrees competition heads. It is for serious 1,000-plus-hp race Rats, and no, it won't fit under the hood of your 1969 El Camino! (Photo Courtesy Don Cooper/RMRE)

Even General Motors gets into single-plane manifolds for serious horsepower big-blocks. GMPP PN 88961161 is standard issue on the 572/620 crate engine. (Photo Courtesy GMPP)

Brodix Big Duke intake manifold matches the Big Duke spread port cylinder heads for serious drag racing.

Edelbrock's Super Victor CNC has been CNC ported by Reher-Morrison Racing Engines for rectangular port big-blocks with 4500 series carbs like the Holley Dominator or Quick Fuel Technology QFX carbs. (Photo Courtesy Edelbrock)

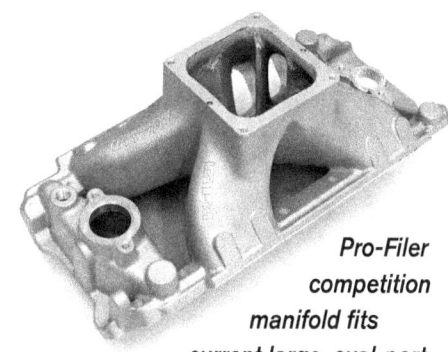

Pro-Filer competition manifold fits current large, oval-port siamesed-port big-block heads like the Sniper 24 degree, Brodix 383 Head Hunter, Edelbrock/Musi Victor 24 degree, and similar competition heads.

Stock Big-Block Chevy Aluminum Intake Manifold Casting Numbers

Casting #	Years	Engine size	Factory HP, RPO, Configuration
3866963	1965	396	375, 425 L37
3885069	1966–1968	396	375 L78
3886093	1967	427	430 L88
3894374	1967	427	435 3x2 L71
3894382	1967	427	400 3x2 L68, oval port
3919849	1968	427	390 L-36, oval port, Q-jet
3919850	1968	427	400 3x2 L68, oval port
3919852	1968	427	435 3x2 L71
3919878	1968	396	375 L78
3933163	1968–1969	396	375 L78/L89
3933198	1968–1969	427	430 L88/ZL1
3937793	1968	427	390 L36, oval port, Q-jet, Late
3937795	1969	427	400 3x2 L68, oval port
3937797	1969	427	435 3x2 L71
3947801	1969	427	390 L36, oval port, Q-jet
3963569	1970–1971	396/402	375 L78/L89
3967474	1971	454	425

All big-block rectangular port intake manifolds were cast aluminum, like this 3933163 for 1968–1969 375-hp 396 engines. Dual-plane manifold has slight reduction in the center divider for more top end power. (Photo Courtesy George Kettler)

these tend to be very pricey. Hardcore racing firms like Hogan's and CFE can make whatever you want in an intake manifold if you are willing to pay for it, and these so-called sheet-metal intakes are the norm in NHRA Pro Stock and other unlimited classes of drag racing.

Carburetor Spacers and Adapters

A common racer's trick that has been around for decades is to use carburetor spacers between the carb and manifold. If the spacer is open, it becomes merely an extension of the plenum chamber in the manifold and may offer more top end power potential. There are also four-hole carb spacers, which do not add to the plenum volume, but become extensions of the carb's throttle bores and help to combat reversion. These spacers

Intake Manifold Milling

If your heads or deck have been milled to raise compression, it may be necessary to mill the intake manifold flanges to restore proper fitment. Use the chart to get your manifold back in line for proper port alignment and gasket seal. Thinner head gaskets my also require milling the intake manifold.

The chart is handy if you know that your block and heads were stock to begin with, but when using parts with an unknown history, you can mock-up the assembly using shim stock of various thicknesses between the manifold and head, then visually check port and bolt-hole alignment if you are using a single-plane intake manifold. You have to know the thickness of the intake gaskets that you are using, and then deduct the shim thickness from the gasket thickness to yield the amount of material removal necessary. For instance, most intake gaskets are 1/16 inch (.062) thick, so if your ports align with .040-inch shims, you need to mill .022 inch from the manifold (.062 – .040 = .022).

The intake manifold bottom dimension is not too critical as long as you make sure there is some clearance (usually 1/16 to 1/8 inch) between the manifold and the manifold sealing surfaces on the block, then use RTV silicone sealant instead of factory-style end gaskets. If there is no clearance at the ends of the manifold, the manifold bottoms out against the block before you have proper gasket crush and you can expect leaks, oil consumption, and other problems.

The flip side of the coin is when the intake ports in the heads are higher than your manifold port exits, which is common with many Bowtie and other Rat motor aluminum heads. Many performance gasket makers offer 1/8-inch-thick gaskets that should bring everything into alignment, and most aftermarket competition-style manifolds have reduced port exits to accommodate port matching to slightly raised runners.

Since the intake manifold also locates the distributor, be sure to check distributor engagement in the oil pump driveshaft after milling the manifold or adding thick gaskets.

If the distributor doesn't seat on the manifold, use distributor spacers to gain clearance. If oil pump driveshaft engagement is insufficient, a slip-collar distributor can be adjusted to increase the engagement.

Note: Although the chart below from Chevrolet starts at only .005 inch of deck reduction, it is usually not necessary to mill aftermarket manifolds to correct for such a small change in deck height. It is smart to test fit your manifold before any machining is done, even if you know for sure how much was milled from the deck and heads.

Deck Surface (inch)	Manifold Intake Flange (inch)	Manifold Bottom (inch)
.005	.004	.010
.010	.007	.019
.015	.011	.029
.020	.014	.038
.025	.018	.048
.030	.021	.058

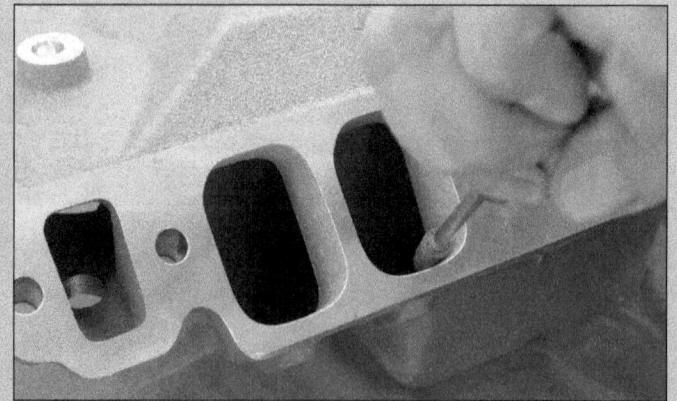

Racing manifolds should be port matched to the cylinder heads, leaving the port exit about .050 inch smaller than the intake gasket.

INDUCTION SYSTEMS

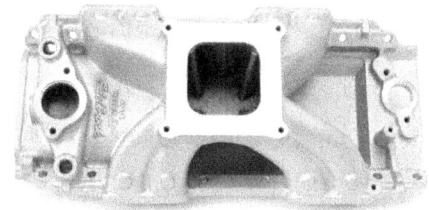

Many aftermarket racing manifolds are intended to be used with a 1-inch-or-more open carb spacer, but are designed to fit under the hood of a typical high-performance car that may not have the necessary carb-to-hood clearance for such a tall combination. If an open carb spacer won't fit your vehicle, it may be desirable to switch to a larger carburetor to reduce the exit speed of the air/fuel mixture as it enters the manifold's plenum chamber. (Photo Courtesy Edelbrock)

Carb spacers, like this 1-inch open Edelbrock spacer, are relatively inexpensive and easy to change, so their effect on performance can easily be tested at the dragstrip. Remember that spacers change the signal to the carb and may require re-jetting or re-calibration of the fuel metering circuits. (Photo Courtesy Edelbrock)

are frequently used to improve throttle response and low-end torque.

Remember that spacers change the signal to the carb and may require re-jetting or re-calibration of the fuel metering circuits. Carb spacers are usually made from aluminum, but there are also versions produced from phenolic plastics and wood laminates, which do a good job of isolating the carb from engine heat. Typical carb spacers range from 1 to 2 inches thick, though other sizes are available if desired.

Carb adapters are used to mate non-standard carb/manifold combinations together, and are generally to be avoided like the plague. One possible exception is the combination of a spread-bore Quadrajet carb, required by racing organization rules, on a square-bore competition-style intake manifold. There are commercially available adapters for this application, but many top Super Stock drag racers have modified existing adapters or just made their own to reposition the carb over the plenum chamber for optimum air/fuel distribution.

Tunnel Ram Intake Manifolds

Tunnel ram manifolds are simply large single-plane intakes designed to mount multiple carburetors, usually two 4-barrel carbs. One of the advantages of using eight barrels to feed eight cylinders is the possibility of fine tuning each cylinder separately, if necessary. The necessary large plenum chamber does an outstanding job of absorbing reversion pulses at high RPM, but also reduces the signal to the carbs so effectively that low-end performance suffers dramatically, making them a poor choice for any street-driven vehicle. Tunnel ram manifolds should only be used on drag race vehicles that typically see no less than 5,500 rpm on the starting line, and climb to 8,000 rpm or more in the quarter-mile.

From a power producing standpoint, one of the main benefits to the tunnel ram design is that each carb throttle bore can be positioned almost directly over the intake port runner for maximum airflow potential, and all eight intake ports can be made to the same length, a situation not possible with eight runners converging into a smaller plenum as with traditional single-carb manifolds. Some tunnel ram manifolds mount the carbs angled so that the right pair of carb throttle bores is slightly forward, due to the offset arrangement of each pair of intake runners.

To further refine this feature, ultra-high-end racers have resorted to running split Dominator series carbs, in which

Reher-Morrison Racing Engines makes this two-piece anti-reversion carb spacer for 4500 series carbs, featuring CNC-machined throttle bore extensions. It broadens the power curve and improves the signal to the carburetor, and has been shown to be worth 8 to 10 hp on typical 555-ci big-block racing engines, depending on the combination of parts used. This bottom view shows what the intake manifold sees; from the top it just looks like a four-hole spacer.

Although tunnel ram manifolds like this Weiand topped with two Holley 4-barrel carbs, are not usually needed on a street car, their "wow" factor is undeniable. Keeping carb sizes small, around 450 to 600 cfm, helps drivablility. Note the hole in the hood to let the Hilborn-style aluminum scoop get a good look at the outside world. Don't drive this one in the rain.

CHAPTER 7

these large 4-barrel carburetors are cut in half to produce four 2-barrel carbs that are positioned directly over their matching pair of runners. This has become so popular with mountain motor racers that Braswell carburetors has even introduced its own version of these giant 2-barrel carbs (PN 7520) that is ready to race as delivered.

Rochester Quadrajet Carburetors

The vast majority of standard performance big-block Chevys with oval port heads came equipped with a Rochester Quadrajet 4-barrel carburetor from the factory, while the high-performance rectangular port head engines were usually topped with one of the popular Holley modular carburetors.

The Quadrajet is a spread-bore design with two small primary throttle bores (1⅜ or 1½ inches) and two large secondary throttle bores (2 inches). The secondary barrels are activated mechanically via a progressive linkage arrangement, but airflow is controlled by a large air valve that opens as the engine demands more airflow at higher speeds. Quadrajets are rated at 750 or 795 cfm, and there are versions with modified air valves that flow 850 cfm. These large Q-Jets are extremely well suited for use on street-driven big-blocks, as the small primaries deliver excellent low-speed throttle response and fuel economy (not usually that important to the big-block driver), and the giant secondaries deliver sufficient air/fuel flow for engines up to about 500 hp.

Q-Jets are very sophisticated and reliable carbs, but modifying them for true high-performance applications requires quite a bit of knowledge and experience; you can't just change the fuel circuit calibrations with off-the-shelf parts like you can with the Holley and other modular design carbs. Because the last Chevy truck equipped with a Q-Jet rolled off the assembly line in 1987, and Rochester only made new replacements for a few years thereafter, most Q-Jets are more than 30 years old and are in need of some serious mechanical love if they are to function properly on a high-performance machine.

Edelbrock marketed new Q-Jet carbs made on the original Rochester tooling as recently as 2005, including the aforementioned 850-cfm carb (PN 1910), which makes an outstanding street carb for moderate performance big-blocks. If you're starting with one of the old OEM Q-Jets and are intent upon making it provide good power, there are a number of good carb shops across the country that specialize in the Quadrajet. Contact JET (Jones Electronic Technology), Hedworth Racing Carburetors, SMI (Sean Murphy Induction), The Carb Shop, and I'm sure many others who can tune your Q-Jet to your satisfaction. Holley also makes spread-bore carbs as replacements for the Quadrajet (models 4165 and 4175), but their performance potential is not as good as the more commonly used square-bore Holley carbs, and they are typically used only for very mild, low-RPM big-blocks when a stock replacement carb is needed to fit the OEM spread-bore intake manifold.

Holley-Style Modular Carburetors

The most popular choices for high-performance and racing big-blocks by far are the Holley modular-design carburetors (models 4150, 4160, and 4500) and their offspring, including Braswell, Demon, Quick Fuel Technology, and others based on the original Holley design. The advantage to this design is its vast flexibility in airflow capacity, fuel capacity, and fuel circuit calibration.

Most street models have vacuum operated secondaries, which are opened by a vacuum diaphragm that senses airflow through the primary venturi, so that total airflow through the carb is always closely matched to the engine's needs at various throttle positions and loads. The double-pumper series have mechanically opened secondaries with a second accelerator pump to cover up the momentary bog that occurs when the throttles are suddenly opened.

So-called square-bore carbs or standard-flange carbs have the same (or close to it) throttle bore diameters for all four holes, with a maximum throttle bore diameter of 1.750 inches (unmodified), but their bolt pattern is a rectangular 5.15 inches by 5.625 inches where it mounts to the intake manifold. The large 4500 series carbs, known as

The Q-Jet carb on this NHRA stock class big-block Camaro may not look like much, but this baby runs the quarter-mile in 10 seconds, far quicker than most of the spit 'n polish show cars at your local cruise night. Beauty is in the eye of the beholder.

INDUCTION SYSTEMS

Holley carbs have always been a mainstay on high-performance big-block Chevys, and vacuum secondary models of 650, 750, 770, 850, or 870 cfm are a great choice for 90 percent of the street-driven Rat motors on the road. This one features a shiny finish, center-pivot floats, dual fuel inlets, and an electric choke for civilized street manners. (Photo Courtesy GMPP)

Holley double-pumper carbs are the stuff of legend, ensuring that when you stand on the gas you're going to get plenty of it. They are available in a host of sizes from 600 to 1,000 cfm. This one features a shiny finish, dual-feed center-pivot float bowls, mechanical secondaries and twin accelerator pumps (that's why it's called a double-pumper), and electric choke. (Photo Courtesy GMPP)

APD makes this highly modified 1,250-cfm Dominator carb for serious race Rats. It features billet aluminum metering blocks, annular discharge boosters, changeable air bleeds, and adjustable secondary linkage.

Dominators, King Demons, and a host of other names, are standard fare on any very high-performance or racing big-block. With 2-plus-inch throttle bores and a minimum of $1^{11}/_{16}$-inch venturi, airflow rates start at 1,050 cfm and climb to 1,150, 1,250, and higher. Whether or not you really need that much carburetor depends on the air/fuel appetite of your big-block, but when you're packing more than 600 ci and putting out more than 1,000 hp, one of these hefty carbs is the only logical choice.

Make no mistake; all of the 4500 series carbs are competition oriented and a poor choice for street-driven vehicles. Since they are tuned for drag racing use only, very few were offered with Power Valves, meaning that even during light throttle cruise mode, you run on the main fuel circuit with maximum enrichment; not good for throttle response, fuel economy (ha!), or long spark plug life. Oddly enough, the 4500 series carbs were never called square-bore carbs, even though they richly deserve it: all four throttle bores are the same diameter, and the mounting flange bolt pattern is square at $5^3/_8$ inches on each side.

For really monstrous motors, Braswell has raised the bar even higher by super-sizing the 4500 series concept to produce its 7390 and 7395 carbs. After a certain point, rating the carburetor size in CFM becomes almost more of an advertising issue than a true measure of flow capacity, so Braswell simply markets these carbs by their throttle bore and venturi specifications.

Carter/Weber/Edelbrock Square-Bore Carburetors

Introduced in the 1960s, the Carter AFB (aluminum four barrel) carbs were produced in sizes ranging from 400 to 750 cfm. Only the 750-cfm size is of interest to the big-block Chevy performance buff, and it is well suited to the task of mixing air and fuel reliably on a modest performance engine. As on the Quadrajet, the secondaries are mechanically linked to the primary barrels, and airflow through the secondary side is controlled by an air valve positioned above the secondaries.

Braswell Carburetion makes this giant model 7395 4-barrel carb for single carb engines producing up to 1,200 hp. It is similar to the 4500 series Dominator carb design, only bigger in every respect. It has a 5.5-inch x 5.5-inch bolt pattern, and an 8-inch air horn, compared to the Dominator's 7-inch air horn. It features four-circuit fuel metering, spread throttle bores, longer venturies, and throttle bores from 2.200 to 2.500 inches. The stock Holley 1250 carbs measure 2.125 inches. This is the "big dog" of carburetors. Model 7390 is designed for two 4-barrel applications making up to 2,200 hp or more. This is mountain motor stuff.

CHAPTER 7

Edelbrock Performer Series 750-cfm carb with manual choke is a solid, reliable street performance carb for mild big-blocks. (Photo Courtesy Edelbrock)

Edelbrock Thunder Series AVS 800-cfm carb with electric choke features an adjustable secondary air valve for easy tuning to suit various applications. (Photo Courtesy Edelbrock)

The ABF differs from the Q-Jet in that the secondary air valve is a non-adjustable counter weighted assembly, so changes in the secondary activation rate can only be accomplished by lightening the counterweights (to open sooner) or changing to an air valve with heavier weights to delay the opening. Air valves with heavier counterweights were typically used on marine versions of these carbs, and are still available through Edelbrock.

The Carter AVS (adjustable valve secondary) design adds the sophistication of an adjustable secondary spring that permits easy changes of the opening rate to suit various performance parameters. For instance, a warmed-over 454 with modest performance improvements uses a slow opening rate in a heavy vehicle with "highway" gears (around 3.23:1). But in a lighter car with 4.11:1 rear gears, the secondaries can be adjusted to open much sooner to provide more air and fuel to the rapidly accelerating engine. Carter carburetors are no longer produced but, beginning in 1987, Edelbrock contracted with Weber USA to reproduce this solid street-performance carburetor under the Edelbrock banner.

Edelbrock Performer Series carburetors are similar to the original Carter design, but not identical. Nearly every metering circuit in the carb was revamped and improved to work with Edelbrock's extensive line of high-performance intake manifolds, essentially making them a "tuned up" version of the aging AFB. Edelbrock eventually added the AVS design to its arsenal, with an attending increase in airflow capacity to 800 cfm, and these carbs are popular on medium-

Carburetor Size Formula

The formula for calculating carburetor flow capacity for high-performance big-block engines is:

$$\text{Engine Size} \times \text{Maximum RPM} \div 3456 \times \text{VE}$$

Where:
Engine size = measured in cubic inches
VE = volumetric efficiency

Most street high-performance engines have a VE of 85 percent (0.85). Competition single 4-barrel engines that are operated primarily at WOT have a VE of 100 percent (1.0). Extremely modified and dual 4-barrel competition engines may achieve a VE of 105 percent (1.05) to 110 percent (1.1). Here are a couple examples:

454 ci with a top engine speed of 6,000 rpm on a street engine
$(454 \times 6{,}000) \div 3{,}456 \times .85 = 669.9$ cfm

You could use a 650-cfm engine for great low-end throttle response, but I usually recommend going up to a 700-cfm carb with mechanical secondaries, or the popular 750-cfm size with vacuum secondaries. The vacuum secondaries open as needed, so the chance of over-carbureting is diminished. Note that most factory stock Quadrajet carbs were either 750 or 795 cfm.

565 ci with a top engine speed of 7,500 rpm
on a single 4-barrel race engine
$(565 \times 7{,}500) \div 3{,}456 \times 1.0 = 1{,}226.1$ cfm

Holley and other carb manufacturers offer 1,150- and 1,250-cfm double-pumper competition carbs, and either one is a good choice. If the car competes in one of NHRA's Super classes such as Super Gas or Super Comp with a set index, most racers use a throttle stop to "hit the number," and the smaller 1,150-cfm carb usually responds better to the throttle-control device.

INDUCTION SYSTEMS

performance big-blocks, which are primarily driven on the street.

Air Cleaners

Modern air cleaner designs not only filter out damaging particles, but they can also be a source of increased power through proper airflow management. The original factory high-performance engines were equipped with 14-inch-diameter low-restriction air filters, usually 3 inches tall, sandwiched between the stamped metal base and a shiny chrome lid that was a good place to put the engine badge proclaiming to the world that this was a 375-hp 396 (or whatever).

That same basic design is available today from a number of sources, including GM Performance Parts (PN 12342079), and usually comes with a standard perforated paper filter element. K&N Performance has taken air cleaner technology to the next plateau with its excellent washable/reusable oiled-cotton elements, which can be ordered in just about any size you desire. They also produce an air cleaner assembly that utilizes that same cotton/gauze filter medium for the air cleaner lid as well as around the perimeter for virtually unrestricted airflow potential.

Air cleaners for standard flange carbs all fit the standard 5⅛-inch air horn found on Holley, Carter/Edelbrock, and Quadrajet carbs. Most 14-inch air cleaners have a dropped base to provide additional hood clearance, but you'd better check to ensure that the base clears your electric choke assembly (if so equipped), your fuel lines, and any other possible sources of interference. Of course you can always modify the base yourself with a ball-peen hammer, and some manufacturers offer air cleaners with additional height built into the base. Be sure to check for adequate clearance before slamming the hood if you are using one of these raised air cleaners.

The 4500 series carbs come with a larger 7-inch-diameter air horn and there are a limited number of air cleaners available for them, as well. Check with K&N Performance; the company offers 14- and 16-inch cleaners with a variety of filter heights, plus specialized air cleaners for use with popular competition hood scoops.

If your big-block is destined for marine use, note that Coast Guard requirements, as well as common sense, dictate that an appropriately designed flame arrestor and marine carburetor be used.

Fuel Pumps

All of the factory carbureted big-blocks received their supply of fuel from a mechanical fuel pump mounted on the lower right side of the engine block. Traditional mechanical fuel pumps use a rubberized diaphragm and a series of one-way valves to pump the fuel, and the reciprocating motion is supplied by a fuel pump pushrod that is operated by the fuel pump eccentric on the camshaft. The stock fuel pump is generally adequate for feeding big-blocks up to 400 hp, but most high-performance street and all racing applications can benefit from a better fuel delivery source, whether mechanical or electric. Remember that Gen V and some Gen VI blocks did not have the fuel

K&N Filters makes a 14-inch-diameter air cleaner with a high-flow cotton/gauze filter medium for the air cleaner lid, as well as around the perimeter, for virtually unrestricted airflow potential. (Photo Courtesy K&N)

You think your flow bench moves a lot of air? K&N test fixture showed that this competition filter flowed 2,200 cfm with no restriction. A large collection grid at the bottom of the pyramid collects any debris for analysis.

K&N also makes this traditional-style 14-inch air cleaner with chrome lid for carbs with standard 5⅛-inch air horn. (Photo Courtesy K&N)

Competition cars deserve clean air too. K&N makes a filter for just about any application you can think of.

pump mounting provision, so an electric fuel pump becomes the only option if you are using one of those blocks.

There are a number of aftermarket sources for good fuel pumps and most suppliers list the pump's flow rating in gallons per hour (gph). That is useful information, but only if the pressure rating is listed as well. The free-flow rate is almost meaningless; your carburetor needs to see at least 4 pounds of fuel pressure under load, and more is better. The formula for determining fuel flow requirements is pretty straightforward: you need about 1/2-pound of gasoline per hour for 1 hp. This is known as the Brake Specific Fuel Consumption (BSFC). Alcohol-fueled engines require double that, or about 1 pound of alcohol per horsepower per hour.

So to feed a 500-hp gasoline-burning engine, you need 250 pounds (1/2 x 500) of gasoline per hour, and since there are about 6 pounds of gasoline in a gallon, that becomes 250 ÷ 6 = 41.67 gph. That doesn't sound like much, but that is with a minimum of 4 pounds of pressure; the free-flow rate is substantially higher. I can hear all you old-timers shaking your head and remarking that you always set your fuel pressure between 6 and 8 psi (pounds per square inch), and that is the correct pressure setting for most carburetors at idle.

The pressure drops at WOT in high gear, and that is the important number.

Now that we know that even a 1,000-hp engine only requires about 84 gph at 4 psi, why are there so many performance enthusiasts who insist upon packing the latest 250- to 500-gph fuel pump? Because other forces such as resistance to flow in lengthy fuel lines and the inertia of the car's forward acceleration pushing the fuel away from the carburetor (if the fuel tank is behind the engine) all work against the goal of keeping the carb supplied with fuel.

Competition fuel pumps typically deliver around 15 psi at zero flow (deadhead pressure), and that much pressure quickly overpowers the needles and seats in the carb and leads to flooding. Fuel pressure regulators are absolutely required with any pump that makes more than 7 or 8 pounds of pressure, and a good regulator also helps to even out the flow by dampening some of the pulses from the pump.

If you switch to an electric fuel pump for your Rat motor, be sure to mount it as close as possible to the fuel tank and low enough that it is gravity-fed by the tank. These pumps are designed to push the fuel through a fuel line, and they are not very good at pulling fuel through a lengthy section of fuel line from the tank. While the stock steel fuel line may be good for feeding up to a 500-hp engine, it is prudent to use 1/2-inch or -8 AN lines to and from the fuel pump. From the regulator to the carb(s), 3/8-inch or -6 AN lines are recommended.

It should go without saying that an electric fuel pump should only receive power when the engine is on, so be sure yours is wired to a switched source of electric power. Some companies offer fuel pump safety switches that monitor engine oil pressure, so that your pump receives electrical power only when the engine is running. Good idea. High-capacity electric pumps pull a lot of amps, so most manufacturers also recommend the use of a relay to handle the high electric current flow to the pump.

Don't forget fuel filters. Fuel pumps and carburetors really don't like stuff in them other than pure liquid fuel, and little metal shavings, dirt, and other contaminants cause more carburetor and fuel system problems than anything else. There are plenty of good high-flow fuel filters on the market.

Fuel Injection

In contrast to carburetors, which sense the pressure differential through a venturi to draw fuel into the engine, fuel injection systems, as their name implies, inject the fuel under pressure regardless of the airflow through the system. There must be some means of controlling the ratio of fuel injected to the airflow into the engine, and that problem is solved either with mechanical fuel metering circuits or with sophisticated electronic controls.

Mechanical Fuel Injection Systems

Early fuel injection systems like the popular Hilborn, Crower, and Enderle

Edelbrock billet aluminum mechanical fuel pump has a free-flow rate of 170 gph. (Photo Courtesy Edelbrock)

Edelbrock electric fuel pump has a free-flow rate of 160 gph and can feed a 1,000-hp Rat motor. (Photo Courtesy Edelbrock)

All carburetors deserve clean fuel, so make sure you use a fuel filter of sufficient flow capacity for your engine. (Photo Courtesy Edelbrock)

INDUCTION SYSTEMS

Brake-Specific Fuel Consumption

In calculating the fuel requirements for a big-block, I frequently refer to the amount of fuel needed to make 1 hp per hour as "1/2 pound per hour." This is an approximation of the exact Brake Specific Fuel Consumption (BSFC), which can only be determined accurately on an engine dynamometer. Many of us don't have access to a dyno, but after years of engine testing, some common numbers have surfaced, which you can refer to for guidance. Most stock engines have a BSFC of around .5 pound per horsepower/hour, and high-performance engines are typically between .45 and .55 pound per horsepower/hour. Note that the lower the BSFC, the more efficient the engine is at turning fuel into work (horsepower). Gasoline-burning engines with nitrous oxide injection usually require more fuel, and have a BSFC around .55 pound per horsepower/hour. Supercharged engines tend to run about .60 pound per horsepower/hour. If alcohol is used for fuel, it takes more than twice as much, due to alcohol's stoiciometric ratio of 6:1 (air to fuel ratio) versus gasoline's ratio of 14.7:1.

If you do know the exact BSFC for your engine, you can plug that number into the formula to determine fuel flow requirements, but remember that you should have more fuel available than the minimum requirement. If you provide a safety margin of 20 percent more than the calculated fuel flow requirement, you have adequate fuel available to account for minor changes in the BSFC, as well as other physical impediments to fuel flow.

The bottom line: go ahead and use 1/2 pound per horsepower/hour for gasoline, and 1 pound per horsepower/hour for alcohol, then make sure your fuel delivery system exceeds minimum fuel flow specs by 20 percent. Done.

competition fuel injections used a barrel valve, which is a variable fuel metering valve. This simple constant-flow design progressively metered more fuel as the throttle position increased from idle to WOT, and was tuned by the use of an adjustable linkage between the throttle blades and the barrel valve, plus "pills," which are simple metering orifices that bleed off excessive fuel and return it to the tank or inlet side of the high-pressure fuel pump. Since these systems had no way of sensing throttle transition from steady state cruise to WOT, they were normally calibrated much richer than necessary (more fuel than chemically needed to combust with a given amount of air) to cover up the bog that otherwise occurs during sudden throttle opening.

Additional tuning was provided by a "high-speed lean-out," which is a pressure-sensitive valve that can be adjusted to bleed-off fuel at a predetermined pressure, thereby leaning out the air/fuel ratio to the ideal or stoichiometric air/fuel ratio for maximum power at high engine speeds. All mechanical fuel injection systems require an engine-driven high-pressure fuel pump, which supplies additional fuel flow as engine speeds increase. The interaction between the fuel pump, barrel valve, throttle blades, pills, and high-speed lean-out requires a serious amount of tuning and coordination to achieve proper performance.

The good news is that when all of these variables are just right, the throttle response and top-end power produced by these units is nothing short of amazing. Throttle response is instantaneous, and the airflow path is wide open because there is no need for a flow-reducing venturi. Today's mechanical fuel injection systems have changed little since their introduction in the 1960s, but they still provide amazing performance on a big-block Chevy used exclusively for drag racing.

The Hilborn and Crower systems are true independent runner (IR) systems with no common plenum chamber, and as a result, they typically have much larger throttle bores than are necessary in a carbureted setup. The Enderle "hat" type of fuel injection was initially developed to sit atop a GMC supercharger, and the Bugcatcher, Birdcatcher, and Buzzardcatcher injectors were developed to provide increasingly larger volumes of air/fuel delivery as power production increased.

An interesting development for big-block Chevys is the adaptation of the Enderle injector hat for use on top of a traditional tunnel ram intake manifold base. These systems offer all the performance of traditional fuel injection with the added benefit of a plenum chamber to combat reversion and provide adequate air/fuel flow with smaller injectors.

Electronic Fuel Injection

EFI is the most sophisticated and versatile of all the induction systems currently available, and has been the only choice for air/fuel control offered by Chevrolet on production vehicles since 1987. EFI systems all use high-pressure electronic fuel injectors that receive a signal from a computerized control unit—with various names including electronic control unit (ECU), electronic control module (ECM), and powertrain control module (PCM)—which controls engine and transmission operation.

The first OEM system on big-block Chevys was TBI, which was used from 1987 to 1995. It was little more than a large 2-barrel throttle body on top of a cast-iron intake manifold with two large injectors positioned above the throttle blades, and the overall operation and performance of this system was very similar to an electronically controlled carburetor. This method simplified the changeover from carburetors to EFI on the assembly line, and was more economical to produce than multi-point injection systems that use one injector for each cylinder.

TBI had very little performance potential. Since it was only used on big-blocks found in trucks and Suburbans, there are few performance options for these vehicles.

In 1996 Chevrolet changed the big-block's induction system to central port fuel injection (CPFI), a design that used tubes with poppet valves to spray fuel at each intake port, offering some of the benefits of MPFI without the expense of eight individual injectors. These systems offered good performance on stock engines, but are not suitable for adaptation to a true high-performance environment.

Aftermarket EFI Systems

Fortunately, the aftermarket manufacturers have really stepped up to the plate by offering high-flow, high-performance EFI systems for big-blocks in just about any configuration you can imagine. There are plug-and-play kits that include everything you need to add EFI to street performance vehicles making up to 625 hp, although they do require computer programming to get everything just right for your particular engine combination. Many companies offer pre-programmed computer chips that may be plugged into the ECM supplied with the kit, and others require the use of a laptop computer to make the necessary programming changes.

On the other end of the spectrum, you can piece together an EFI system that feeds your 1,000-plus-hp normally aspirated big-block, or even higher output supercharged engines. There are a host of aftermarket EFI manufacturers, some offering complete kits, while others specialize in individual components such as the ECU or injectors. They include Accel DFI, Bosch, Edelbrock, EFI Technology, Fuel Air Spark Technology (FAST), Holley, Mototron, MSD, Pro-M, and many others.

The key components found in most EFI systems include the ECU, the fuel injectors, a throttle body to control airflow, a throttle position sensor (TPS), an idle air controller (IAC), a manifold absolute pressure (MAP) sensor, air and coolant temperature sensors, O_2 sensors, which are also known as exhaust gas oxygen (EGO) sensors, sometimes a knock sensor, a high-pressure fuel pump (usually 40 to 60 psi), and return-style fuel pressure regulator. Systems that use the mass air flow (MAF) method of fuel management also require a MAF sensor, or meter. Ancillary pieces include the fuel rails and stands, an intake manifold designed to position the injectors for best air/fuel atomization, a fuel return line to the gas tank, and a high-flow air cleaner. Additionally, most ECUs also control the ignition spark advance curve, which requires a special distributor containing both a reluctor wheel and a cam position sensor to indicate when the engine is approaching TDC of the number-1 cylinder.

This seems like a lot of complicated hardware, yet the purpose of all these sensors is merely to feed information to the ECU so that it signals to the injectors the exact amount of fuel needed at that particular throttle opening and

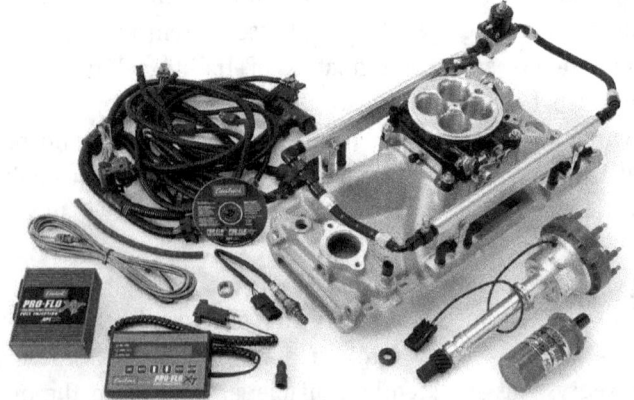

Edelbrock Pro-Flo 2 Multi-Point EFI System for rectangular port big-blocks is the same system used on Edelbrock's 675-hp 555-ci crate engine. (Photo Courtesy Edelbrock)

Accel's DFI Super-Ram system has runner lengths tuned for power in the 3,500- to 6,500-rpm range. The 30 lb/hour injectors provide enough fuel to feed 450 horses.

INDUCTION SYSTEMS

engine load. The ECU sorts all this information by means of "look-up tables" that are programmed into its memory, and modifying these tables to suit your exact engine and vehicle has become a kind of black art that EFI tuners have to master in order to achieve maximum performance, fuel economy, and throttle response.

A common misconception is that electronic fuel injectors vary the flow rate of the fuel to the engine—they do not. They are either open or closed, and the ECU triggers more or less fuel by changing the length of time they are held open. This signal is known as the injector pulse width, or "duty cycle," and is simply the amount of time, expressed in the percentage that the injector is turned on. Most sources agree that 80 to 90 percent should be the maximum duty cycle for a high-performance engine. At 100 percent, the injector never closes, and becomes a constant flow nozzle, similar to the old mechanical fuel injectors. That's not necessarily a bad thing, unless something changes (weather, operating conditions, or engine wear), and your engine needs a bit more fuel.

Fuel injectors are available in many different flow rates, from 19 lbs/hour to more than 60 lbs/hour, and the correct injector size is one of the most critical aspects of setting up a high-performance or competition EFI system. Avoid the temptation to select the largest injectors you can find. Just as carburetor size must be matched to the engine's operating parameters, so too must the injectors be matched. Overly large injectors do not have the ability to accurately meter fuel at the low end of the fuel requirement scale, such as during engine idle.

What's Your Tuning Strategy?

Currently, there are three tuning strategies used to control the injector pulse width.

Mass Air Flow (MAF)

The mass air flow system uses a MAF sensor positioned ahead of the throttle body to measure the volume of air ingested by the engine, making it the only tuning strategy that computes fuel requirements based on the engine's actual air consumption. Because of this feature, MAF systems are able to compensate for some changes in the engine configuration, and they respond well to traditional hot rodding such as cam changes, better flowing cylinder heads, etc. This makes them the best choice for street performance and supercharged or turbocharged engines.

The downside of this approach is that the MAF sensor itself needs to be small enough to accurately measure airflow, and it can become a flow restriction on higher-horsepower engines. For this reason, some ECUs include compatibility with two MAF sensors, and may offer a combination of MAF and MAP so that the MAF sensor(s) may be removed after initial programming. MAF is the OEM tuning strategy for the GM LS1 small-block V-8, as well as "Blue Oval" high-performance V-8s.

Speed/Density (S/D)

Speed/Density systems are the most popular in the aftermarket and are applicable to engines from stock to serious high-performance street and mild race applications. The primary players in this system are the TPS and the MAP sensors. The ECU compares engine speed and throttle position to the manifold vacuum information from the MAP sensor, and determines the injector pulse width based on look-up tables programmed into the ECU. Since it doesn't know what "normal" manifold vacuum is for your engine, the ECU must be programmed to take into account all the variables that affect manifold vacuum (actually, manifold absolute pressure) including cam timing, port volume, spark advance, throttle body size, and even the exhaust system. If any of these components are changed, a new fuel map must be used by the ECU, requiring either a different computer chip or reprogramming with a lap-top computer; sometimes both are required. Since manifold absolute pressure is so critical with Speed/Density systems, they generally work best with camshafts that develop at least 10 inches Hg of vacuum at idle.

Alpha-N

Alpha-N systems are the crudest form of fuel management, simply comparing the throttle position to the engine speed. They lack the sophistication offered by MAF and S/D strategies, making them a poor choice for street-driven vehicles, but because they ignore manifold absolute pressure, they can be used with radical race-only camshafts that produce low manifold vacuum at low engine speeds. Obviously, individual fuel maps must be created for your exact engine configuration, and the tuner's ability to program the ECU is critical to proper performance with Alpha-N systems.

In terms of physical size, most EFI systems for the big-block Chevy use one of two injector sizes, either the compact Pico or the larger Bosch style. Competition systems favor the Bosch design, because larger injectors can supply more fuel to feed a higher-horsepower engine, but the Pico-sized injectors fit into a physically smaller space, lending more flexibility in the injector positioning for best spray pattern disbursement. Don't get overly creative here; use the injectors that your system was designed for, unless you know more than the engineers who designed it.

All OEM EFI systems and most street performance systems include the use of oxygen (O_2) sensors, also known as exhaust gas oxygen (EGO) sensors in the exhaust pipe(s) to measure the O_2 content of the exhaust gases. This information is digested by the ECU, which either ignores it (during certain operating conditions such as heavy acceleration), or uses the info to adjust the injector pulse width to correct readings that are too rich or too lean. "Closed loop" is the term used to describe the system when the ECU is responding to input from the O_2 sensor, and "open loop" is when the ECU is ignoring O_2 sensor input, such as during WOT operation.

First generation O_2 sensors were narrow band sensors that produced an exponential voltage signal (0 to 1.0 volt), so they had a very narrow range of useable sensitivity. Wide band O_2 sensors (0 to 5 volts) are popular with most aftermarket EFI manufacturers, as their linear response is capable of sensing a wider range of air/fuel ratios, which are typically present with a high-performance EFI system. Most original-equipment EFI systems now use heated exhaust gas oxygen (HEGO) sensors, also known as universal exhaust gas oxygen (UEGO) sensors, which incorporate a heater circuit to bring the sensor up to proper operating temperatures quicker for more precise feedback to the computer.

Nitrous Oxide Injection

Nitrous oxide injection has become one of the most popular and cost-effective modifications you can make to your big-block either for street performance or all-out racing. Just don't call it NOS unless you are using a system from Nitrous Oxide Systems, the company that really got the ball rolling with the introduction of nitrous oxide to the domestic motorsports community in the 1970s. If you must refer to the gas as a three-digit term, use N_2O, the correct chemical expression of this compound containing two parts nitrogen and one part oxygen (36-percent oxygen by weight).

Nitrous oxide acts as an oxidizer in the combustion process, and must be mixed with additional fuel when burned in an engine, so the process is most accurately described as nitrous oxide/fuel injection. The higher-than-atmospheric oxygen concentration in nitrous oxide gas (only 20.95 percent of dry air is oxygen, and even less when humidity is factored in) causes very lean air/fuel ratios and extremely high combustion temperatures if injected without the correct amount of added fuel, so the balance of nitrous and fuel is extremely critical to maximize horsepower gains and engine component life. Most commercial nitrous systems use interchangeable jets with precisely machined orifices, similar to the jets in your carburetor, to control both the nitrous and the fuel delivery.

Although nitrous oxide is used as an oxidizer in engines, it is a very stable compound under normal atmospheric conditions, and the oxygen molecules aren't released until the temperature reaches 572 degrees F, which occurs inside the combustion chamber. Additionally, the remaining nitrogen acts as a buffer to dampen the rapidly increasing cylinder pressure and helps to control detonation.

With a boiling point of –88.48 degrees C (about –191 degrees F), nitrous oxide is a clear gas at normal temperatures and standard atmospheric pressure. It remains a liquid under high pressure, and commercially produced nitrous bottles are designed to safely handle the 1,000-plus-psi pressure of liquid N_2O. Similarly, nitrous valves, solenoids, lines, fittings and nozzles must all be properly designed and manufactured to withstand this high level of pressure. The nitrous remains in liquid form until it is released into the engine, and the rapid expansion of the gas has a tremendous cooling effect that provides additional performance gains by producing a cold, dense intake charge with more fuel and oxygen available for combustion.

ZEX Perimeter Plate nitrous system uses a carb plate with 12 injection points around the perimeter for even distribution of nitrous and fuel. This system for standard flange carbs is tunable for 100- to 300-hp increases. (Photo Courtesy ZEX)

INDUCTION SYSTEMS

Since nitrous injection introduces added fuel and oxygen to the combustion chamber, its effect on the engine is quite similar to a supercharger, and many of the same engine enhancements needed for a blown engine apply to a nitrous motor as well. At the low end of the scale, nitrous systems that produce an additional 100 to 200 hp should only be used on engines with forged pistons, rods, and crankshafts designed to handle the added stress. Additional engine mods in the form of high-energy ignition systems, colder spark plugs, reduced ignition timing, a free-flowing exhaust system and a high-quality fuel delivery system are all wise investments for your bottle-fed Rat Motor and should be considered when calculating the overall cost of using nitrous oxide.

As we move up the power scale, using nitrous on a competition engine demands specific changes to the engine build compared to a similar non-nitrous motor. For instance, adding a 400 hp unit to a single 4-barrel drag race engine capable of 800 to 1,000 hp without the squeeze dictates the use of pistons and rings with thicker decks and a lower ring location. The ring end gaps have to be increased to prevent damage from the higher cylinder pressure and heat, and aluminum connecting rods are frequently needed to prevent the severe shock loads from being transferred to the crankshaft. A competition nitrous camshaft has more exhaust lift and timing to evacuate the added combustion gases, and usually features a very wide lobe separation angle to reduce valve overlap and reversion.

Even cylinder head selection is nitrous sensitive. While this type of competition engine generally calls for the use of Big Chief or other spread port heads with 12- to 14-degree valve angles, nitrous motors seem to like valve angles no smaller than 18 degrees. Remember that as valve angles are reduced, the combustion chamber becomes shallower and smaller, and the added volume of fuel and oxygen from nitrous injection requires a larger chamber to allow adequate room for the mixture to prevent hydraulic lock.

Nitrous systems are divided into two categories: wet and dry. Wet systems include both nitrous and fuel solenoids to deliver the correct ratio of fuel and oxidizer, while dry systems deliver nitrous oxide only and integrate with the vehicle's fuel management system to provide additional fuel through the fuel injector nozzles. Obviously, dry systems are only for vehicles with computer-controlled EFI induction systems. Except for the Mercury Marine engines, there were no original-equipment high-performance EFI-equipped big-blocks, so dry nitrous systems are only of interest if your Rat motor features one of the high-performance aftermarket EFI induction systems. Even then, remember that the added fuel is limited by the injector size, so power increases with dry nitrous systems are normally less than 100 hp.

The vast majority of street or race big-blocks require a wet nitrous system with both nitrous and fuel solenoids. For most carbureted engines, the easiest way to accomplish this goal is by using one of the many nitrous plate systems that feature a spacer plate, usually between 1/2 and 1 inch thick, sandwiched between the carb and the intake manifold. Most of these nitrous plates have two brass or stainless steel tubes with precisely drilled discharge orifices to inject the nitrous oxide and additional fuel directly into the intake manifold in a "V" pattern, providing even distribution to the left and right bank of cylinders. Although some of these plates are advertised as being compatible with dual-plane manifolds, it is usually best to use a single-plane intake with any plate system producing more than 100 hp. There are also plate systems with additional spray bars (usually in a cross or "X" configuration), and some with peripheral discharge orifices machined directly into the spacer plate.

At the high end of the nitrous spectrum, direct port nitrous systems are the choice of serious racers who are coaxing 400 or more additional horsepower from their engine. Direct port nitrous systems are very similar in design concept to multi-point fuel injection systems. Single-stage systems feature eight nitrous/fuel nozzles plumbed directly into the port runners of the intake manifold, usually about 1 inch from the port exit of the manifold. The nitrous/fuel spray is aimed directly into the port opening of the cylinder head, which produces a very responsive system that can be individually adjusted to tune each cylinder as required. For really high flow volumes, two-stage and sometimes even three-stage systems can be plumbed into the manifold, though very few big-blocks really need that much nitrous, or can even handle the power of such systems.

The heart of direct port systems is the nozzle itself, and every manufacturer has a slightly different approach to producing a spray pattern that they feel produces the best fuel atomization and mixture

Edelbrock direct port two-stage nitrous system installed in a Hogan's sheet-metal manifold for spread port heads. Note two nozzles in every intake runner: each stage is capable of adding 400-plus hp, though most racers use a nitrous controller to bring the power on progressively as the car traverses the quarter-mile. (Photo Courtesy Edelbrock)

with the liquid nitrous. Most nozzles are a 90-degree design, whereby the nitrous and fuel exit at right angles to the axis of the nozzle, which makes installation in the intake manifold much easier. Some designs feature an in-line spray pattern, which complicates installation, though some users like the improved flow capability of such a design.

Superchargers

A supercharger is any device that pressurizes the air ingested by an engine to higher than atmospheric levels, so that when the intake valve opens, the air/fuel mixture is forced into the combustion chamber, rather than relying on the pressure differential created by the piston's downward movement to draw it in. As more air and fuel is packed into the combustion chamber, power rises dramatically, and supercharged engines can easily make 30- to 40-percent more power than normally aspirated engines.

At the high end of the scale, competition big-blocks can produce double the power of non-supercharged engines, cranking out more than 2,000 hp. Of course, this puts far more stress on all of the engine's components, so building an engine strong enough to survive the power generated by supercharging is a critical step in planning a boosted engine's construction. Steel four-bolt main caps and aluminum connecting rods are standard fare for supercharged engines, and at the high end of the scale, Unlimited class racers use billet aluminum engine blocks with cross-bolted mains and billet steel cranks to survive the pounding of 2,000-plus hp.

All superchargers increase the dynamic compression ratio of the engine, so static compression ratios must be lower than non-boosted engines of similar configuration. This works out well when using small street-type blowers on cars with about 8:1 compression, except that most of those engines come with cast pistons that do not hold up well with the additional power. Forged pistons are a must in supercharged engines, and fuels with a higher octane rating. Some aftermarket companies offer water/alcohol injection systems designed specifically to eliminate detonation when using unleaded pump gas in supercharged engines.

Like all performance parts for your big-block, there are many different sizes and options when it comes to selecting the right supercharger for your engine, so contact the manufacturer of your choice for their recommendations.

There are three types of superchargers available for your Rat motor: positive displacement superchargers, mechanically driven centrifugal superchargers, and turbochargers.

Positive Displacement Superchargers (Blowers)

The GMC-style positive displacement Roots blower was originally designed to pump fresh air into coal mines, and adapted to large truck engines produced by GMC. Early hot rodders began mounting them on their engines. The nomenclature 6-71, 8-71, etc., refers to their original application on truck engines. A 6-71 blower was designed for a six-cylinder Diesel, with each cylinder displacing 71 ci.

A positive displacement blower is really a pretty simple piece of machinery comprised of two interlocking impellers and a case with end plates to hold the impeller bearings and gears that spin them. As the interlocking three-lobe impellers rotate, air is trapped between the impeller and the case on the inlet side of the blower. When the lobes mesh at the bottom of the blower, the air is positively forced out of the blower and into the intake manifold. The impellers are turned by a pulley and large cogged belt, usually 3 inches wide, which is driven by a pulley attached to the crankshaft. Most big-block cranks for blown engines have two large keyways to prevent the harmonic dampener or blower hub from shearing off the stock single woodruff key. An adjustable idler pulley keeps the belt tension just right, which means not too tight.

One of the first rookie mistakes a new blower owner can make is to adjust the belt with tension on it, as with a fan belt. As the engine gets hot, the growth of the block, heads, and manifold overstretches the belt, either breaking the belt or wiping out the bearings. The speed that the blower turns relative to the engine speed is dictated by the size of the crank pulley and the blower pulley. A larger crank pulley or smaller blower pulley spins the blower faster, thus creating more boost pressure, and vice-versa. If both pulleys have the same number of teeth, the blower is driven 1-to-1.

Typical street blowers are set up to generate 5 to 7 psi of boost, while competition blowers may be tuned to deliver 25 psi or more. Note that normal atmospheric pressure is 14.7 psi, and some manufacturers state blower boost in "atmospheres," i.e., 1 atmosphere = 14.7 pounds of boost.

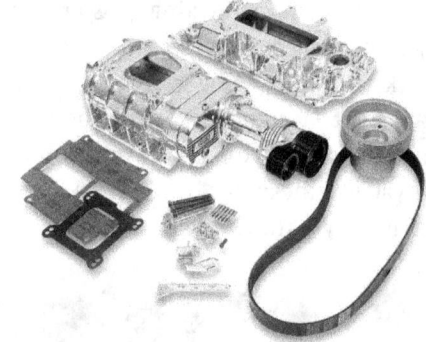

Weiand 174 Series low-profile supercharger kit is engineered to provide 25- to 40-percent more power on mild street big-blocks with a single 4-barrel carb. Overall height is just 8.25 inches. (Photo Courtesy Weiand)

INDUCTION SYSTEMS

Weiand 6-71 blower topped with two Holley carbs is big, obnoxious, noisy, and moves a lot of air—exactly what you want for a no-compromise, take-no-prisoners radical street and strip or race-only big-block. This one has nitrous too. If some is good, more is better, and too much is just right.

This 6-71 blower is topped with a Hilborn fuel injector hat. Boat guys love blowers, maybe because there are no speed limit signs once you get past the marina. This flat-bottom speedboat gives new meaning to the advice "hang on to your hat."

Some manufacturers offer relatively small blowers specifically designed for street applications, such as the Weiand 177 series. These units are usually low enough to fit under stock hoods or hoods with a modest scoop, and have a carb mount pad to accept a single carburetor. Their smaller displacement reduces load on the crankshaft and the rest of the engine, and they offer a solid increase in power at normal street RPM ranges.

The larger 6-71 and 8-71 pattern blowers are big, obnoxious, noisy, and move a lot of air—exactly what you want for a no-compromise, take-no-prisoners radical street and strip or race-only big-block. They are typically topped with a pair of 4-barrel carburetors or a mechanical fuel injection system such as those offered by Enderle, Crower, and Hilborn. Blower Drive Service (BDS) specializes in GMC-style superchargers, offering an electronic fuel injection system specifically designed for use with its blowers.

While other types of superchargers are designed to move dry air only, blowers are perfectly happy ingesting the air/fuel mixture and the fuel helps to seal the impellers to the case more efficiently. However, since the blower is filled with a combustible mixture of air and fuel, a simple backfire can cause it to explode, so proper tuning of a blown engine is very important. Many street blowers have pop-off valves in the blower manifold to relieve excessive pressure from over-boosting or backfires, and competition blowers must be mounted to the intake manifold with aluminum studs that are designed to shear off in the event of a serious backfire, thus saving the blower from catastrophic damage.

Centrifugal Superchargers

Centrifugal superchargers are belt-drive rotary blowers. The compressor turbine is similar to those used in turbocharged engines, but is driven by a belt from a crankshaft pulley, similar to the GMC-style blowers. While a turbo uses exhaust gases to spin the turbine to 50,000 rpm or more, centrifugal blowers use internal gears to multiply the pulley RPM by 5 or 6 to generate as much as 30 psi of boost in race trim. Centrifugal blowers have less parasitic drag on the engine than positive displacement blowers and usually are driven with serpentine belts, although high-output racing versions resort to a cogged belt to eliminate slippage.

Another one of the virtues of centrifugal blowers is that, because of their remote mounting location, the pressurized output can be routed through an intercooler before feeding the engine, and the cooler inlet charge has much

Cutaway view of the ProCharger F-3 centrifugal supercharger showing the 7075 T-6 billet aluminum impellers and 5.10 to 6.24 step-up gears. The housing is machine from 6061 billet aluminum and the drive system uses either an 8- or 14-mm cogged belt. This unit is capable of generating more than 22 pounds of boost, and has made as much as 2,600 hp from a 565-ci big-block. (Photo Courtesy ProCharger)

 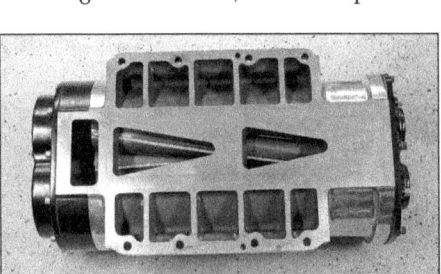

Blower Drive Service 14-71 blower with Air-Lock rotors that reduce internal temperatures compared to original GMC-style rotors. Heat build-up is a major concern with positive displacement superchargers; a cooler charge makes more power. Bottom of the blower (right) reveals unique outlet design to provide a more even distribution of the air/fuel mixture into the intake manifold.

more power potential than the hot compressed air from a positive displacement supercharger.

Turbochargers

Turbochargers have been a part of the automotive racing scene for decades, typically used on small-displacement engines in cars that turn left and right. That stigma has kept turbos from being used as a viable form of supercharging for big-block Chevys in the past. In the late 1960s and early 1970s, some brave souls experimented with turbos on Unlimited class big-block drag race cars, but problems with turbo lag kept them from being competitive in an environment where instant throttle response is crucial. Turbo lag is the delay in throttle response caused by the fact that turbos use engine exhaust heat and pressure to spin the compressor section, so they don't produce boost until the exhaust flow increases as a result of wide-open throttle.

That was then, this is now. Modern electronic engine management systems are capable of altering fuel and spark curves to largely eliminate turbo lag, typically by dumping in excess fuel and retarding the timing when the TPS (throttle position sensor) senses sudden throttle opening, or by using an external signal from the transbrake button on drag racing cars with an automatic transmission. The extreme heat from too much fuel and too little spark advance really gets the turbo spinning in a hurry, so "spool up" time is much quicker. Modern competition turbocharged big-blocks typically use twin turbos, one attached to each exhaust header, and many are capable of exceeding 2,000 hp in race trim.

Since turbos are driven by engine exhaust, some proponents of "hairdryers" claim that turbos produce free boost, but that is not entirely true, since the exhaust flow restriction is very high. As with any supercharged engine, that makes camshaft selection extremely important with a turbocharged engine. Typical lobe separation angles are wider than normal to reduce valve overlap, and the exhaust lift curve must be carefully tailored to the application. Intake timing can be more conservative, since boost on the intake side quickly fills the cylinder with less lift and duration than a normally aspirated engine requires.

Extreme exhaust temperatures require stainless steel headers, and a waste gate must be used to bleed off exhaust flow to the turbo when boost pressure is too high. On the pressure side of the turbo, blow-off valves are also necessary to relieve excessive inlet pressure when the throttle is suddenly closed and the turbine blades are still spinning at up to 100,000 rpm.

One of the most important components of competitive turbo systems is the intercooler, which is similar in construction and principle to a large radiator. Also known as heat exchangers, they simply cool the very hot pressurized air from the turbocharger before routing it into the engine, which not only produces a denser intake charge, it also lessens the chance of detonation in the combustion chamber. Intercoolers are just as important on any street-driven turbo car, since unleaded pump gas has a relatively low octane rating and little resistance to detonation with high dynamic compression ratios.

One of the reasons you don't see more turbocharged big-blocks on the street is because they require so much custom plumbing to integrate the turbocharger with a specific vehicle. Stainless steel headers, a custom exhaust system, custom bent inlet tubing and intercooler, and specialized engine fuel and spark management systems make it difficult to package everything you need in a "turbo kit" for your 1968 Camaro with a Rat motor. Turbo manufacturers like Garret and Turbonetics offer excellent products with decades of product development and application experience, but you need to find a shop that really knows the score to piece everything together for you.

This big-block 1968 Camaro drag car uses a massive ProCharger centrifugal supercharger and EFI to push it into the 6-second zone in the quarter-mile. (Photo Courtesy ProCharger)

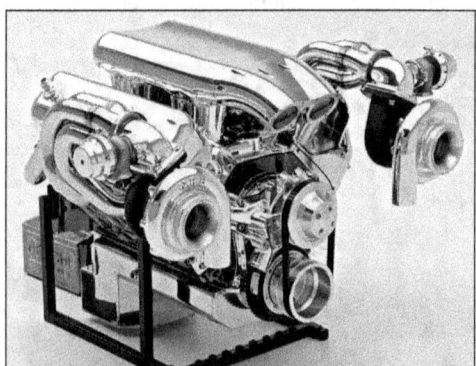

Nelson Racing Engines builds what might be described as the most beautiful, most powerful street engines anywhere. The Twin Turbo 572-ci "Daily Driver" series uses two 76-mm Turbonetics tangential turbos with intercoolers and lots of NRE components, including the unique Alien billet-aluminum intake manifold. The intake boasts two injectors per cylinder: one for pump gas, and one for race gas fed from a separate tank. It makes 1,190 hp on pump gas and 1,600 horses with race gas. That'll get you to the grocery store in a hurry. (Photo Courtesy Nelson Racing Engines)

CHAPTER 8

EXHAUST SYSTEMS

Bigger carbs, manifolds, heads, and cams all are designed to let the engine take in as much air and fuel as possible, but the byproducts of combustion must be vacated quickly to make room for more of the good stuff (fresh air and fuel) on the next intake stroke. So why not just bolt on the biggest exhaust headers (in terms of primary tube diameter) with the largest collector you can find, and call it good? If 2½-inch tailpipes are good and 3-inch pipes are better, then why not go to 4-inch pipes? Heck, let's try 5-inch tailpipes. Import guys seem to think their four-banger engines need 'em, so why shouldn't we? If you answered "to keep the exhaust flow velocity up," that's correct, but why does velocity matter?

Remember, the only event that actually produces power in your four-stroke engine is the power stroke, so how can the exhaust system create more cylinder pressure on the piston top? The key to this riddle is the effect that the exhaust gas flow has on the intake flow during valve overlap, the time when both exhaust and intake valves are open. If not for valve overlap, the bigger the exhaust pipe the better; just dump out all of that nasty combustion residue and be done with it. But because of valve overlap, a properly tuned exhaust system actually helps to activate the intake flow earlier in the cycle due to the scavenging effect of the exhaust gases flowing out the exhaust valve. With a header that is too large for the size of your engine and RPM range you need, all of the exhaust gases indeed get dumped out quickly; so quickly that there is little or nothing left to help pull in fresh air and fuel when the intake valve opens. As engine speed increases, even the larger header pipes have some amount of residual flow during valve overlap, which is why high-RPM racing engines are best served with larger header sizes.

OEM Exhaust Manifolds

Enough theory; let's talk nuts and bolts. All production big-blocks use cast-iron exhaust manifolds, which are little more than sturdy chambers with four short legs attached to each exhaust port

Equal length four-into-one headers help to extract maximum power from a big-block.

CHAPTER 8

exit, dumping into a head pipe with a three-bolt flange. The primary virtue of cast-iron exhaust manifolds is that they are durable, and the heavy casting does a good job of dampening exhaust noise, a major consideration for your aunt Matilda.

Tubular Headers

Headers are frequently the first and most cost-effective performance upgrade that most gearheads make to their vehicle, and the more power your big-block is capable of, the greater the need for an exhaust system that matches the other performance parts in the engine. Most tubular exhaust headers are a four-into-one design, meaning that four individual primary tubes (one for each cylinder on that side of the engine) merge into a single collector. Street-driven vehicles also must have exhaust pipes that are typically 2½ or 3 inches in diameter feeding two low-restriction mufflers. Most street headers have primary tube sizes of 1¾ inches or 2 inches dumping into a 3- or 3½-inch collector, and typical competition headers start with 2¼-inch primaries feeding a 4-inch collector and go up from there, depending of the size of that monster mill under your hood.

Some competition headers feature a stepped design, where primary pipe diameter is increased before each pipe enters the collector, typically from 2¼ to 2⅜ inches, or 2⅜ to 2½ inches. The stepped design is said to minimize reversion, which is a negative pressure wave that travels back up the header pipe after the initial exhaust pulse exits the primary tube. If the pipe length is just right, the timing of these pulses serve to help pull along the next exhaust pulse for a super scavenging affect; motorcycle racers refer to this as being "on the pipe." Not all racing engine builders embrace the stepped header design, pointing out that the increasing diameter also slows the exhaust gas velocity.

The primary pipe diameter must be large enough to accommodate the volume of exhaust flow, so a larger displacement or an improvement in the volumetric efficiency of the engine calls for an increase in the diameter of the pipe, while primary pipe length is dictated by engine RPM; a short pipe becomes resonant at a higher frequency (thus a higher RPM) than a longer pipe.

Competition headers should have equal length primary tubes, usually from 28 to 30 inches long, so that all eight cylinders produce their peak power at the same RPM. Street headers may have a vast difference in primary pipe length due to cramped engine compartments, manufacturing considerations, and other variables. It's really not that big a deal for most street applications, since the exhaust must be routed through tailpipes and mufflers anyway, which tends to negate the advantages of true equal length headers.

A variation of this theme was popular some time ago with the design of tri-Y headers, in which each pair of primary tubes are joined in a "Y" connection, and those two pipes are then joined in a similar "Y" connection at the collector. This design is excellent for producing good power at relatively low engine speeds, and could be just the ticket for tow trucks, RVs, or other low-speed, high-torque applications. A variation of the tri-Y design is the 4-2-1 header collector offered by some manufacturers. It joins each pair of primary tubes into a two-into-one connection; then those two pipes are merged into the final collector. While it is an interesting approach to exhaust tuning, it has not found favor with most professional-level racers.

Most tubular exhaust headers are made from mild steel, though more expensive sets are often manufactured from stainless steel for its better strength, corrosion resistance, lower coefficient of thermal conductivity, and appearance. Many companies offer high-temperature coatings, usually a ceramic-based chemical, for their mild steel tubes. When properly applied, these coatings offer complete protection from corrosion and act as a thermal barrier to reduce the heat

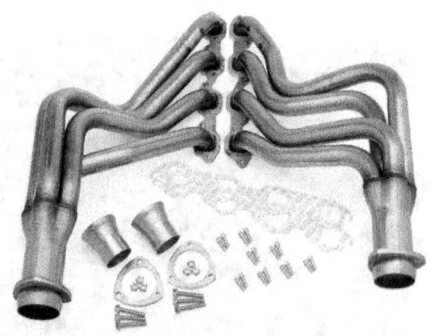

A good set of headers is often the first and most cost-effective modification you can make to your big-block Chevy. This 304 stainless steel Hedman Hedder has 1¾-inch primary pipes dumping into 3-inch collectors. It fits first-generation Camaros and Novas, and is also available in painted or coated mild steel. (Photo Courtesy Hedman)

Many companies offer high-temperature ceramic-based coatings that offer complete protection from corrosion and act as a thermal barrier to reduce the heat radiated from the pipes. (Photo Courtesy Hedman)

radiated from the pipes. Also, header pipe diameters are measured on the outside, so the internal dimensions are smaller by the wall thickness. Most bargain-priced headers use 18-gauge steel, while more expensive sets may go up to 14 gauge.

Competition headers lead a pampered life compared to their street-driven compadres; so many racing headers are also made from 18-gauge tubing to reduce weight. The thickness of the header flange where it bolts to the cylinder heads can be as thin as 1/4 inch or as heavy as 3/8 inch for the more pricey headers. Thicker flanges are always better since they are less likely to bend and distort while tightening, and they offer a better gasket seal and longer life. You can improve the chances of gasket survival by regularly re-tightening the header bolts, since high heat and vibration tend to loosen them.

Mufflers and Exhaust Pipes

All street cars and some competition cars have to be equipped with noise-reducing mufflers, and the aftermarket performance industry has responded with an impressive selection of high-flow mufflers and exhaust systems. Today's selection of performance mufflers have evolved into scientifically designed sound-reducing chambers with baffles, sound wave deflection chambers, unequal length passages to reduce or cancel harmonic resonance, and other advanced engineering features. Some still incorporate perforated steel passages with a packing material to absorb sound waves, while others rely on solid steel construction with no packing material that might blow out.

Typical performance mufflers for your big-block feature 2½- or 3-inch inlets and outlets; racing mufflers are available up to 5 inches in inlet/outlet sizes. For best performance, the entire exhaust system should match the diameter of the mufflers' inlet and outlet. The minimum size for any big-block is 2½ inches, and that is on the small side. Serious street performance big-blocks need 3-inch pipes and mufflers.

A crossover tube between the left and right banks of your exhaust system is beneficial for both more power and quieter operation. Traditionally, the cross-over tube is placed behind the header collectors and in front of the mufflers in an "H" pipe configuration, but many more modern systems use an "X" configuration where each head pipe is curved inward to meet its mate from the other side, with a substantial opening where the two are welded together. When a single pulse from one side of the engine exits the header collector and heads toward the mufflers, it now has two low-pressure passages available: one from the muffler straight ahead, and one from the crossover pipe leading to the other bank of the exhaust system. Because the flow path through the crossover is a little longer than the flow path to the muffler on the same side as the header, the split pulse exits the two tailpipes at different times, and you hear a higher frequency with less booming and harmonic resonance than an isolated dual exhaust produces.

An Exhausting Summary

The majority of street performance big-blocks are miles ahead with even a modest set of tubular exhaust headers dumping into 3-inch pipes and mufflers, again with a crossover pipe. Two-inch primary tubes provide excellent power for most high-performance street engines and support more than 550 hp, if that's what your Rat motor is capable of producing. Larger diameter exhaust pipes not only flow more, they are also louder, so if your objective is to build a "stealth" street machine, don't go too large on the exhaust pipe size; 2½-inch pipes may be best.

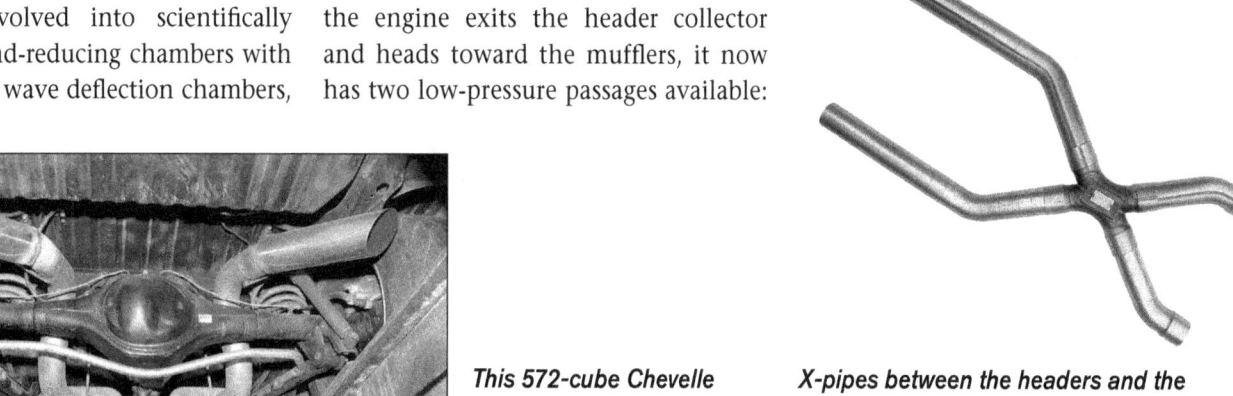

This 572-cube Chevelle uses two 3-inch Flowmaster mufflers and 3-inch mandrel-bent pipes to evacuate the exhaust from 620 hp.

X-pipes between the headers and the mufflers improve the flow capacity of the exhaust system and tame-down annoying harmonic vibrations and booming. This Hedman cross-pipe is offered in 2½ and 3-inch sizes. (Photo Courtesy Hedman)

CHAPTER 8

Competition machines usually are allowed to run open headers, and primary tube size starts at 2¼ inches and goes up from there. Consider step headers for large-displacement and/or high-RPM engines, and consult the manufacturer for specific recommendations.

So-called street car racing organizations and classes are really designed for full-on racing vehicles with mufflers, but the good news is that there are competition mufflers and exhaust systems big enough to handle 1,000-plus-hp engines. Several manufacturers offer header collector mufflers that simply replace the existing collector on a set of racing headers.

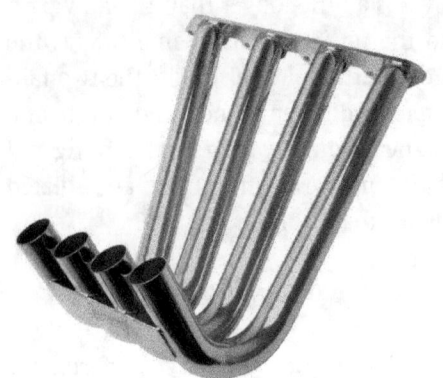

Pan-evacuation kit from Moroso includes the exhaust probes, anti-backfire valves, valve cover breathers, and grommets. (Photo Courtesy Moroso)

Zoomies are the simplest type of competition headers; four individual primary pipes with no collector. They are usually found on the most powerful supercharged engines, and most folks think that they don't have collectors because those engines are so powerful that they don't need the additional mid-range torque that collectors help to generate. That's not true. Of course, tubing diameter and length must still be matched to the engine's flow volume and RPM range for best power.

Serious engines need serious pipes. This all-aluminum Rat motor has spread port heads, sheet-metal intake manifold, and two stages of direct port nitrous. Fabshop 2½-inch headers feed into a merge collector where an O_2 sensor gathers data for tuning.

Pan evacuators take advantage of exhaust flow to create a low-pressure signal to the crankcase breathers in the valve covers, which can be good for as much as 10 more horsepower. Although they have largely fallen out of favor with today's professional racers since belt-driven vacuum pumps are far more efficient, they still offer a good bang for the buck for many Sportsman and Bracket racers. Pan evacuators are only for open exhaust headers and should not be used on street-driven vehicles with mufflers.

These Borla stainless steel race headers have a muffler built into the collector for racing organizations that have maximum noise restrictions. They are also useful in bracket-style drag racing, allowing you to "sneak up" on your competitor if you have the faster car.

CHAPTER 9

IGNITION SYSTEMS

According to some trendy types, you can never be too rich or too thin. If you're a torque wrench-wielding big-block enthusiast, add that you can never have too much ignition power. Today's hot rodder can choose from three basic levels of sophistication for the ignition system:

1. Traditional distributor and a spark box
2. Crank trigger and a spark box (the distributor merely acts as a rotary spark switch to feed the juice to each plug wire)
3. Fully computerized using either a distributor with a cam synch sensor or a crank trigger, which still requires a cam synch sensor and distributor to function as a rotary switch

Ninety percent of you are perfectly served with the first option, especially if the car is driven on the street, and the crank trigger option number-2 is good for the 9 percent of you racing your big-block at the dragstrip with engine speeds up to 8,500 rpm. The computerized system gets the call when you go Unlimited drag racing in classes like NHRA Competition Eliminator or Pro Stock, or if you have an aftermarket EFI induction system.

Distributors, Coils and Spark Plug Wires

Stock big-blocks came with cast-iron Delco-Remy distributors until 1969 (Corvettes until 1974); then the switch was made to aluminum-bodied point distributors. In 1974, the HEI was introduced and was standard issue until computer-controlled EFI systems came out in 1987. The HEI is a unitized distributor with magnetic reluctors to trigger its internal control module and an ignition coil built into the large-diameter cap. It was and still is a very good design for most high-performance big-blocks, offering more precise timing control than point distributors, and the larger cap lessened the possibility of cross-firing with the higher voltage that it generates. The coil-in-cap was changed from the old oil-filled cylindrical design to a more effective

Precision aftermarket distributor and high-quality ignition components ensure that your big-block delivers all the performance it is capable of.

HOW TO BUILD KILLER BIG-BLOCK CHEVY ENGINES

CHAPTER 9

Crank trigger ignition systems offer rock-solid timing stability and are the best choice for drag racing. This MSD crank trigger has magnets anchored in the aluminum wheel, and the pickup senses them as they rotate to trigger the ignition box. Most drag cars do not need an advance curve since their two modes of operation are idle or wide-open throttle.

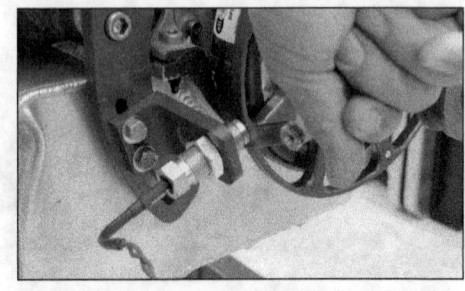

Crank-trigger-wheel-to-sensor gap should be checked any time you loosen or adjust the pickup. The standard gap is .050 inch.

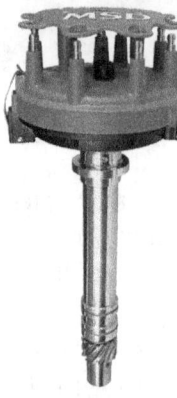

Crank trigger distributors have no advance weights, no pickups, and no wires, except for the plug wires in the cap. They simply act as a rotary switch, directing the high-voltage spark from the coil wire to the appropriate plug wire, and drive the oil pump in a wet sump system. Turning the distributor does not change timing, but it must be phased so that the rotor is pointing at the number-1 spark plug terminal when the ignition fires. Note the bronze gear needed for compatibility with steel roller lifter camshafts. (Photo Courtesy MSD)

Front drive distributors are popular in full-bodied drag cars due to the lack of room at the rear of the engine. They are driven with a small cog belt driven by the camshaft, and are usually designed to work with cam belt drives used in higher-level racing engines. (Photo Courtesy MSD)

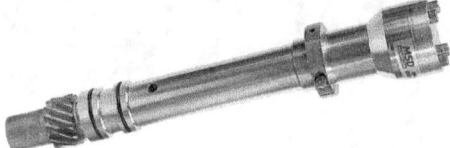

If a front-drive distributor is used on an engine with a wet sump oil system, an oil pump drive must be installed in place of the original distributor. (Photo Courtesy MSD)

Distributor with a cam synch sensor must be used with computerized ignition systems and EFI. (Photo Courtesy MSD)

The HEI is a unitized distributor with magnetic reluctors to trigger its internal control module and an ignition coil built into the large-diameter cap. Note that small-block and big-block Chevy distributors are interchangeable. (Photo Courtesy GMPP)

transformer design, and most modern aftermarket coils have followed suit.

Although General Motors called it a "high energy" ignition system, it did not supply adequate spark intensity to turn more than 5,500 or 6,000 rpm, which is fine for most people, but not for any self-respecting performance enthusiast. Simply removing the stock ignition module and using one of today's modern ignition boxes, like those offered by Accel, Mallory, or MSD (the popular 6-AL), provides all the ignition performance you need until you get into the race-only systems. The downside to this approach is that most old HEI distributors are quite likely mechanically worn out, exhibiting excessive shaft-to-bearing wear, corroded and sticking advance weights, and leaky or sticky vacuum advance canisters.

If your HEI is worn out, you can buy a new version from GMPP or the aftermarket, or switch to an aftermarket distributor with a smaller cap and remote coil. The small-cap distributors are much easier to service when the big factory HEI distributor cap barely clears the firewall, as is the case with most muscle cars.

IGNITION SYSTEMS

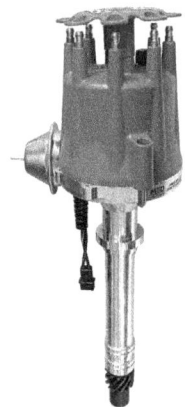

Aftermarket electronic distributors with vacuum advance are ideal for street and strip Rat motors This Street Pro-Billet distributor (PN 8361) from MSD features a small cap for improved firewall clearance. (Photo Courtesy MSD)

OEM wires have very high resistance, but modern high-performance plug wires are designed to cancel EMI (electromagnetic interference) with as little as 50 ohms of resistance per foot. There are several good sources of high-performance plug wires, such as these from MSD (left) and Moroso (right). Check your plug wires with an ohmmeter after you make them, and periodically to make sure they are in good condition. (Photos Courtesy MSD and Moroso)

Spark plug wires are the critical connection from your distributor cap to the plugs, and all modern wires have some amount of electrical resistance to lessen radio frequency (RF) interference with the other electronic circuits in your car. Even racing plug wires need this resistance due to the wide-spread use of sophisticated ignition systems, automatic shifters, data acquisition computers, etc. While stock resistor wires use simple non-metallic conductors to cut down on RF, high-performance wire sets are much more sophisticated. Many use wire wound around a central core to cut down RF interference. "Fat" wires (8.5 and 9 mm are popular) with heat-resistant silicon jackets and other advanced features are a good investment for your high-performance engine.

Ignition Controllers

The ignition box senses the very low current signal from your distributor or crank trigger and amplifies the voltage considerably, sending a powerful current to the coil where it is amplified again to produce 50,000-plus volts to the spark plugs. While the old point distributors sent a 12-volt signal to the coil, some modern ignition boxes send as much as 460 to 580 volts to the coil. Obviously, the coil must be matched to the ignition controller. Many ignition controllers offer options such as rev limiting to

The MSD Digital-6 Plus features a two-step rev limiter, start retard, and a high-speed retard that is useful with nitrous. (Photo Courtesy MSD)

MSD 6AL (left) and 6AL-2 (right) ignition boxes are classic choices for high-performance big-blocks, offering multiple sparks at lower RPM and ample voltage for high-RPM power. The 6AL has a rev limiter that accepts various RPM chips, and the 6AL-2 has a two-step rev limiter that is useful for controlling launch RPM on the drag strip. (Photos Courtesy MSD)

HVC coil uses an E-core winding design to produce high voltage with high current with any of MSD's 7- or 8-series professional racing ignitions. (Photo Courtesy MSD)

Advance Curves and Timing

Most performance distributors come with a good curve designed into them, or are adjustable to suit your needs. If you are upgrading a stock Delco-Remy or HEI distributor, there are plenty of curve kits on the market with a variety of springs, weights, and stop bushings to tailor your distributor to your needs. So what should your curve be? The answer is that different engines and vehicles, as well as different driving styles, all require a different advance curve, but there are some basic concepts that help you zero-in on the right curve.

The spark plug must be fired before TDC because it takes time for the air/fuel mixture in your combustion chamber to burn, and the ideal amount of spark advance produces maximum combustion pressure when your piston and connecting rod have the greatest leverage angle on the crankshaft. Spark advance is most influenced by three factors: the efficiency of your combustion chamber design, the burn rate of your air/fuel mixture, and the load on the engine. Remember that the combustion chamber is more than just that cavity in your cylinder head; the floor of the combustion chamber is your piston top, and domed pistons require more spark advance than flat top pistons since the flame front has to "climb over" the dome.

Efficiency

Here's the first general rule regarding ignition advance: the more efficient your combustion chamber design, the less spark advance is required. Typical open-chamber racing engines with high-octane fuel should run best with total ignition timing of 32 to 36 degrees of advance. Closed chamber heads on a similar engine usually need about 40 degrees of timing advance, and super-efficient spread port heads with small chambers and flat top pistons typically only need 28 to 30 degrees, sometimes less if it's a really good engine.

These figures are all based upon the use of high-octane racing fuels, and assume that the air/fuel ratio is correct. Typical drag racing engines are only operated at idle or wide-open throttle, so part throttle and cruise timing are not a factor. No advance curve is generally needed, as evidenced by the fact that crank trigger wheels offer no spark advance curve, yet their on-track performance is perfect for drag racing. The only caveat to this rule is that less than full advance makes it easier to start these engines without kickback, which damages or breaks your starter and ring gear on the flywheel/flexplate. Most competition ignition boxes have a start retard feature.

Burn Rate

The second general rule in determining total timing concerns the air/fuel ratio. If your fuel mixture is excessively rich, it takes longer to burn in the chamber so ignition advance must be increased. Conversely, a mixture that is too lean burns with explosive combustion speed, and detonation can occur, which quickly damages your pistons, rings, and bearings. Retarded timing cures the symptom (detonation), but to cure the cause you need to richen the air/fuel mixture.

Engine Load

The third general rule is that higher engine loads reduce the amount of timing an engine tolerates, so total timing is limited to what your engine accepts in high gear, when it is working the hardest. This is why computerized systems can be programmed to provide different advance curves in each gear for optimum performance on the drag strip.

Street-driven cars running on unleaded fuel do need advance curves due to the wide variety of operating conditions on the street. The centrifugal curve is controlled by movable weights and springs, which simply increase timing as the engine speed increases. A vacuum canister provides more spark advance under light throttle conditions, such as steady-state cruise or idle, which pays dividends of better fuel economy and less carbon build-up in the combustion chamber.

Procedure

To work up the curves in a street car, check your mechanical advance mechanism with a timing light (vacuum advance disconnected) to determine at what RPM total advanced is achieved, and set the total timing to a conservative number, say, about 30 degrees. Disconnect the vacuum advance hose from the distributor and plug it to prevent a vacuum leak. Find a long stretch of deserted highway to conduct your timing tests, and gradually bring the engine speed in high gear up to the RPM that gives you total advance (typically around 2,000 to 2,500 rpm), then stand on the throttle. If you have a fully automatic transmission, you have to unhook the kick-down linkage at the carburetor to keep the tranny in high gear.

If the engine starts to "rattle," you're already over-advanced, so back out of the throttle before you hurt the motor. Repeat the test, but this time gradually increase engine speed by 500 rpm and see if the rattle disappears at the higher speed. If not,

IGNITION SYSTEMS

reduce total timing and test again. If it does disappear, this is the RPM for your total mechanical advance. Heavier springs in the distributor delay maximum timing, and lighter springs bring it in sooner. With a few test runs, you should be able to determine exactly what RPM your engine can take full advance, and what total timing gives the best results.

After you've finalized the mechanical advance, hook up the vacuum advance and test to make sure that part throttle acceleration does not produce detonation. If it does, you need to limit the vacuum advance, or disconnect it.

Checking total timing requires a harmonic dampener that is marked up to at least 45 degrees, which is standard on all aftermarket dampeners. You can buy timing tapes for your stock dampener, too.

Distributor curve kits, like this one from TransDapt, include advance weights, different springs, bushings, and a new mechanical advance cam. (Photo Courtesy TransDapt)

Checking total timing requires a harmonic dampener with degree markings.

prevent engine damage from a missed shift or broken drivetrain components, start retard to ease the load on your starter, and even digital ignition curves to replace the mechanical weights and springs in your distributor.

Spark Plugs

The early cast-iron and all-aluminum heads used 3/4-inch-reach gasketed spark plugs with a 13/16-inch hex, while most 1970-and-later iron heads switched to the smaller taper seat "peanut" plugs with a 5/8-inch hex. Many gearheads use anti-seize compound on the plugs in aluminum heads. Some spark plug experts say that anti-seize should not be used because it inhibits the plug's ability to conduct heat away from the combustion chamber, but I've been using it for years and my motors didn't know they weren't supposed to like it. Whatever you use, make sure that the plug threads are lubricated, especially with aluminum heads.

With high-compression domed pistons, it's important to index the plugs so that the electrode is in the upper half of the chamber when tightened, to avoid contact with the piston. Use a felt-tip marker to indicate the electrode's position on the porcelain and keep switching the plugs around until all eight have the mark facing away from the piston domes. Moroso offers a plug indexing kit with copper gaskets of various thicknesses to help get all eight plugs pointing in the right direction, but these affect the heat range of the plug and should not be used unless absolutely necessary to get proper indexing. High-compression ratios and high-RPM operation requires plugs with a colder than stock heat range, and most competition engines should not use extended tip plugs, which are used on stock engines to extend the service life of the plug.

A typical plug gap is .035 inch, though some HEI systems fire with gaps up to .045 inch, producing a hotter spark. Very high compression ratios may require reducing the gap to .025 inch. Defective spark plugs are rare, but it does occur. Checking for high internal resistance with an ohmmeter before you install them is always a good idea.

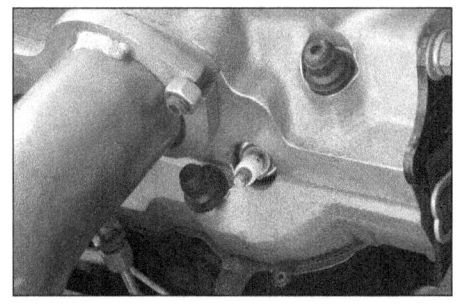

With high-compression domed pistons, spark plugs should be installed so that the electrode faces up, away from the piston when seated.

CHAPTER 9

Moroso offers plug indexing washers of various thicknesses to help you obtain the desired electrode orientation. These are for tapered seat plugs. (Photo Courtesy Moroso)

You should check with the manufacturer for recommendations, but spark plugs recommended as either stock replacement or by aftermarket cylinder head manufacturers for typical applications. At right is a list of some.

Batteries and Cables

If you relocate the battery to the trunk for better weight distribution, make sure to use larger-than-stock gauge cables to compensate for the extra length, and run a separate ground cable from the battery to the engine block, as well as to the chassis. Heavy-gauge battery cables are available from Meziere Enterprises, Painless Performance, and other sources. Twelve-volt automotive systems are actually designed to work with 14.7 volts supplied by the alternator, so if you are running a drag race car with no alternator, I highly recommend the use of a 16-volt battery like the TurboStart by Axion Power. The 16-volt batteries are compatible with all aftermarket ignition systems and starters, and there are resistors available to drop the current to 12 volts for sensitive electronic devices, such as throttle controllers or the ECU for computer-controlled EFI systems. TurboStart 16-volt batteries with a third 12-volt terminal are also available for the same purpose.

Choosing Spark Plugs

Usage	Spark Plugs
Stock replacement	3/4-inch gasketed: NGK BR5ES, GR5; Champion RN14YC; AC 44XL
	Tapered seat: AC R44TS, R44T, Champion RV17YC
High-performance street, pump gas	3/4-inch gasketed: NGK BR8ES; Champion RN12YC, RC12YC; AC 43XL; Autolite 3935
	Tapered seat: AC R43TS, R43T, Champion RV12YC
Competition, high-compression with race gas	3/4-inch gasketed: NGK R5671A-8, NGK R5671A-9, Champion C59C, C57C, C55C, AC R42T, Autolite 3932
	Tapered seat: AC R42T, Champion V57C

Spark plugs for high-performance and competition big-blocks run much colder than stock plugs; note that none of these have a projected tip, which is used to provide long service life on street engines. Left to right: NGK R5671-A9, NGK B8ES, Champion N5C, Champion BL57 with a tapered seat, and Autolite AR 3932. The Champion N series and the NGK B series have a 13/16-inch hex; all others are 5/8 inch. Pre-1970 big-block heads were machined for the larger 13/16-inch plugs, but they do not fit later cylinder heads or most aftermarket heads. The Champion C series or NGK R56 series work in early or late heads, and provide additional clearance with headers.

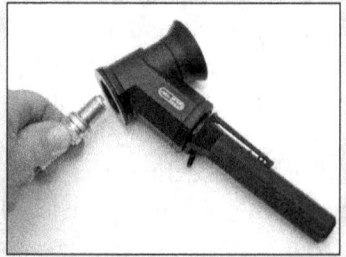

A lighted plug inspection tool reveals any problems, such as aluminum specs on the insulator from melted piston tops, and the location of the "fire ring" where the color changes inside the plug. Reading plugs is a science in itself, and is complicated by high energy ignitions and fuels with different properties.

On any drag race car without a charging system, a 16-volt battery like the TurboStart is highly recommended. They are available in full size and lightweight models, and require a dedicated 16-volt battery charger. Although charging between rounds is always a good idea, you can race an entire day at the drags without charging if necessary. (Photo Courtesy Axion Power)

CHAPTER 10

COOLING SYSTEMS

You may be building a hot rod to serve as a home for your big-block powerplant, but for maximum performance you have to keep your cool. An overheated engine can have far more serious consequences than just an embarrassing stop along the roadside to let things cool off—blown head gaskets, burned or tuliped valves, scuffed bores, and burnished piston rings are all possible if you keep driving when the temp gauge gets to the far side of "H." The cooling system is usually the last thing on any performance enthusiast's list of things to upgrade, but if you design and execute your system with a bit of forethought and knowledge, it does more than just keep you from overheating while cruising the local car show; it helps your Rat motor make more power.

I again reference the Kings of Carbureted Big-Blocks, NHRA Pro Stock racers, to illustrate the value of proper engine cooling. Pro Stock racers do everything in their power to keep the engine cool before an assault on the quarter-mile. They use heat exchangers and portable refrigeration units in the pits to bring water temperatures down to 50 or 60 degrees F before each pass, and only run the engine long enough to drive it to the staging lanes, as required by the rules.

It's an old wives' tale (more likely an old husbands' tale) that your engine has to be thoroughly warmed up to make maximum horsepower. That used to be true when all cars had stock carburetors that were jetted as lean as possible for best fuel economy, and before the introduction of synthetic motor oils. A cold engine requires a richer air/fuel ratio than a hot one, and that's why street carburetors have chokes. The purpose of a choke is to richen the air/fuel mixture, and blade-type chokes do this by restricting the amount of air ingested. Low-speed drivability is poor only because the carb is tuned for the proper air/fuel ratio when the engine is thoroughly warmed up. Modern high-performance and racing carbs are calibrated richer than stock, and EFI systems have coolant temperature sensors that richen the fuel delivery when temps are low.

Conventional motor oils are thick when they are cold, and the spinning crank and other internal engine parts have to wade through a pool of this thick liquid in the crankcase, so that warm, thinned oil offers less resistance than cold oil.

Synthetic motor oils can provide the lubrication necessary for even the most powerful big-blocks with much less viscosity, which reduces the parasitic drag on engine components. Less drag, combined with superior lubrication properties, make synthetics the oil of choice for any professional racer, (after proper engine break-in with conventional oil), and synthetic oils don't need to be "hot" to yield maximum power from your Rat motor.

There is no such thing as keeping the engine "too cool" for best performance, so let's look at how your cooling system can be designed to meet that challenge.

(Photo Courtesy Be Cool)

CHAPTER 10

Water Pumps

Big-block Chevy water pumps were produced in two lengths, short and long. Short-style pumps were used in passenger cars through 1968 and in Corvettes through 1974, while light-duty trucks had them until 1972. Long-style pumps were all standard rotation until 1988, when the serpentine drive belts were introduced. Serpentine belts rotate the water pump in a counter-clockwise direction, so the water pump impellers are curved the opposite direction of standard rotation pumps. If you are going to use one of the aftermarket billet aluminum serpentine belt pulley sets, you must switch to a reverse-rotation pump from a 1988-or-newer big-block.

Many aftermarket water pumps are more than just lightweight versions of the stock pump. They flow more water at a higher pressure and are able to cool your hot Rat motor better than the stock pump.

Electric water pumps offer several benefits for drag racing. First of all, they eliminate water pump drag on your engine. This may be as much as 15 hp, depending on the pump and pulley system used. The biggest advantage of electric pumps is that the engine does not have to be running to cool off after a pass down the quarter-mile, when temperatures are at their highest. Shut the engine off, leave the electric pump and fans running, and you'll be ready for the next round of eliminations in a few minutes.

Most street cars use belt-driven water pumps, and the stock Chevy crankshaft and water pump pulleys work fine if you already have them. If you're piecing your big-block together, it may be easier to find matching pulleys from the aftermarket industry. Companies like Billet Specialties, March, Moroso, and Tru Trac all offer aluminum pulleys for the big-block Chevy. Remember to use a reverse-rotation water pump if you go with one of the serpentine belt systems.

This Edelbrock short-style water pump fits early muscle cars and 1969–1970 Corvettes, and offers improved cooling along with less weight. Edelbrock pumps are available as-cast, polished, or with their chrome-like EnduraShine finish for you show-and-shine guys. (Photo Courtesy Edelbrock)

When you make more power, you need an improved cooling system. Many good aluminum radiators are available from the aftermarket. Be Cool offers a line of original replacement aluminum radiators that drop right into your big-block muscle car. They are even painted black to disguise their alloy origins from unsuspecting onlookers. (Photo Courtesy Be Cool)

Here you can see a Be Cool aluminum dragster radiator mounted horizontally behind a 555-cube Rat motor. Because the radiator is not at the highest point in the cooling system, water filling is accomplished with a Moroso extended fill tube bolted to the waterneck pad on the intake manifold. A Meziere billet aluminum electric water pump bolted to the front of the engine handles coolant circulation.

Tru Trac billet-aluminum pulley and bracket kit adds a lot of class to this 572-ci big-block in a 1969 El Camino. Serpentine belt requires the use of a reverse-rotation water pump for a 1988-and-newer engine.

This CSR billet aluminum electric water pump is mounted on the front of a 565-ci drag racing big-block.

CHAPTER 11

Gaskets and Fasteners

In a high-performance engine, the gaskets and hardware are the soldiers on the front line of power production. Your $6,000 CNC-ported cylinder heads aren't going to make enough power to pull a fat kid off a tricycle if the head gaskets can't handle the pressure of combustion, and your high-dollar aluminum engine block is soon going to be ventilated if the connecting rod bolts decide to take a break (pardon the pun).

Of course there's no such thing as parts that are too good for your engine, but the fact is you can get away with budget bolts and gaskets for certain parts of your Rat motor, but the cylinder heads, rotating assembly, and valvetrain are not among them. Even if your intake manifold is happy with hardware store Grade-5 bolts, you are going to be happier with precision reduced-head or 12-point manifold bolts that are designed for proper tool clearance when it comes time to snug them down.

Cylinder Head Gaskets

Head gaskets are the most important gaskets in your engine; they have the responsibility of sealing very high combustion chamber pressures. Any leakage does not only reduce your power output, it also quickly leads to expensive damage

Good gaskets and fasteners are critical to proper power production from your engine.

Stainless steel 3/8-inch 12-point head intake bolts provide clearance for a box-end wrench with aftermarket intake manifolds. Stock 9/16-inch head bolts might not fit, and you couldn't get anything other than an open-end wrench on them. Some big-block intake manifold bolts line up with the intake pushrods, and if the bolt is too long it hits the pushrod. You need to visually check bolt-to-pushrod clearance on your engine.

HOW TO BUILD KILLER BIG-BLOCK CHEVY ENGINES

CHAPTER 11

This Mark IV block has been O-ringed with stainless steel wire around each bore for use with copper head gaskets.

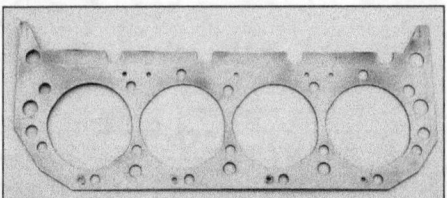

Copper head gaskets are extremely tough—able to seal supercharged and nitrous race engines. They are available in custom configurations for just about any block and head combination you can come up with.

Fel-Pro Perma Torque gasket (PN 1027) for Mark IV blocks has a 4.370-inch bore and is .039 inch thick with a pre-flattened copper wire around the combustion chamber. It's a good choice for 454 and smaller engines with aluminum heads.

to the head and/or block from the hot exhaust gases eroding away the deck surfaces with cutting-torch temperatures.

Other than proper gasket selection, the most important factor in achieving a good head gasket seal is that both the block and head deck surfaces be clean and flat. Standard specs call for no more than .0025 inch of warpage, and some gaskets require even less run-out. Additionally, some gaskets require a specific surface finish, or RA (roughness average), for a proper seal. This is especially critical with iron block/aluminum head combinations because of the different rates of expansion as the two dissimilar metals heat up.

There are three general types of head gaskets: solid metal (included embossed

Fel-Pro Perma Torque gasket PN 1093 is designed for large-bore engines with aftermarket cylinder heads. It is .051 inch thick and has a pre-flattened steel ring around the combustion chamber.

steel and dead-soft copper), composition, and multi-layered steel (MLS).

Embossed steel shim gaskets should only be used on cast-iron blocks with cast-iron heads. The best thing about steel shim gaskets is that they are thin, usually around .020 inch compared to the stock gasket's thickness of about .040 inch, and represent a quick and easy way to increase the compression ratio on your street performance big-block. Depending on your combination of piston dome and combustion chamber size, this could amount to at least one-half point of com-

Fel-Pro Perma Torque gasket PN 1017-1 for Mark IV and aftermarket blocks has a 4.540-inch bore and is .041 inch thick with a pre-flattened steel ring around the combustion chamber. Here it is being test fitted on a Gen V 502 block, and it works on this particular block with aftermarket cylinder heads. Safer choices are Fel-Pro PN 1047, GMPP PN 12363411, Cometic PN C5333-040 (MLS), and Mr. Gasket PN 5804G or PN 3157G (MLS), which are all designed for the Gen V 502 big-block.

pression increase, typically from 8.5:1 to about 9.2:1. Remember that this also reduces piston-to-valve clearance, so you need to recheck that if you are using a high-lift cam. Mr. Gasket still offers a .020-inch-thick elastomer-coated steel-shim head gasket (PN 1131G) for Mark IV engines with bores up to 4.370 inches and iron heads.

Dead soft copper gaskets used to be the exclusive choice of Top Fuel and other extremely high-horsepower engines due to their robust construction, but they were hard to seal.

Things have improved today, and there are several specialty companies offering copper head gaskets with elastomer coatings that seal the water passages quite well, and some incorporate steel O-rings into the gasket itself, requiring no special machine work to the heads or block. With modern manufacturing techniques, they can be custom-made to fit whatever application you want. You can get them from Copper Head, Clark, Milodon, SCE, Hussey, and others.

Composition gaskets have good sealing properties for the coolant passages and formed stainless steel around each bore to handle combustion pressure. Most head gaskets you get from the local auto supply store fall into this category, but the performance gaskets from Fel-Pro, GMPP, Mahle/Victor Reinz, Mr. Gasket, and SCE are well suited for

GASKETS AND FASTENERS

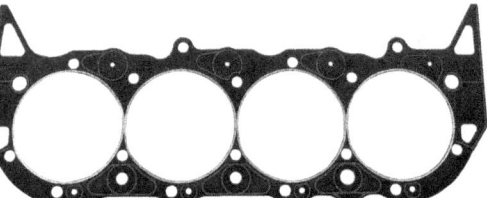

GMPP gasket PN 88961561 is a .030-inch-thick composition gasket with pre-flattened wire rings for Gen VI 572 crate engines. (Photo Courtesy GMPP)

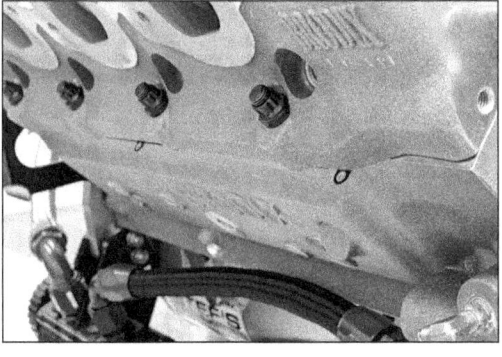

This 1,000-plus-hp all-aluminum big-block racing engine is equipped with MLS head gaskets. You can tell by the tabs sticking out between the block and heads: the three piece MLS gaskets are riveted together, and the rivet tabs must be outside of the head and block mating surfaces.

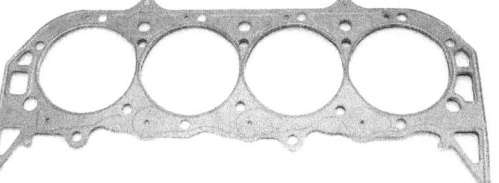

Cometic MLS head gasket PN C5816-040 for Mark IV engines has a bore of 4.320 inches, and is .040 inch thick. It has two water passages on each end, and the lower three are open between each bore. (Photo Courtesy Cometic Gasket)

high-performance big-blocks up to around 14:1 compression. Some companies, such as Edelbrock, offer composition gaskets specifically designed to fit their products for street high-performance applications.

Multi-layered steel (MLS) gaskets are the latest design in head gasket technology, and utilize three layers of stainless steel sandwiched together. The outer layers usually have some sort of elastomer or other sealing agent for a positive seal around all coolant passages. High-performance MLS gaskets are able to withstand very high compression ratios, and do not need O-rings. Surface preparation is crucial, but that has always been the case with very-high-compression engines. A surface finish of RA 50 or better is required for MLS gaskets. MLS head gaskets for Mark IV and Gen V/VI big-blocks are available from Cometic, Fel-Pro, Mahle/Victor Reinz, and Mr. Gasket.

Big-Block Engine Gaskets and Seals

Mark IV engines require a two-piece rear main seal such as Fel-Pro PN 2904 and PN 2918, and 1990-and-later Gen V and Gen VI motors use a one-piece seal such as Fel-Pro PN 2920.

Most oil pan gasket sets are the traditional four-piece set with cork/composition side gaskets and formed rubber end seals, such as Fel-Pro PN 1804 for Mark IV oil pans. I prefer the new one-piece pan gaskets, especially if you have to

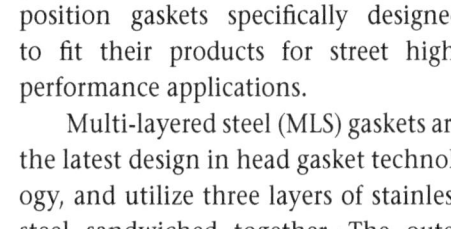

Cometic MLS head gasket pattern for Brodix Big Duke and Big Brodie heads with two added bolt-holes on the intake side and bores from 4.310 to 4.630 inches. (Photo Courtesy Cometic Gasket)

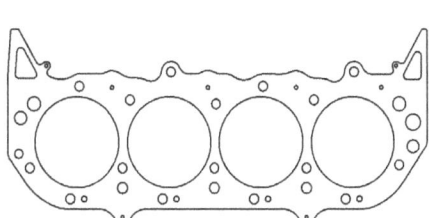

Cometic MLS head gasket pattern for ZL1 with bores from 4.250 to 4.375 inches. (Photo Courtesy Cometic Gasket)

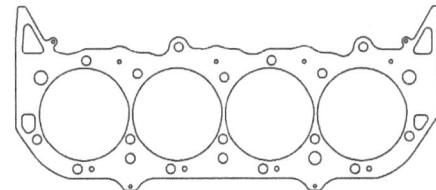

Cometic MLS head gasket pattern for Gen V and Gen VI 396 through 502 big-blocks has one water passage on each end, and the lower three open between each bore. (Photo Courtesy Cometic Gasket)

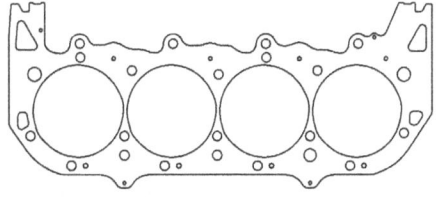

Cometic MLS head gasket pattern for Mercury Marine Mark IV, Gen V, and Gen VI big-blocks with four added bolt-holes on the intake side and bores from 4.500 to 4.600 inches. (Photo Courtesy Cometic Gasket)

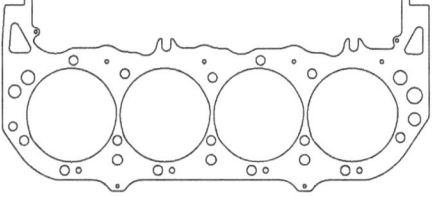

Cometic MLS head gasket pattern for Mercury Marine 1050 Mark IV and Dart blocks with two added bolt-holes on the intake side and bores from 4.500 to 4.600 inches. (Photo Courtesy Cometic Gasket)

CHAPTER 11

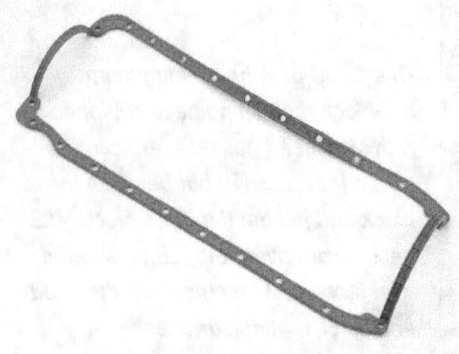

One-piece oil pan gaskets are much easier to install and less likely to leak than the old four-piece pan gaskets.

RTV sealant should be used around the water ports in the heads and on the end seals of the block prior to intake manifold installation.

Head studs are the best choice for secure gasket clamping on high-horsepower big-blocks.

High-quality main cap studs are a wise investment for your Rat motor. These studs have a hex in the end to allow installation with splayed-bolt main caps.

change gaskets with the engine installed in the vehicle. Fel-Pro PN 1884R and SCE PN 213090 are formed one-piece gaskets that fit Mark IV pans. GMPP offers a one-piece pan gasket for Gen V/VI engines, PN 10106407. SCE also makes one-piece pan gaskets for Gen V/VI engines, plus exotic blocks like the DRCE/Merlin, AJPE 481X, KB Olds/New Century, and the Donovan 700.

There are as many intake flange gaskets as there are cylinder heads, so refer to the head manufacturer for recommendations. For production 1974-and-earlier large oval-port heads, Fel-Pro PN 1212 or Mr. Gasket PN 5827 are readily available. For production rectangular port heads with a center bolt-hole between each pair of runners, Fel-Pro PN 1211 or Mr. Gasket PN 5828 are popular choices.

Fasteners

Stock Chevy main cap bolts, head bolts, and 7/16-inch connecting rod bolts are adequate for most street performance applications up to 600 hp, but higher-output engines need to upgrade to aftermarket hardware to keep everything where it belongs. Stock 3/8-inch connecting rod bolts should be upgraded as soon as possible for anything other than a very mild Rat motor. ARP makes excellent fasteners for all forms of motorsports competition, and replacement WaveLok connecting rod bolts are on my list of things to procure as soon as possible for a 3/8-inch rod motor.

All stock big-blocks use bolts to attach the heads and main caps to the block, but for high-horsepower engines studs should be used for their superior clamping power. Stud kits are available from A1 Technologies, ARP, Milodon, Mr. Gasket, and several cylinder head and block manufacturers, which offer kits specifically for their products. Studs should only be tightened to a snug fit in the block using either a thread lubricant like oil for blind holes, or a thread sealer for through holes that open into the water jacket, such as head-bolt holes on a production block.

Also note that many head stud kits cause interference with the header flange and the four short studs on the outside of the head. You may have to shorten those studs to clear your headers, and that's much easier to do if you test fit your headers on the engine before you install it in the car.

GASKETS AND FASTENERS

Stock Chevy Bolt Torque and Lubricants

Part	Thread	Torque	Lubricant
Main Cap Bolts	1/2-13	110 ft-lbs	Oil
Connecting Rod Nuts	7/16-20	67–73 ft-lbs or .007-inch stretch	Moly Lube
Connecting Rod Nuts	3/8-16	45–50 ft-lbs or .0055-inch stretch	Moly Lube
Oil Pump Bolt	7/16-14	65 ft-lbs	Oil
Oil Pump Cover Bolts	1/4-20	80 inch-lbs Loctite 242	
Flywheel/Flexplate Bolts	7/16-20	60 ft-lbs	Loctite 242
Harmonic Dampener Bolt	1/2-20	85 ft-lbs	Oil
Cam Sprocket Bolts	5/16-18	20 ft-lbs	Loctite 242
Cylinder Head Bolts	7/16-14	75 ft-lbs (long), 65 ft-lbs (short)	Sealant (oil with blind holes)
Cylinder Head Studs	7/16-20	65 ft-lbs (long), 55 ft-lbs (short)	Sealant (oil with blind holes)
Rocker Arm Studs	7/16-14	50 ft-lbs	Sealant (oil in blind holes)
Pressure Plate Bolts	3/8-16	35 ft-lbs	Locktite 242
Intake Manifold Bolts	3/8-16	25 ft-lbs (aluminum)	Sealant (oil in blind holes)
Intake Manifold Bolts	3/8-16	35 ft-lbs (iron)	Sealant (oil in blind holes)
Exhaust Manifold Bolts	3/8-16	25 ft-lbs (aluminum heads)	Anti-seize
Exhaust Manifold Bolts	3/8-16	35 ft-lbs (iron heads)	Anti-seize
Bellhousing Bolts	3/8-16	35 ft-lbs	Oil
Distributor Clamp Bolt	3/8-16	25 ft-lbs	Oil (anti-seize w/ aluminum manifold)
Oil Pan Bolts	5/16-18	165 inch/lbs	Oil
Oil Pan to Front Cover Bolts	1/4-20	80 inch/lbs	Oil
Front Cover Bolts	1/4-20	75 inch/lbs	Oil
Valve Cover Bolts	1/4-20	25 inch/lbs	Oil
Water Pump Bolts	3/8-16	30 ft-lbs	Oil

For aftermarket parts such as aluminum cylinder heads and stud kits, use the manufacturer's recommended torque values and lubricants. Most aftermarket connecting rods have a higher torque requirement than stock, and many call for the use of a specific lubricant. Rod bolt stretch is always the preferred method of measuring rod bolt torque.

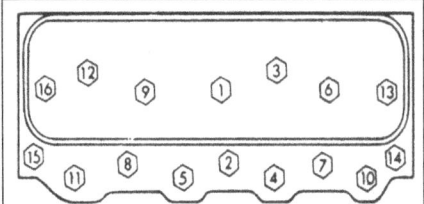

Cylinder head torque sequence. Note: Some aftermarket and Bowtie blocks have two additional bolt bosses in the lifter valley. These may be tightened after full torque is applied to the 16 top bolts. If you are using aluminum heads on a block without these additional bolt bosses, be sure to plug the threaded holes in the bottom of the heads to prevent leaks.

Studs that are installed in blind bolt-holes should have a blunt nose on the end to prevent damage to the threads when they are seated.

Apply gasket sealer to the intake flange on the head (above) and the side of the gasket (left) that goes against the head to hold the gasket in place during manifold installation.

CHAPTER 12

ENGINE BUILD-UP

This 598-ci all-aluminum big-block made 1,097 hp at 7,300 rpm and 852 ft-lbs of torque at 6,400 rpm with a single 4-barrel carb on race gas.

Putting It All Together

Project: 598-ci All-Aluminum Big-Block
Application: Competition only, NHRA Top Dragster/Top Sportsman, fast brackets (Quick 16, etc.)
Target Power Level: 1,100 hp

This engine is owned by K&N engineer Jonathon Fiello, who competes in the NHRA's Top Dragster class. It has run as quick as 6.8 seconds in the quarter-mile at more than 200 mph with a single 4-barrel carburetor on race gasoline with no power adders. Follow along as I show you how Jonathon and John Reedy, K&N race shop's expert engine builder and dyno operator, assembled this heavy-hitting, lightweight Rat. And check out the complete specification list.

Short-Block Assembly

1 The heart of this alloy animal is a Brodix cast aluminum tall-deck (10.2 inches) block with splayed-bolt billet steel main caps and traditional Mark IV bore spacing (4.840 inches). Its cast-iron cylinder liners were bored to 4.600 inches, and the .400-inch raised cam bore is sized for installation of 2.125-inch (460 Ford spec) Babbitt cam bearings.

HOW TO BUILD KILLER BIG-BLOCK CHEVY ENGINES

ENGINE BUILD-UP

2 Prior to installation of the cam bearings, the block was heated to 150 degrees F in this large curing oven to open up the bearing bores and ease installation.

3 While the block is still hot, the special 2.125-inch Babbitt bearings (Comp Cams PN 3521) are hammered into position using a cam bearing installation tool. Note the white tapered alignment cone, which ensures that the bearings are driven in straight. Plain (Babbitt) cam bearings have an oil hole that must be aligned with the matching oil supply hole in the block during installation.

4 The cam bearings must be pinned with these special anti-rotation bolts to prevent them from spinning in their bores when the aluminum block expands during operation. The bolts are installed in the lifter valley of the block.

5 After bearing installation, the cam is installed using two long 5/16-18 bolts to make sure everything is straight and properly aligned. Note the step on the front of the camshaft. The face of the cam is machined to standard big-block specs for compatibility with the cam drive sprocket. Although it looks similar to the design of OEM Gen VI cams, this step is not for thrust containment. The thrust clearance is adjusted with the Jesel belt drive assembly. The block does have bosses for the OEM-style thrust plate, which can be drilled and tapped if you desire.

6 Jonathon used this special bearing micrometer with a spherical anvil for precise measurement of the bearing insert thicknesses. After measuring the main bore diameters in the block, you can quickly determine main-bearing-to-crankshaft clearances with this tool.

7 This exotic all-aluminum Rat motor uses the same two-piece rear main seals as your budget 454.

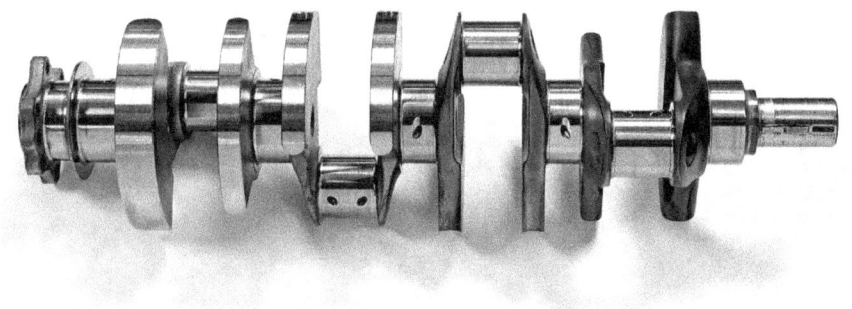

8 The crankshaft is a fully-counterweighted 4340 forged steel ultra-light Crower with a 4.500-inch stroke and 2.100-inch (small-block Chevy) rod journals.

HOW TO BUILD KILLER BIG-BLOCK CHEVY ENGINES

CHAPTER 12

9 After installing the upper main bearing shells in the block, the crank and bearings are coated with engine assembly lube and the crank is carefully laid on the bearings. The main caps engage dowels in the block to prevent cap "walk" and are a tight fit, so a hammer is used to seat the caps. Don't forget to install the upper rear main seal in the block before dropping in the crank!

10 A very thin layer of silicone RTV sealant is applied between the block and the rear main cap to prevent oil seepage.

11 You must install the rear main cap before the RTV sealant starts to harden. Of course, the lower main bearing shells are snapped into the main caps and coated with assembly lube before the main caps are installed.

12 While most splayed-bolt main caps use bolts in the angled outboard locations, Jonathon used these ARP studs, which have a hex for easy installation and superior clamping. Studs are always preferred over bolts for high-stress junctions such as main caps and cylinder head installation.

13 In addition to oiling the stud threads, the hardened washers and the mating surfaces of the nuts should also be lubricated to ensure proper torque readings. Also note that different lubricants may require different torque specifications.

14 The main studs are torqued to 95 ft-lbs (inner studs) and 85 ft-lbs (outer studs) in four steps (45, 65, 85, and 95) starting with the center cap and working out toward each end.

15 Crankshaft thrust clearance can be measured several ways, but one of the quickest and easiest is to use a feeler gage between the thrust surface of the crank and the rear main cap. Clearance should be .005 to .007 inch.

ENGINE BUILD-UP

16 Since this engine uses a dry sump oil system, the oil pump mounting pad on the rear main cap is blocked off with this plate. There is no need to install an oil pump driveshaft in the block through the rear main cap, either.

17 Before installing the pistons and rods, the bores are cleaned one last time with a lint-free cloth and lightweight oil.

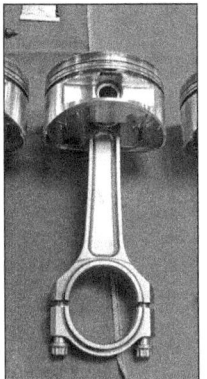

18 Crower 4340 steel connecting rods are 6.800 inches long (+.665 inch) and sized for small-block Chevy (2.100 inches) bearings. The custom JE pistons are forged from 2618 aluminum alloy and feature vertical gas ports to help seal the top ring. Ring package is .043-inch Total Seal gapless top ring with a .170-inch backcut; .043-inch napier second ring with a .170-inch backcut, and 3-mm oil control rings, which must be used with a vacuum pump or dry sump oil pump for proper oil control. Tool steel wrist pins are standard .990-inch diameter.

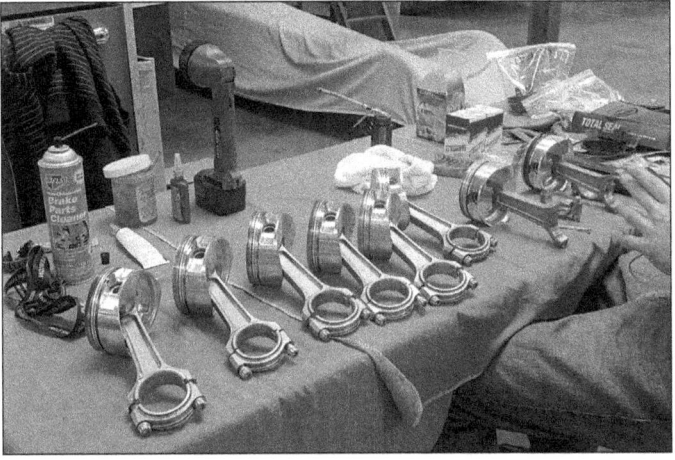

19 Lay out all the pistons, rods, rings, wristpins and rod bearing in a clean organized area for the time-consuming task of "hanging the rods" on the pistons. Before this step, the rings have been file-fitted to their bores, bearing clearances checked and verified, and piston domes have been hand finished to the desired shape. And of course, all of that had to be completed before the parts were sent out to be balanced.

20 After oiling the bores, piston skirts, and rings, the piston and rod assemblies are ready for installation. A bore-specific tapered ring compressor makes it extremely easy to install the fresh piston/rod assemblies. Many times you can push the pistons in with just your thumbs, although the old trick of using the wooden handle of a hammer helps to move things along. After you use one of these tapered ring compressors, you'll never go back to old-school "ring squeezers" again. By turning the block until the deck is level, the rods hang straight down, simplifying alignment of the rod bearings and crankshaft journals.

21 After installing all eight piston/rod assemblies, turn the engine over and torque the rod bolts. The final torque depends on the lubricant you use on the rod bolt threads, and many top engine builders measure bolt stretch with a rod bolt stretch gage to ensure proper preload. Whichever method you choose, follow the manufacturer's recommendations and be sure to double- or triple-check to be absolutely certain all eight pairs of rod bolts are properly torqued.

CHAPTER 12

22 The Jesel belt drive front cover is installed in the same manner as a stock front timing cover, except that RTV silicone sealer is used instead of a gasket. Because the camshaft thrust clearance is so critical and different gaskets may vary in thickness, installing the front cover metal-to-metal ensures that you have the same clearance every time the unit is removed and re-installed. This Jesel belt drive unit is made specifically for the .400-inch raised cam location. Cover bolts are torqued to 12 ft-lbs.

23 After slipping the rear bronze thrust washer over the cam, the cam adaptor is torqued to the camshaft using this spanner wrench (supplied with the belt drive) to hold the unit while tightening with a torque wrench to 28 to 30 ft-lbs. It's a good idea to use non-permanent thread-locking compound on these bolts. Cam is a custom 4-7 swap Comp Cams roller with 2⅛-inch journals, 285/306 degree (intake/exhaust) duration at .050-inch checking clearance, .948/.928-inch lift at the valve with 1.8:1 rocker arms, and a 116-degree lobe separation angle.

24 As the cam is installed into the block, assembly lube is applied to the cam journals. Jonathon applies assembly lube to the cam lobes after the cam is in the block, although many prefer to do so at this point. This is especially critical with flat-tappet cams, which must have a moly-disulfide lube on every lobe, plus the bottoms of the lifters. Moly-disulfide lube should not be applied to the cam journals; use only assembly lube, as shown here. Don't forget to lube both sides of the thrust washer, too.

25 Next the outer thrust washer is lubed and placed over the cam adaptor, and then the thrust shims and thrust plate are installed.

26 Install the thrust plate nuts, then set up a dial indicator and check cam fore and aft movement. Jonathon is using a screwdriver to move the cam back and forth while watching the indicator. Proper clearance is .005 to .010 inch. The Jesel belt drive comes with an assortment of thrust shims that you can add or subtract as needed.

27 After verifying correct cam thrust clearance, the thrust plate nuts are torqued to 18 ft-lbs.

28 Then the crank pulley is driven on with a hammer and sleeve. The nose of the crankshaft must be coated with a thin layer of anti-seize to make the pulley installation and later removal easier.

136 HOW TO BUILD KILLER BIG-BLOCK CHEVY ENGINES

ENGINE BUILD-UP

29 The cam pulley and timing belt are installed next. The timing marks on the upper and lower pulleys must be aligned with the engine at TDC of the number-6 cylinder (same crank position as TDC of number-1 cylinder). The upper pulley bolt is left-hand thread and must be tightened to 70 ft-lbs.

30 The 7-inch-diameter ATI Super Damper is installed with a dampener puller/installation tool. The crank snout must be coated with a thin layer of anti-seize to help installation and ease future disassembly.

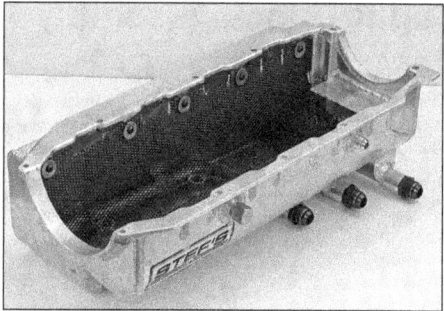

31 The Stef's dry sump oil pan is fabricated from aluminum and features built-in windage tray/screen, multiple scavenge connections, and a full right-side kick-out.

32 Connecting rod side clearance is checked with a .016-inch feeler gage. This is just a final check, as you must determine if you need to change the clearance before final assembly. If too small, the rod sides can be narrowed; if too large, either different rods or crank must be used.

33 Oil pan gaskets and end seals are sealed with RTV silicone, and then the pan is lowered onto the block, being careful not to push the gaskets out of place.

34 Jonathon prefers studs and nuts to attach the pan, so he uses a little grease to hold the nuts in the socket while he installs them through the access holes on the kick-out side of the pan. The bolt access holes are then sealed with pipe plugs.

35 This special oil filter adapter for dry sump systems includes the main oil pressure feed fitting. Note that the block was relieved to clear the fitting.

36 The complete short-block is rotated on the engine stand for installation of the heads and final assembly. The crank trigger wheel and dry sump/vacuum pump belt drive mandrel are bolted to the harmonic dampener.

37 Jonathon installed the Barnes four-stage (one pressure section plus three scavenge sections) dry sump oil pump and CSR electric water pump. The 1/4-inch-thick aluminum front motor plate, which is sandwiched between the water pump and the block, also serves as a mounting bracket for the dry sump oil tank.

HOW TO BUILD KILLER BIG-BLOCK CHEVY ENGINES

CHAPTER 12

Long-Block Assembly

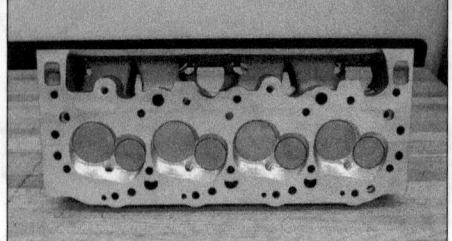

1 The fully CNC ported Brodix PB 1200 Big Duke cylinder heads are the key to big horsepower gains. They feature 12-degree intake valve angles, high-flow oval intake ports, and titanium 2.520-inch intake and 1.860-inch exhaust valves with 11/32-inch stems.

2 These heads came from Brodix completely assembled, but K&N's John Reedy disassembled them to double-check all clearances and component specs. All good engine builders do this; don't assume anything!

3 Valvesprings are checked for correct seat pressure and open pressure on this Rimac spring tester.

4 Coil bind is also verified by squeezing the springs solid in a vice. The valvespring retainer must be used for accurate results because of the steps that position the inner valvesprings. Some people are afraid to squeeze the springs solid, but John says that if they can't take this operation, they won't last long in a race engine anyway. These Manley titanium valves and triple valvesprings are the key to high-RPM valvetrain stability. The springs have 350 pounds of pressure on the seat and 1,010 pounds at full lift!

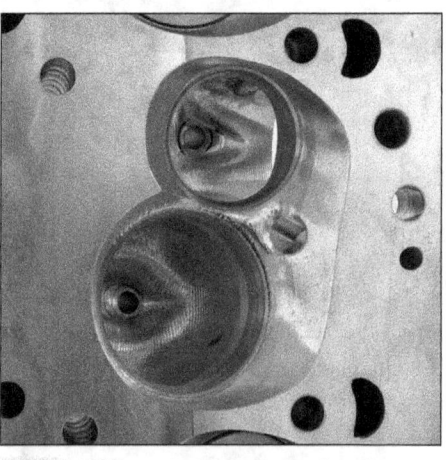

5 CNC-ported 68-cc combustion chambers with copper/beryllium valve seats feature 55-degree seat angles for improved flow at high valve lifts.

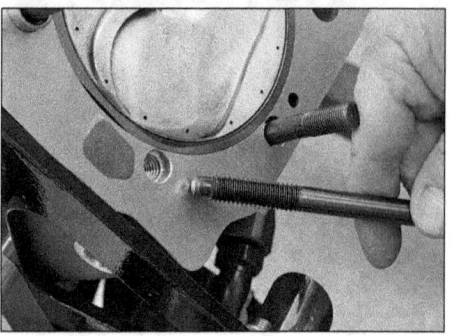

6 The head studs have a bullet-shaped nose that bottom-out in the blind head-bolt holes without damaging the threads. After oiling the threads, studs are very lightly tightened into the block. No sealer is necessary with blind head-bolt holes.

7 Before bolting the heads to the block, test-fit them to check for any interference. You can see that the shaft rocker stand comes very close to hitting the top of this stud, but there is adequate clearance to proceed with installation. Another source of possible interference is the header-flange-to-head-stud clearance. The time to shorten any studs that need it is now, not after the heads are bolted on.

ENGINE BUILD-UP

8 After fitting the number-1 intake and exhaust valves with lightweight checking springs, piston-to-valve clearance is verified using a dial indicator. With the engine rotated to the valve overlap position, check exhaust valve clearance at 10 degrees BTDC and intake valve clearance at 10 degrees ATDC. Once again, this is only a final verification; you must check this before the engine is assembled, as any valve pocket machining must be done prior to piston balancing and installation. Minimum clearance is usually .080 inch for the intake and .100 inch for the exhaust. The measured clearance was .146 inch on the intake and .150 inch for the exhaust, which is enough to allow for variations in cam timing.

9 After placing the MLS head gaskets on the block, the re-assembled cylinder heads are ready for installation. Head studs make this much easier, but you need to verify that you have adequate room in your engine compartment for in-car head removal, if necessary. Many full-bodied cars lack sufficient room for studs because the head might hit the brake master cylinder or other obstructions in the engine bay. Some companies, such as ARP, offer hex-head studs that can be removed and installed through the cylinder head with a hex wrench, making them the best choice for full-bodied cars.

10 After placing the hardened washers and nuts on all the studs, oil the threads and washers then torque to 75 ft-lbs in three steps: 40, 60, and 75 ft-lbs. If you use ARP's special moly thread lube, reduce torque to 70 ft-lbs. The proper torque sequence is to start with the center bolt-hole and work out in a spiral pattern.

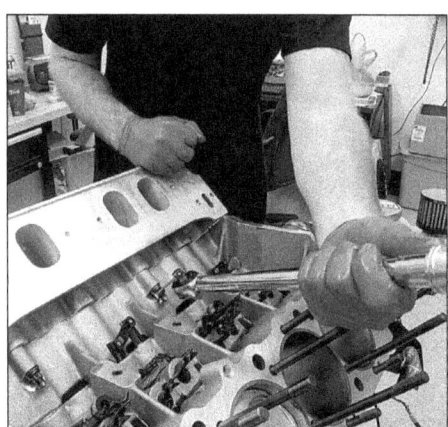

11 The Brodix block has two additional head bolt bosses per side in the lifter valley for additional head gasket clamping. After installing the studs, nuts, and washers, these were torqued using a 1/2-inch combination wrench. You must reduce the torque wrench setting by about 10 ft-lbs to compensate for the added leverage provided by the 1/2-inch wrench.

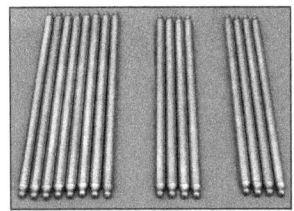

12 Brodix Big Duke heads require three different-length pushrods. All eight of the exhaust pushrods are 10.700 inches long, and the intake pushrods are 10.375 and 10.435 inches long. The longer pushrods are needed for the severe offset of the intake rocker arms of cylinders 1, 5, 4, and 8. Manton supplied these bulletproof 7/16-inch chrome-moly pushrods.

13 After installing the T&D rocker stand, assembly lube was applied to the valvestem tips and pushrod tips where they contact the rocker arms.

14 As the rocker arms are installed on the rocker stand studs, rotate the engine so that the lifter is on the base circle of the cam to prevent valvespring preload from "tweaking" things. The rocker arm nuts are torqued to 25 ft-lbs using oil as a lubricant.

HOW TO BUILD KILLER BIG-BLOCK CHEVY ENGINES

CHAPTER 12

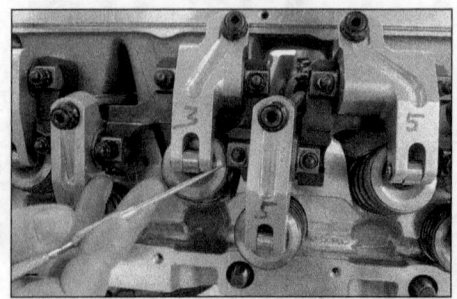

15 When the T&D shaft rocker arms were installed, John noticed that there was insufficient clearance between the number-5 exhaust rocker shaft and the number-3 intake valvespring. A quick trip to the belt sander provided clearance for the offending rocker shaft.

16 After the rocker arms have been installed and the valve lash adjusted to "cold" specs, these intake manifold end seal spacers are glued to the block with weatherstrip adhesive.

17 The Brodix Big Duke manifold is a perfect match for the Brodix PB 1200 heads.

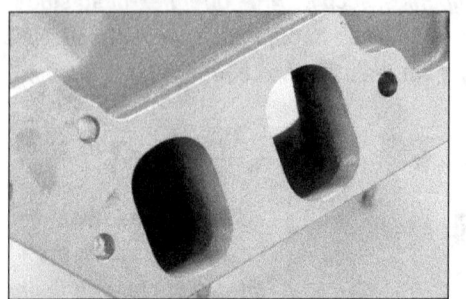

18 The manifold runner exits have been port matched to the oval intake ports in the PB 1200 heads.

19 The intake gaskets are placed on the heads and RTV silicone sealant is used around the water passages and on each end seal.

20 The intake manifold is lowered straight down onto the engine, being careful not to disturb the gasket alignment.

21 All manifold bolts are started by hand before any are tightened. Manifold bolt torque is listed as 25 ft-lbs, but you can't get a torque wrench on most of them, so every good engine builder develops a feel for how hard to tug on the box-end wrench used with these 12-point bolts. Manifold bolts are tightened from the center out and side-to-side in several steps. It's a good idea to go over all 12 bolts as many as four or five times, snugging every bolt a little tighter each time. Note that some of the manifold bolts are in line with the pushrods, so be sure to use the correct length bolts and check with a flashlight to be sure that the pushrods are not pinched by the bolts.

22 Now that the full valvetrain is assembled, intake opening at .050 inch is re-checked. With the pressure of all 16 triple valvesprings, the cam timing belt usually stretches a bit, but the Jesel belt drive unit is easily adjusted to achieve the correct timing.

23 With valve lash adjusted to 0.000 inch, a dial indicator was used to measure valve lift on the number-1 intake and exhaust valves. Since the cam was already checked for correct lobe lift, this check is mainly used to verify rocker arm ratios. These T&D 1.8:1 rockers were right on the money.

ENGINE BUILD-UP

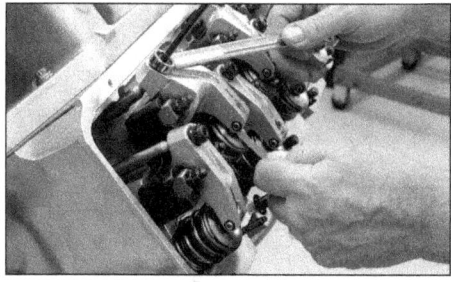

24 Final valve lash is adjusted using feeler gages to measure the clearance between the top of the valvestem and the roller tip on the rocker arm. Cold valve lash settings for an all-aluminum engine are usually the hot lash minus .012 inch, or .012 inch (.024 minus .012 inch) for the intakes and .018 inch (.030 minus .012 inch) for the exhaust valves.

Final Accessory Installation

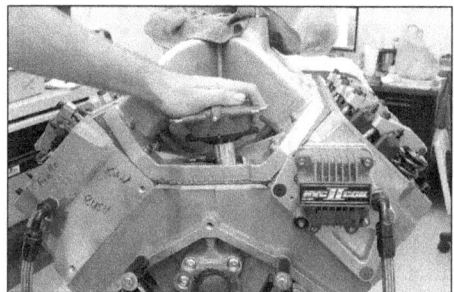

1 After rotating the engine to 30 degrees BTDC on the compression stroke of the number-1 cylinder, the billet aluminum MSD crank trigger distributor dropped right into place, since this dry-sump-equipped engine has no internal oil pump to align with the bottom of the distributor shaft. This view also shows why the manifold end spacers had to be fabricated to seal the ends of the intake manifold. It's common practice on tall-deck blocks, or any engine with competition heads and manifold.

2 The valve covers and vacuum pump were then bolted on and the vacuum line from the pump to the valve covers installed. The carb pad on the intake manifold was taped up to prevent anything from falling into the engine as it was moved onto the dyno for final assembly and testing.

3 The 1,250-cfm APD three-circuit carb features billet metering blocks, annular boosters, adjustable air bleeds, and adjustable secondary throttle linkage.

4 This two-piece Reher-Morrison Racing Engines anti-reversion plate fits between the carb and manifold. Viewed from the bottom (manifold side), you can see the throttle bore extensions, which help to improve throttle response and mid-range torque.

5 The Fel-Pro exhaust gaskets are a perfect match for the Edelbrock 2⅜-inch header tubes. You can see how the exhaust ports are flattened on the bottom to improve exhaust flow on the "short side" of the runner, and brass tubes seal the head-bolt holes adjacent to the exhaust ports.

6 With the headers installed and all fluid lines connected, the engine's lubrication system is easily primed by unhooking the oil pump drive belt and spinning the pump with a speed wrench—one more advantage of a dry sump system!

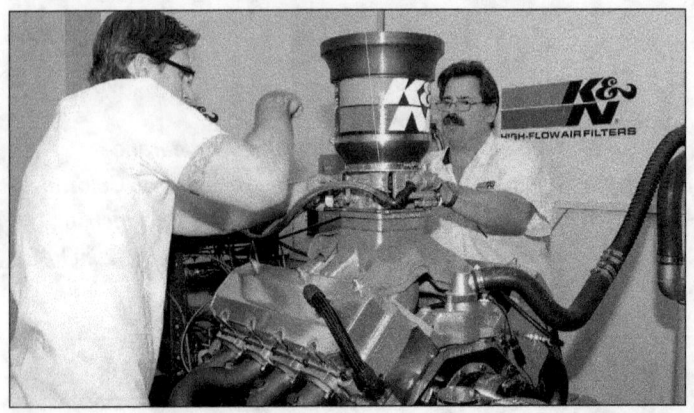

7 Steve Williams (right), K&N's Vice President of Marketing and a multiple NHRA Super Comp national and divisional event winner, stopped by to help with the tune-up. After several carb jet and air bleed changes, plus some cam timing changes, the engine made an impressive 1,097 hp at 7,300 rpm with 852 ft-lbs of torque at 6,400 rpm.

8 Jonathon Fiello (left) and John Reedy (right) are all smiles after their newborn Rat motor made nearly 1,100 hp on K&N's dyno.

ENGINE

Displacement: 598 ci

Bore x Stroke: 4.600 inches x 4.500 inches

Block: Brodix aluminum, 10.2-inch deck height, four-bolt billet steel main caps, .400-inch raised-cam location, 2.125-inch cam bearings (460 Ford diameter, special Comp Cams bearings)

Crank: Crower 4340 forged steel, 4.500-inch stroke, fully counterweighted, 2.750-inch mains, 2.100-inch rod journals

Rods: Crower 4340 forged steel, 6.800 inches long

Bearings: Clevite, MS-829 VN (mains), CB-663 VN (rods, small-block Chevy)

Harmonic Dampener: ATI 7-inch diameter, neutral balance, meets SFI specs 18-1

Pistons: JE 2618 aluminum, 4.594-inch diameter, 15:1 compression ratio, vertical gas ports, .990-inch tool steel wrist pins

Rings: Top: .043-inch Total Seal, .170-inch backcut; Second: .043-inch Napier, .170-inch backcut; Oil: 3 mm

Lubrication System: Stef's aluminum dry sump oil pan, Barnes four-stage dry sump oil pump, Star Machine vacuum pump, K&N PN 3002 oil filter

Camshaft: Comp Cams grind number CB 47 2074RE/1878RE R 116.0, 4-7 swap firing order (1-8-7-3-6-5-4-2)

Duration at .050 inch: 285 degrees/306 degrees (intake/exhaust)

Lift at lobe: .5270 inch/.5160 inch (intake/exhaust)

Lift at valve with 1.8:1/1.8:1 rockers (theoretical): .948 inch/.928 inch (intake/exhaust)

Lift at valve (measured, with lash): .927 inch/.908 inch (intake/exhaust)

LSA: 116 degrees

Intake Centerline: 114 degrees

Cam Drive: Jesel belt drive

Rocker Arms: T&D shaft rockers, 1.8:1/1.8:1 (intake/exhaust)

Valvesprings and Retainers: Manley triple PN 221448, 1.677-inch diameter, 2.100- inches installed height, 350 lbs seat pressure, 1,010 lbs at full lift, 733 lbs/inch spring rate, 1.142 inch coil bind, Manley titanium retainers, Comp Cams 7-degree machined steel valve locks

Lifters: Comp Cams .903-inch-diameter tie-bar roller lifters

Pushrods: Manton 7/16- inch diameter, 10.700 inches (exhaust, 8), 10.375 inches (intake, 4), 10.435 inches (intake, 4)

Heads: Brodix Big Duke PB 1200, A-356 virgin aluminum, 12-degrees intake valve angle, fully CNC ported, raised oval intake ports, 55-degree seat angle, copper/beryllium valve seats, 483-cc intake port volume, 120-cc exhaust port volume, 68-cc combustion chamber volume

Valves: Brodix/Manley titanium, 2.520 inches/1.860 inches (intake/exhaust), 11/32-inch stem diameter, 55-degree seat angle, length: 6.920 inches/6.620 inches (intake/exhaust)

Intake Manifold: Brodix Big Duke PN 1917 for 10.200-inch tall-deck engines, port matched to intake gaskets, fabricated 1/4-inch aluminum end seal spacers

Carburetor: APD Dominator-style 4-barrel, 1250 CFM, 3-circuit, 2.125-inch throttle bores, 1.88-inch venturi diameters, annular discharge booster venturis, changeable screw-in air bleeds, adjustable secondary-throttle linkage ratio, billet aluminum metering plates

ENGINE BUILD-UP

Ignition System: MSD crank trigger and billet aluminum distributor, Accel 8.8-mm spark plug wires
Headers: Edelbrock stainless steel step headers, 2 3/8-inch to 2 1/2-inch primaries, merge collector, 5-inch collector exit
Spark Plugs: NGK R5671A-9 (PN 5238), .045-inch gap
Valve Covers: Jeff Johnston's Billet Fabrication aluminum sheet metal

GASKETS

Head: Fel-Pro PN 1077, MLS, .040-inch thick
Intake: Brodix/Mr. Gasket PN 2015, 1/16-inch thick
Exhaust: Brodix/Mr. Gasket PN 2005 or Fel-Pro PN 1490
Oil Pan: Fel-Pro PN 1893
Valve Cover: Brodix/Mr. Gasket PN 2016

FASTENER TORQUE

Main Cap Studs: 95 ft-lbs inner, 85 ft-lbs outer (oil)
Rod Bolts: 75 ft-lbs (moly disulfide)
Oil Pump Block-off Plate Bolt: 50 ft-lbs (oil)
Head Studs: 75 ft-lbs (oil), or 70 ft-lbs (moly disulfide)
Rocker Stand Bolts: 50 ft-lbs (oil)
Rocker Shaft Nuts: 25 ft-lbs (oil)

CLEARANCES

Main Bearings: .003 inch
Rod Bearings: .003 inch
Rod Side Clearance: .014 inch
Crank End Thrust: .007 inch
Piston to Valve: .146 inch (intake), .150 inch (exhaust)
Piston to Deck: .000 inch
Piston to Cylinder Wall: .007 inch
Ring End Gaps: .046 (top), .042 (second), .018 inch (oil ring rails)
Ring Side Gaps: .001 to .002 inch
Piston to Wrist Pin: .0015 inch (with vacuum pump)
Cam End Thrust: .005 inch
Valve Lash: .024/.030 inch (intake/exhaust, hot)

SOURCE GUIDE

Aerospace Components
2625 75th Street North
Saint Petersburg, FL 33710
727-347-9915
www.aerospacecomponents.com

Air Flow Research
28611 W. Industry Drive
Valencia, CA 91355
661-257-8124
Toll Free: 877-892-8844
www.airflowresearch.com

ARP
1863 Eastman Avenue
Ventura, CA 93003
800-826-3045
www.arpfasteners.com

ATI Performance Products
6747 Whitestone Road
Baltimore, MD 21207
Order Line: 877-298-5039
Tech Help: 877-298-4343
www.atiracing.com

Brodix, Inc.
301 Maple
P.O. Box 1347
Mena, AR 71953
479-394-1075
www.brodix.com

Callies Performance Products
901 South Union Street
Fostoria, OH 44830
419-435-2711
www.callies.com

COMP Cams
3406 Democrat Road
Memphis, TN 38118
Order Line: 901-795-2400
Tech Support: 800-999-0853
www.compcams.com

CN Blocks
291 North FM 3549
Rockwall, TX 75087
972-722-8333
www.cnblocks.com

Crower Cams & Equipment
6180 Business Center Court
San Diego, CA 92154-5604
619-661-6477
www.crower.com

Dart Machinery
353 Oliver Street
Troy, MI 48084
248-362-1188
www.dartheads.com

Donovan Engineering
   Corporation
2305 Border Avenue
Torrance CA 90501
310-320-3772
www.donovanengineering.com

Edelbrock Corporation
2700 California Street
Torrance, CA 90503
310-781-2222
Tech Line: 800-416-8628
www.edelbrock/com

GM Performance Parts
www.gmperformanceparts.com

Holley / Weiand / NOS
1801 Russellville Road
Bowling Green, KY 42101
270-782-2900
Tech Line: 270 781-9741
www.holley.com

JE Pistons
15312 Connector Lane
Huntington Beach, CA 92649
714-898-9764
www.jepistons.com

Manley Performance Products,
   Inc.
1960 Swarthmore Avenue
Lakewood, NJ 08701
732-905-3366
www.manleyperformance.com

Meziere Enterprises
220 S. Hale Avenue
Escondido, CA 92029
800-208-1755
www.meziere.com

Milodon, Inc.
2250 Agate Court
Simi Valley, CA 93065
805-577-5950
www.milodon.com

Probe Industries
2555 West 237th Street
Torrance, CA 90505
Toll-free: 866-249-9142
www.probeindustries.com

Pro-Filer Performance Products
P.O. Box 217
New Carlisle, OH 45344
937-846-1333
www.profilerperformance.com

Quick Fuel Technology
129 Dishman Lane
Bowling Green, KY 42101
270-793-0900
www.quickfueltechnology.com

Reher/Morrison Racing Engines
1120 Enterprise Place
Arlington, TX 76001
817-467-7171
www.rehermorrison.com

Rollmaster Performance Products
25-31 Innes Road
Windsor Gardens, SA 5087
Austrailia
61+8-8261-7222
www.romac.com/au

Scat Enterprises, Inc.
1400 Kingsdale Avenue
Redondo Beach, CA 90278
310-370-5501
www.scatcrankshafts.com

Shaver Racing Engines
20608 Earl Street
Torrance, CA 90503
310-370-6941
www.myspace.com/
   shaverracingengines

Speed-O-Motive
131 North Lang Avenue
West Covina, CA 91790
626-869-0270
www.speedomotive.com

Star Machine LLC
6618 Blackhead Road
Baltimore, MD 21220
410-335-4316
www.starvacuumpumps.com

TCI Automotive
151 Industrial Drive
Ashland, MS 38603
Toll Free: 888-776-9824
www.tciauto.com

World Products
51 Trade Zone Court
Ronkonkoma, NY 11779
631-981-1918
www.worldcastings.com

www.ingramcontent.com/pod-product-compliance
Lightning Source LLC
Chambersburg PA
CBHW051413070526
44584CB00023B/3415